Two Ohmans

The backgrounds of the front cover and back cover

of this book show a ledger page from the

LIST OR MANIFEST OF ALIEN PASSENGERS

FOR THE UNITED STATES

IMMIGRATION OFFICER AT PORT OF ARRIVAL.

Incoming immigrants processed on Ellis Island, New York City,

were asked thirty-three assessment questions.

Kristina Ohman's responses on March 16, 1920,

are on line 30, the last entry of this document.

Two Ohmans

A Complexity of Immigration

Stina E. Ohman

Leonard G. Ohman

Janet Ohman Lindsay

Translations by Eva Ohman Johansson

NIBOLOLA PRESS
Two Ohmans: A Complexity of Immigration—Stina E. Ohman and
Leonard G. Ohman.
Janet K. Lindsay, author. Translations by Eva Johansson

Copy Consultant: Therese Trotochaud
Cover Design: Janet K. Lindsay
Interior Design: Janet K. Lindsay

Published in the United States by Nibolola Press
ISBN 978-1-7357672-0-8

Version 1
Printed by KDP.Amazon, On-Demand Publishing

My father Leonard (Lennart) Gordon Ohman

and his mother Stina (Kristina) Evelyn Ohman

were victims of circumstance due to immigration.

Both lacked a sense of belonging.

The content of the letters was unknown for 100 years.

May my father now rest in peace.

Two Ohmans

A Complexity of Immigration

Preface

Map of Hälsingland

"Dearest Little Stina!"

December 1916 - June 1954

"Dear Mother:"

September 1938 - June 1940

To the Reader

Preface

Preface

I'm the one who knew her. There is no one living who knew her better than I. There is no other person who can write this story. No one. It is a story that must be told.

It was a different time with different values of family pride. It is a story of rejection on several levels: social, spousal, and parental. A pregnant daughter is sent across the Atlantic to begin a new life in a foreign country. There is infidelity across all spectrums and a mother who rejects her child as he interferes with her lifestyle.

This anthology is the story of two Ohmans, two languages, two cultures, and two continents. Seventy-eight letters received by my grandmother, Stina, remained dormant for over 100 years, unread and hidden, due to the language barrier.

My father, Leonard, never knew his father. His mother, Stina, was a private, secretive person. I did not think my father and grandmother were loved. I did not know there was a bond of devotion and family regret. If only my father had known this. It may have stifled his lifelong stigma of rejection. I grieve over his years of mental distress.

As I begin to write, I am reminded of an afternoon long ago. I realize now, it may have been the pivotal moment that determined the fate of the letters. That is, whether Stina kept the letters or destroyed them. I remember that day. It was 1958. I was nine years old, and Grandma Stina was visiting us. Much of her belongings were in trunks, barrels, and crates being stored in our basement. She had little storage at her apartment, so many of the items she had brought from Sweden were in storage at our house. She had set this date to visit and had fully planned to go through some of her personal items at this time. She told my parents that she did not want to be bothered and that she would be busy most of the afternoon in our basement. My parents relayed this information to me, and I was to stay away and not bother her. I busied myself for what seemed to be several hours and then decided she'd had enough time to get the job done. So that she knew I was coming, I loudly clogged down the basement steps to announce my arrival. She was sitting on a stool reading a letter. I assumed she had been reading letters for some time. There were several piles of letters. Deep in thought, she lifted her head from reading to look at me. Our eyes met and locked. She quietly zeroed in.

"Can you read Swedish?" she inquired with a far away voice. This surprised me.

"Can you read this?" she asked as she handed me a letter. She knew I was not literate in the Swedish language, but I replied anyway, shaking my head,

"I can't read this."

She continued her intense stare as if evaluating the situation. Then she looked down and continued to read. I scanned the room noticing she had been digging and sorting through several trunks. I skipped and jumped around the basement a bit and then ran back upstairs. I realized that Grandma Stina was engaged in important work and that she should not be disturbed. I believe this may have been the defining moment when Stina decided to leave the letters intact and allow them to remain in their home in the transatlantic trunk that had carried her precious keepsakes from Edsbyn to Minneapolis. I did not know until after her death that they still remained in her trunk, untouched by anyone other than Stina, herself.

Grandma Stina did not often hug me or touch me. Perhaps it was the Swedish way, not to be affectionate. As a young child, upon seeing her, I was often told, "Now go give Farmor (Father's Mother) a big hug," at which I would shuffle reluctantly over to her and complete the task. I didn't like visiting her. She had no toys, and I was taught that I couldn't touch anything in her apartment. There was nothing to do at her house.

I remember a time that I visited her alone, which actually rarely happened because she lived in south Minneapolis and our home was in Brooklyn Park, a northern suburb. I was probably about eight years old. We were in her apartment, and she sat quietly pondering at her desk. I was near her, and I watched her. I could tell that she was somewhere far away. Her eyes were closed. She was in a distant daydream, unaware of my nearby presence.

She slowly opened her eyes and very quietly said, "You know, there is a little girl about your age far away in Sweden. She's nicer than you, but you might like her." I was very surprised by this! I didn't know there was a little girl in Sweden my age. I thought, "If this girl is nicer than me, she must *really* be nice, because I think I'm an okay nice girl."

"What is her name?" I asked.

"Her name is Eva," my grandmother replied.

I thought about this for several moments. Then I asked, "Who is she?"

"She is my brother Göthe's daughter. In fact, you are kind of cousins," she replied.

My spirits lifted, but only for a short time. I thought Eva may not like me because I wasn't as nice as she was. I felt badly, but I didn't say anything to my grandmother—I just thought about this for a long time.

I was an only child the first nine years of my life. I desperately wanted a sibling to play with. This idea, that there was a girl my age, a kind of cousin in Sweden, was a wonderful revelation! Eva's last name was the same as mine, "Ohman!" What an exciting stroke of luck! I could hardly believe this magnificent news.

Months later, when my grandmother and I were alone again, I asked her if she thought I might be able to write a letter to Eva. She became silent, considering my request.

"It might be okay."

"But I don't know her address. How can I send her a letter?" I asked.

"I have her address. She lives with her mother and father, who is my brother, and I have their address," Grandma Stina replied.

And so I wrote, and our friendship began:

Dear Eva,

My name is Janet Kaye Ohman. My grandmother is your father's sister. I am nine years old. I live in Minneapolis, Minnesota. I have an Irish setter dog named Toots. Please write back. Do you speak English? I do not speak Swedish.

A kind of cousin,

Janet

From then on, Eva and I corresponded with one another several times a year. I decided at an early age that I would start saving my money to go visit Eva some day. I talked to my parents about my dream trip to meet Eva. The perfect time would be during a summer when I was home from college. I would be old enough then to travel alone, and, hopefully, smart enough to maneuver a foreign country. I figured Eva would meet me at the airport in Stockholm.

I was excited about my plan! After several years of saving money, I told my parents that I thought I would go the summer between my freshman and sophomore year of college. I knew my father would be pleased that I planned to visit his family, and, of course, I would stay with his aunt and uncle, Eva's parents.

I guess this trip was "all in my head" and never taken seriously by my parents. I believe, now, they simply humored me all of those years, just to keep me quiet. When the real plans began to move quickly, the spring of my freshman year, the trip came to an abrupt end.

With a firm resolve, my father said, "You're not going."

"What?" my jaw dropped.

He repeated, more firmly, "You're not going."

"Why?" I exhaled and became smaller.

Decisively, my father replied, "Sweden is a country of free love. If you go to Sweden you will never come back."

"What?" I dissolved in disbelief.

With a final, decisive resolute, my father said, "You're not going."

Wide eyed with shock, I left the room.

I was crushed. I cried for days. That was the end of that.

Four years later, the night of our wedding, I told my husband, Jerry, that I wanted our first big trip to be to Sweden. Having never left the farm, he, like my father, thought I had a loose screw. Since I did not let the subject lie or die, after our first year of marriage, in

1974, my dream came true. Jerry and I went to Sweden. We had a remarkable meeting with Eva. I cannot write or think of it without tears. Eva and I had written to one another for sixteen years. We knew one another well. We had exchanged many photos of each other, so we knew what the other one looked like. As Jerry and I entered the station in Bollnäs, I saw her from the train window. I stepped off the train, and we ran to each other, tears flowing freely. Finally, so finally, we had met! It seemed more like a reunion. We immediately became sisters as neither of us had one of our own.

In recent years, through our research into our common Ohman family lineage, Eva and I have become even closer, and the pond has become smaller. Our love for one another continues to grow, and now we talk (email) weekly. We have been friends-sisters-cousins for 62 years. Praise and gratitude are given to Eva Ohman Johansson, my second cousin, from Östersund, Sweden, who sat by my side in Macomb, Illinois, and together we translated the 78 letters written in old Swedish to modern English in twelve full days in May 2019. Eva and I interpreted the rich content verbatim. It was a difficult task. Neither of us knew the other's language well. We cried. We laughed. There were late nights and early morning starts. Our collaboration led to the writing of this book.

Two Ohmans consists of two biographical accounts written from the perspective of letters saved by my grandmother, Stina Ohman. The first collection, "Dearest Little Stina!" covers the years 1916 through 1954 and consists of letters written to Stina from family and friends in Sweden. The second, "Dear Mother:" is a series of letters written from 1938 to 1940 by my father, Leonard, to his mother, Stina, while he attended Pillsbury Military Academy in Owatonna,

Minnesota. These two collections are independent of each other, yet together, they are a story of cause and effect. Each account is poignant and speaks for itself.

The first collection contains the original letter translations from Swedish to English and my reflections. Stina wrote two of the letters; the others, she received. Each letter translation is prefaced by a brief introduction explaining where Stina is located, who wrote the letter, and the location from where it was written. Some letters were contained in envelopes and are noted; others were not. For clarification, additional details within the body of a letter are in italics within parentheses. Further comments in italics may be at the bottom of the page.

All credit is given to my grandmother, Stina, for saving the letters she so easily could have destroyed both pre and post immigration. I thank my father, Leonard, who also could have discarded the letters written in Swedish, for he left Sweden too young to learn to read the Swedish language.

To commemorate Stina's immigration occurring 100 years ago in March 1920, the effects on my father, and the immense impact it had on my life, the lives of my children, and those of future generations, I am compelled to write an account of what I learned and know to be true.

I could not keep this story to myself. For the sake of my father, it had to be told. My family needs to know the immigration story of Stina and Lennart Ohman.

The entirety of this life story is non-fiction and authentic.

Janet Ohman Lindsay

May 2019

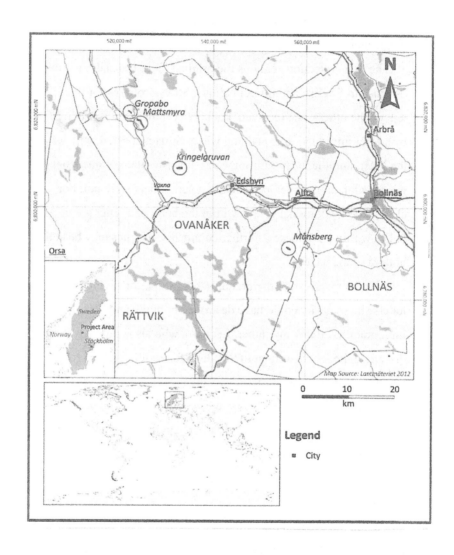

Map of Hälsingland Sweden

(Leading Edge Materials Corp. Public domain: online resource)

"Dearest Little Stina!"

Part One

Letters 1 - 25

21 December 1916 — 25 September 1921

Courtship

Flight

Immigration

Reflections

Note of Clarification

The spellings of Swedish proper names vary extensively. All spellings of names in the first collection, "Dearest Little Stina!" were left intact as they appeared in the Swedish letters. The spelling of "Karl" is interchangeable with "Carl." The same person may use both spellings. "Bengtzon" is spelled many different ways, as the writers of letters to Sven were uncertain of the spelling of his surname. Consequently, a phonetic guess was attempted.

The word "you" is occasionally capitalized in the middle of a sentence. This strategy was used by several of Stina's suitors to emphasize the importance of her role as the influential subject in a desired outcome.

Åke is pronounced (O kEE)

Arvid is pronounced (AR vid)

Bollnäs is pronounced (bull nes)

Edsbyn is pronounced (EEds bin)

Göthe is pronounced (yu ti)

Henrick is pronounced (hen rik)

Hillevi is pronounced (hil a vEE)

Leif is pronounced (LAf)

Lennart is pronounced (len art)

Nisse is pronounced (nis sEE)

Ohman is pronounced (O mun)

Singa is pronounced (sing a)

Stina is pronounced (stEE na)

21 December 1916

Letter 1

21 December 1916. To Stina Ohman, age 22, from Sven Bengtzon, age 21, Edsbyn, Sweden. *Edsbyn (population 4,000) is a small village four hours north of Stockholm. It is where the Carl E. Ohman (Stina's father, my great grandfather) homestead is located.*

Envelope: Fröken (Miss) Stina Ohman

             Edsbyn

B. *(Best)* Stina!

As agreed, we should have met tonight at 9:30.

When we decided this, I did not think how difficult it would be with all things to do so close to Christmas. These last days I have had to be here until 9:30, and the rest of the evenings before Christmas perhaps will be even worse. Please forgive me for postponing our meeting to a more suitable time.

Greetings, Sven

Stina and Sven
Sven is a clerk at the Edsbyn railroad station.

Authentic Letter 2

18 August 1917

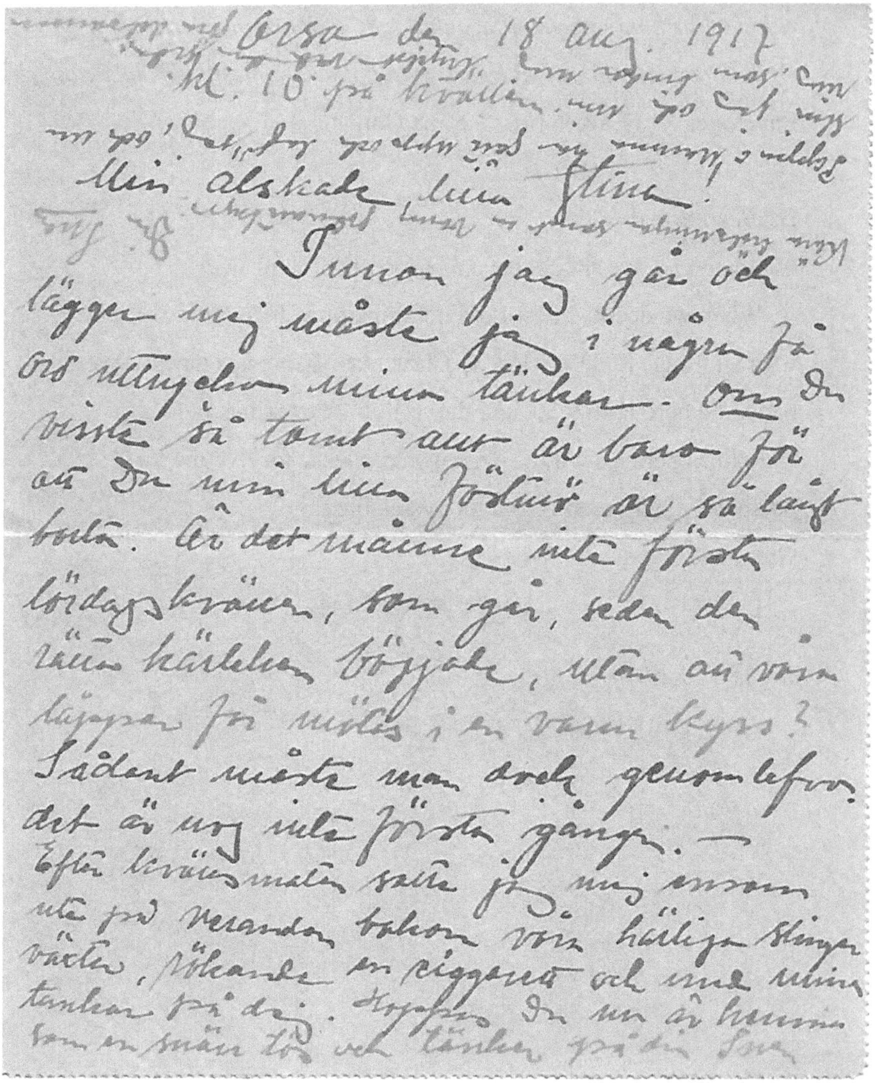
Orsa den 18 aug. 1917

Kl. 10 på kvällen.

Min älskade lilla Stina!

Innan jag går och lägger mig måste jag i några få ord uttrycka mina tankar. Om du visste så tomt allt är bara för att du min lilla fästmö är så långt borta. Är det månne inte första lördagskvällen, som går, sedan den rätta kärleken började, utan att våra läppar får mötas i en varm kyss? Sådant måste man dock genomlefva, det är nog inte första gången. — Efter kvällsmaten satte jag mig ensam ute på verandan bakom våra härliga slingerväxter, rökande en cigarett och vände mina tankar på dig. Kanske du nu är hemma som en snäll tös och tänker på din Sven

Letter 2

18 August 1917. Letter to Stina from Sven, Orsa, 10 PM.

Orsa, Sven's hometown, is a small village in Dalarna, one hour southwest of Edsbyn. Sven is visiting his parents.

Envelope: Fröken Stina Ohman

                 Edsbyn

Before I go to bed, I must express my thoughts in a few words. If you only knew how empty everything is since you, my little fiancé, are so far away. This is the first Saturday night since the real love began without our lips meeting in a warm kiss. Still, this you have to endure, and it might not be the last time.

After supper, I sat alone on the porch, behind our lovely twisted plants, smoking a cigarette. My thoughts were of you. I hope you are now at home like a nice girl, thinking of your Sven.

Ma and Pa have gone to bed, and here I am with my ring that binds me to you.

Dear greetings and a warm good night kiss.

Your Sven

Sven and Stina became engaged on July 12, 1917. They exchanged engagement rings on August 12, 1917.

Letter 3

10 September 1917. Letter to Stina from Sven, Edsbyn.

Envelope: Fröken Stina Ohman

              Edsbyn

My everything, for whom I am living and hoping.

Dearest little girl!

Because of today's strange call/conversation, I only have to tell you that I have to be with you tonight, as I feel this is the most dangerous night of them all. You have to be by my side – or else I cannot be calm. Accordingly, my heartfelt wish is to see you for a little while. I am so tired, but still, we have to work on our happy union day and night because without you, everything is so terrible.

A warm and loving greeting till we meet. I will call you soon.

Yours forever and truly, Sven

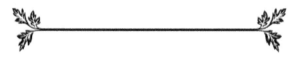

Letter 4

29 September 1917. Letter to Stina from Sven, Edsbyn.

Envelope: Fröken Stina Ohman

              Edsbyn

Dearest little Stina!

Please do not be sad any longer because of me, since you have enough of sad things apart from what happened. It was a little strange of you to so sharply say "good night" and to "thank" me for my expression, and not to hear my call to you, since I did not want to part from you that way. But, is all forgiven? I do not know if I will go home tomorrow or anywhere else. But I will certainly go, wherever it will be. If you do not want to bother with what I asked of you, please tell me, so I can turn elsewhere. The letter to my mother will be sent today no matter what. I am including your and my dear greetings. I am yours forever, whatever is in store for us. Together or apart.

Loving greetings from your Sven

It is unclear what happened to make Stina sad. We can assume Sven and Stina met for a short time and parted abruptly on unfavorable terms. Stina ignored Sven's call for her to return, leaving Sven uncertain of Stina's devotion.

Letter 5

9 October 1917. Letter to Stina from Sven, Edsbyn.

Envelope: Fröken Stina Ohman

                      Edsbyn

Envelope back: From Stina's Sven

(Inside letter, top): Our happy place and place where we got engaged. It is three days before the three-month anniversary of our engagement.

My very dear, beloved, and precious Stina!

How are you today? Your Sven is very good, is healthy but cold. Not because I am forgotten and left by my girl, but because I cannot do the kind of job that keeps me warm. I sent you an ad from the *Svenska Dagbladet* (*Swedish Daily Newspaper)* that is very like you. Don't you think? I will call you about four o'clock this afternoon.

Many dear greetings and even more warm kisses from your forever true, and today, inseparably in love, Sven

Letter 6

9 November 1917. Letter to Stina, from W.T. Heintges, Göteborg, Sweden. *Göteborg is on the southwest coast of Sweden. It is the largest city on Sweden's west coast and the main seaport for shipping goods through the North Sea to the Atlantic Ocean. Göteborg is a seven-hour drive from Edsbyn.*

Envelope: Stina Ohman
            Edsbyn
            Norrland

Envelope back: W.T. Heintges, Göteborg, Edinsgatan 19

Dear Stina!

Thank you so much for you letter! You cannot believe how happy I am that you are not angry with me although you had all the right to be.

The reason why I did not write to you, as I mentioned in my earlier letter, is that I was so sad about the bracelet and hoped I should find it, and not have to tell you about the sad event. You ask how it happened. I had put it in my pocket the night I got it from you. When I arrived to the military barracks in the evening, I put my coat in my wardrobe. In the morning when I went to take it out and return the bracelet, it was gone. You can imagine how upset I was. I immediately made a report to the commander and the police, who started to look for it. I went to the different stores where the thief might have pawned it, but had no luck. I suspect it was stolen at the barracks since both money and valuables had been stolen there. One was arrested for another theft and questioned, but he did not confess. The investigations went on, but so far without results. I really hope it will be found.

Did you really think I would have left for Germany without telling you? No, meine liebchen (*my love*); I could not be that hard. I can see that you are going to Stockholm again. I would have loved to see you there and talk to you, but I am not able to do so because of business. As I mentioned in my last letter, I will come in January (*1918*) again, and it would be nice if we could then meet and revive nice memories.

I have not seen Maggi since you were with us. It is hard to say anything about her because we met for such a short time, as you know. Thank you for kind regards from your sisters. Please send my greetings back to them.

What nice things are you doing during these days? The other day was Gustav Adolf-day, but the weather was terrible here. Have you any pictures that were taken of the group in Stockholm? It would be nice to have some as a memory!

Please send me some notes when you have the time.

Very best regards from your affectionate friend, W. T. Heintges

Gustav Adolf's Day is celebrated in Sweden each November 6 in memory of King Gustavus II Adolphus of Sweden who was killed on that date in 1632 at the Battle of Lutzen in the Thirty Years' War. He led an invasion of the Holy Roman Empire. The King was killed; however, the Swedish armies managed to successfully defeat their enemies. Gustav II Adolf is credited for establishing Sweden as one of the great powers of Europe for the next 100 years. (Wikipedia: online resource.)

Shortly after the above date, Stina went to Stockholm. She lived with the Moden family.

Letter 7

22 November 1917. Letter to Stina, Stockholm, from Sven, Bollnäs.

Bollnäs is a town one-half hour east of Edsbyn.

Envelope: Fröken Stina Ohman

                  c/o Modens

                  Tovastgatan 15

                  Stockholm

Envelope back: Sven Bengtzon

                  Railway Bureau

                  Bollnäs

Dear little Stina!

How are you? I hope you are not sick? I am worried since I have not heard anything from you. I hope you have not forgotten your Sven. That was the last you said, that you should not forget your own Sven. I am longing so much, sweet little Stina. Please can you write something for me here in my loneliness in Bollnäs? I would like to hear how you are. You were not feeling so good when I was there. Is it over now? Please tell me, so I do not have to be worried. Right now I am thinking of several terrible things, worrying and thinking that you are sick.

As you can understand your true Sven has not forgotten his lovely Stina, and *never* will. The most loving greetings and warm kisses from your forever in love and true Sven.

Sven has been promoted to Railway Inspector. He now lives and works in Bollnäs at the Railway Bureau.

Letter 8

24 November 1917. Letter to Stina, Stockholm, from Sven, Bollnäs.

Envelope: Fröken Stina Ohman

              c/o Modens

              Tovastgatan 15

              Stockholm

Envelope back: Sven Bengtzon

              Railway Bureau

              Bollnäs

Dear beloved and missed Stina!

How can you be so hard on me, not to contact me in any way, not a card or letter for over a week? Dear little you, please say something, so I do not have to be this worried. I only think you are sick, but hope for the best. I heard from Jussie that you were not so well, so I am now terribly worried. Are you still living in the same place? Have you received the buttons that you were wishing for? Do you remember your own fiancé? I am longing for a letter, but still more for you, little Stina.

Dearest greetings and many warm kisses from your forever dear and true Sven.

Jussie (Justina) is Stina's younger sister by three years.

Letter 9

26 February 1918. Draft letter to Mr. Mohlen (*not to be confused with the Moden family whom Stina lived with in Stockholm*), Bollnäs, from Sven, Bollnäs. *Sven gave a draft of the letter to Stina. He sent the same letter to Mr. Mohlen.*

DRAFT LETTER:

Mr. Mohlén, Bollnäs

Perhaps you still believe that I do not know about you flirting with my fiancé. I want you to know that I know everything. Other people have told me. I thought you were above such actions and thought you to be a better man. You know that Stina is engaged and also to whom. But you are still having secret meetings with her, even after our sharp conversation and your gentleman's promise to me. Don't you think that I know you have been in Stockholm and also invited her to a ball in Alfta? What do you really mean by this? Can you explain yourself, or do you think that you have a better right and longer love for her than me? I really do not think much of you, and I declare you my biggest enemy on this earth. You think you will succeed in robbing my fiancé away from me, but I will defend her with my life and have a full right to do so, as long as she is mine. It would be best if you avoid me since I cannot answer for what I would do if I met you. It was lucky for you that I could not come to the ball in Alfta, but too bad for me, for had I attended, you would then know whom I really am.

Apart from all this, I also want to mention your telephone calls, letters, and so on. I can now see your weak character. You think I will stand for all this? My patience is over, and a big hate is growing. There is nothing on earth with such a big difference as love and hate. My love for her is still unnaturally great, and my hate for you grows even more.

You really should be very ashamed, as I should be if I had secret meetings with another man's wife or fiancé. You are no longer in secret. Many people know about you. I think you now understand that it is not a good idea for you to share my fiancé, and perhaps wife, with me, your biggest enemy. This would not be good for either of us. Whatever you do, you will not win. STINA IS AND WILL STILL BE MINE. Perhaps in the future she will be my bride. But I suppose you do not understand this, and perhaps you will still continue. This is what I can expect from you.

You only make it difficult for Stina. She says she is not interested at all in you, and we would have a much better life without you interfering. Please mind your own business if you want to be a happy man. This is my advice. Don't ever think that you can be my friend.

Respectfully, Sven Bengtzon, Stina's fiancé

END OF DRAFT LETTER

Letter 10

28 February 1918. Letter to Sven, Bollnäs, from Mr. Mohlen, Bollnäs. *Sven sent this letter to Stina. Sven has written notes in red ink in the margins of this letter, items he wants to discuss with Stina.*

Sven's notes in red ink are in bold face type in the following translation.

Mr. Bengtsson
Bollnäs.

I have received your threat of yesterday. And I understand you think we are now done with this. However, I also have something to say about this matter that might influence you. You think that you are a better person than I, but you are hurting my reputation by accusing me of stealing your fiancé. It is a joke that you accuse me of approaching and flirting with Stina. You should say it is the other way around. At least that is closer to the truth. It is not my fault that you do not have the ability to keep your fiancé's love and faithfulness. If you could, your fiancé would not seek love elsewhere. Even if we say that I am the aggressor, it would be reasonable to assume your fiancé should not encourage another man, as she truly does. She is doing everything she can to attract me and keep me interested.

Stina ought to explain this.

What is meant by this? Is it true, Stina?

Regarding your unnatural love for her, I do not doubt this, yet there is strong evidence of problems in your relationship from both of you: one from a ball in Alfta, and one from an intimate relationship with a woman, a "so-called woman of the night" who was here in Bollnäs not too long ago. If you really love someone highly and purely, especially the one to whom you are betrothed, you do not give yourself to others. It seems, however, this is a common practice for both of you, to seek adventure elsewhere, instead of nurturing you own love for one another. If I were a woman and attracted to such a man who was unfaithful, and things like I mentioned above came to my knowledge while we were engaged, then I could not feel any other way than your fiancé says she feels for you, which is anything but love. The engagement period is the time when you must test your love for one another for the future.

Have you, Stina, described our relationship to Mr. Mohlen? Are you saying these things to Mohlen when you say you love me? Do you still love me when you say such things to Mohlen??

Regarding the letters I have written to your fiancé, please ask Stina for them so that you can read them. Yes, you really should do that. Then you would know a lot about your fiancé and our relationship to each other. Then you would not be able to say, as you assume, that I am pursuing Stina.

It is not necessary for me to see these letters. They are yours to keep.

I am not at all afraid of your threats. They do not impress me. I think they are only childish. Really, what should you do? Should you tell the world that your fiancé is betraying you or that she is silly enough to listen to possible flattery from another man? If so, you would look ridiculous. People in general know Stina too well and sadly enough not exactly from the beautiful side. You have said that I am a man of poor character, but, Sven, I have heard from the ladies in Bollnäs that you are a man of poor character and not popular among the women. Therefore, you are a poor judge of others. Do not judge others, and you will not be judged yourself. This is a very good rule to follow from the Bible. Therefore, you should be ashamed of your own guilt; I will take responsibility for my own acts. You should be ashamed of your fiancé. That is your area of concern.

Stina, I have been concerned about this for a long time, but I have been waiting for things to get better. However, this is not possible.

Your assumption and regret that I am not able to get a fiancé of my own is wrong, since even a woman who is already betrothed is asking for my friendship or even love.

So, you, Stina, are begging him for love and not he begging you for love???

I have no more to say about this. But I have enough proof to clear my name. I respect a woman's honor too much to say anything more.

"respect a woman's honor?" But he seems to hope for my fiancé!

Mr. Mohlen

Stina! Here you see the reason why I have not contacted you these past days. I have been half crazy with anger. Do you see here the result of the interaction between Mohlen (who claims you are asking for his love) and me? I do not want to judge after all of this, for, of course, I should believe my fiancé more than this idiot. You can't blame me for hating such a person. You have to explain and choose between us, so that it will end. I am not surprised if I should lose you (if you have loved another for so long). Actually, I noticed something in your face when we met

last Sunday, and then decided to investigate further, which I am glad I did.

To be continued …..

(Letter continues in red ink and is written on State Railways, Inspector's Expedition stationery. Perhaps Sven is now at his job at the railway station.)

I have understood for some time now that you have not been honest with me, and now I need a decision to know how to act. You may not love three *(?)*, and at the same time, me, as your betrothed. You have to finally decide. I cannot say anything greater than I have said before. My love is and has always been very deep, although this barbarian is trying to hurt me in your eyes. I think he has done this for a very long time and told you lies to make you leave me. Ok, you follow him, and I hope you will be happy. He insinuates that he, and not I, will be able to make you happy.

I had a letter from my mother, asking me to greet "my little, sweet Stina." She wants us to visit during Easter so that she can see you while she is alive. She does not know yet, that I am so unhappy with my Stina, but soon she must know. I have waited and waited for things to get better but now all hope is gone. I hope for your answer, together with the copy of the letter I sent to Mohlen that I absolutely want returned.

Greetings from a sad Sven.

P.S. I want both my and the idiot's letters returned if you are honest with me. I suppose you will call him tomorrow and blab behind the back of your Sven.

It is impossible for us to know to whom Sven is referring in his rebuke of Stina, "You may not love three, and at the same time me." W.T. Heintges appeared earlier as a suitor, and now, Mr. Mohlen may be considered the second. Stina's third suitor is unknown.

Sven was promoted to Railway Stationmaster in Edsbyn in July 1918. He moved to Stockholm for advanced education classes.

Letter 11

August 1918. Typed letter to Stina, Edsbyn, from an anonymous female writer.

Miss Ohman, Edsbyn,

I take the liberty to write a few lines to Miss Ohman. Forgive this question. Do you really believe that you shall win or forever own your "so-called" fiancé, Station Master, Sven Bengtsson, whom you are happy to still own just for fun?

I, and also other people, really suffer very much to see such a sweet and kind boy with such a promising future have such an overwhelming, beyond natural, and sincere love for you. He is truly in love with something that is not good for him. Forgive my eruption of anger, but you are only playing and betraying this poor man who sees nothing and knows nothing. You are playing with him, as well as many of us. Please choose another man, one of lesser worth than this young man.

It is irresponsible of you to fool such a good boy to whom you have been engaged and have owned. Good for you, but not for him. As I have heard, you have been engaged for a full year. If I were you, I would be so ashamed. I would not be able to show my face.

Do you not intend at all to make him happy and be serious with him? If not, let him go, unspoiled. Please let him go before he does something stupid. I will be happy to welcome him, and if I, in the future, may win him, I promise I will do everything possible to make him happy. He is, and will always be, my true, perfect man. So far, he does not know me well, but he will know who I am, and he will also know my decision to make him mine. I hope he will receive me with open arms, and I hope he will hear my warning, since he does not want to hear the warnings from others. I really can't stand to see him suffer and see the look of death on his face. Everyone else can see this as well. It's enough that he is grieving his mother's death very deeply.

You two fit so well together, and he can make you happy. But you don't seem to appreciate him, and you can't seem to behave. I'm sure you will regret this deeply when he is in my arms. It's him or no one.

I hope you do not want to have him. I do. I have been longing for him for so long and have admired him. If I will not meet him here,

I'm sure I will meet him in Stockholm, where I also will go in the beginning of September.

I do not at all have any regrets about this letter since I have studied your relationship and I have found that you do not value him at all. You will not know who I am until we see which of us will win him. Let us remain strangers and rivals. I'm sure you have more rivals than me.

"The one who longs for him and is in love with him."

Letter 12

5 September 1918. Letter to Stina's mother, Kerstin, Edsbyn, from Sven, Stockholm. *Sven is taking classes in Stockholm. His mother died a month ago, in August 1918. The stationery Sven uses is bordered in black as an outward show of mourning. He uses the endearing terms of "Aunt" and "Uncle" when referring to Stina's parents, although the Bengtzon and Ohman families are not related. This letter was in Stina's possession. Kerstin gave it to Stina.*

My dear, little Aunt!

As I suppose my visits to Edsbyn will not continue and we will not meet again, I would just like to convey my heartfelt thanks for everything that we have experienced together. Thank you dear, sweet Aunt! I also ask you to convey my heartfelt thanks to Uncle.

I hope you will not forget me, as Stina seems to be able to do so without any problem. Please do not say a single word to Stina about this, since I, so far, have not been able to find the strength to tell her about my decision. When I leave Bollnäs next Tuesday, I hope I will be strong enough to tell her my decision, which is now becoming more and more clear. I do not want to be unhappy and miserable any more, even if it is very hard to leave Stina forever since I have loved her truly for so long. I think I will be happier if I do this. I do not want to be unhappy, and without happiness, my life is nothing.

She is still seeing this most abominable young man in Edsbyn, the Metalsmith Henning Persson, a person I would never like to know, and such a man with whom your daughter Stina, my fiancé, is involved. This means she does not value her fiancé, me, at all. People say it looks more as if she were engaged to this man and not to me. Every night they are out together. Last night, they sneaked out from their other friends at three o'clock in the morning. I wonder what they did then. I fear the worst.

So my decision is not to force myself any longer on Stina, since she is showing very clearly that she does not love me any longer, but she favors others, perhaps too many.

I cannot be here any longer and be mocked. I am leaving Edsbyn for some other place where they do not know me. It will be hard to forget the girl I have loved for five years, the one I have offered myself to as a true fiancé without the least appreciation for what I have given.

For me, it seems that life should be one sorrow after another. No comfort. No one with whom to share sorrows and burdens. The whole world is making fun of me, the one who has been rejected.

I ask myself each day, <u>why?</u> <u>Why</u> did I ever meet Stina? Why did I give her my young heart? She has not thought about my feelings, but has made fun of me until she now knows that I am deeply in love with her. Stina is afraid of getting caught by me. She decided it was the right time to leave me grieving to my fate and never more acknowledge me. I do not know what I have done wrong. I think I have always been kind and sweet to her. Yes, it will be a hard time now to forget and bury what once was, but I hope my good nature will help. I have to force myself to forget. Everything from yesterday was just a fairy tale. I am sure fate will punish the one who has acted wrongly.

I do not know how I will be able to finish my coursework and education here in Stockholm now with all this sorrow. But perhaps it is also good to have something else on my mind. I hope you will not be sad over this. I do not want that. My heart feels a little easier now that I have told you, but I still have much more to tell, although it is too complicated in a letter. It might be a whole novel. But I did want to tell you since I have always appreciated you so much and can never forget you, or Stina.

I shall follow Stina's life to see if the happy one or perhaps unhappy one will be the person I so much despise. I thought Stina would choose one of the better boys, but apparently not. She apparently loves him much more than the one she has been engaged to for over a year and now has thrown away.

At last and finally, for the last time, thank you for what could have been, and good-bye dear, sweet Aunt.

With sadness and distress,

Sven

Perhaps Henning Persson is the third suitor whom Sven refers to in his letter of 28 February 1918.

Stina and Sven first met in 1913 when Stina was 19 and Sven was 18. Sven has broken their engagement.

Sven thought his drama and heartache with Stina would make a good novel!

Letter 13

1 October 1918. Letter to Kerstin, Stina's mother, from Sven, Stockholm. *This letter was in Stina's possession. Kerstin gave it to Stina. The letter and envelope have a black border. Sven is still mourning his mother's death.*

Envelope: Fru (*Mrs.*) Kerstin Ohman

Edsbyn

Dear Aunt!

Since I am now healthy enough to be able to hold a pen, I would like to write you some lines. Stina has asked me to do so.

Perhaps you do not know that I have been very ill for a week? I have had the Spanish flu. Today is the first day I am not in bed and have also been able to go outside for a while. Stina has visited me a couple of times while I was in bed. But now she is also sick with a temperature of 40 degrees (*104 degrees F*). Too many people have been sick with the Spanish flu lately.

I have just come home from Stina. She is with the Moden family, and they are taking good care of her. Please do not get worried Aunt. I am visiting her at least two times a day and as often as my time allows. If she should get worse, they will tell me immediately, but I should not think so. If it should happen, I will inform you at once via the telegraph. I hope Aunt is not worried. You know that I am here. **I can never forget Stina,** and I am as caring to her as you are.

I myself was very sick but have recovered, and I hope I did not get up too early since the aftereffects can also be bad. It was lucky we did not get sick at the same time. I promise to take care of her as best as I can. Still, I am very much in love with her, and she is the one who means the most to me since my mother died.

My aunt, my mother's sister, who takes care of the house in Dalarna since Mother's death, is here in Stockholm. We will, together, visit Stina tonight about 9:00. She has been in Södertälje for her father's funeral (my grandfather), who was buried last Sunday. I was ill and could not attend. Just think of it, dear Aunt, now I have three close people who have died: Mother, my uncle on Mother's side, and my grandfather. I think it is now enough, one sad thing after another.

Stina is sending her love to her little mama. Also, I send greetings to Uncle.

Yours, Sven

We can assume Sven's family members fell victim to the Spanish flu.
The 1918-1920 pandemic infected 500 million people worldwide,
one-third of the world's population at the time. The death toll is
estimated to have been between 20 and 50 million lives.
(History.com: online resource).

It was a like time. As this book goes to print, one-hundred years
after the Spanish flu pandemic, the coronavirus Covid-19 pandemic
of 2019-2021 has infected millions of people worldwide claiming
over one million deaths. (Elflein. Statista.com: online resource).

Letter 14

28 November 2018. Letter to Stina's mother, Kerstin, from Sven,
Stockholm. *Kerstin gave this letter to Stina.*

Envelope: Fru Kerstin Ohman

                Edsbyn

Envelope back: Sven Bengtzon

                1 Torresgatan 84 III

                Stockholm

Dear little Aunt!

Forgive me for returning to you with my sad things. You must
not look upon this as gossip or upon me as evil, but I think a nice

mother like you has to be told certain things. I think it would not be right to withhold certain things from you.

Since Stina came here, we have not been together for a single moment in happiness and joy. I have informed her that I do not think I can be happy with her and have told her hundreds of times that we need to break our relationship. She has tormented me long enough. I am all destroyed in my head.

She quit her job at Miss Tapper's nearly a month ago, but she is still here. She says she has lent 500 crowns to a person who, to my knowledge, is not a good man. She is out every night in restaurants, and sometimes with different men every night. She smokes and drinks a lot. When I sometimes see her, she looks very tired. Sometimes she contacts me by a call or comes to me, asking me to forgive her. She says I am the only one who can save her. But dear Aunt, I cannot do this anymore. I have been very patient, and I cannot take it anymore. She has no morals. I have been very much in love with her, and she has been forgiven many times, but I cannot stand it anymore. I must forget. I think I will still have to cry many times before I can forget her. I think you will also be sad, but I will be even more, always. I thought she was the girl who would make me happy.

I have seen a sad letter from her correspondence with Henning Persson, and I think everything is getting even sadder. You should only know how much I am grieving over Stina. I do not think I can show myself in Edsbyn. I cannot get the ring back; she is still wearing it. Please, dear Aunt, save Stina from misery. That is my absolute wish.

My heartfelt greetings to Uncle and the girls (*Stina's sisters*).

Sven

Letter 15

1 December 1918 (*three days later*). Letter to Stina's mother, Kerstin, from Sven, Stockholm. *Kerstin gave this letter to Stina.*

Envelope: Fru Kerstin Ohman

              Edsbyn

Dear Aunt!

In regard to my last letter and what has happened since, I feel I would like to add something. Probably to her great luck, this morning Stina has told me that she is going to go live with Anna. Once again, she has succeeded to make me fall for her burning wishes, and because of my love and weakness for her, I will give it a try once more. She has promised me to be forever truthful and to be a good girl and never break up with me again.

I therefore beg you, dear Aunt, for my sake, to keep an eye on her and remind her of her promises to me. You know that I have to travel a lot and I cannot be with her all the time, which, of course, would have been the best. When she comes home, please make her understand my serious, very serious demands. Perhaps we can be happy at last. Stina must be as much in love with me as I am in love with her. We have been together the last two evenings, and she has promised me a lot. If she should play with me again, it will be terrible, and I think I will go mad. So, dear Aunt, you must understand the seriousness of this.

Dear Aunt, please do not mention to Stina what I have told you because then it will be no good. You should punish her, but don't get me involved. I hope you have good news for me the next time we meet. She has said she will now go home and start to seriously plan for our future so that we can soon be married. Please Aunt, help me to be happy if you do not have anything against it. Greetings to Uncle and the others,
Dear greetings, Sven

Sven and Stina renew their love for one another and their fidelity. They once again become engaged.

Anna is Stina's younger sister by five years. Anna lives in Bredgrind, south of Stockholm.

Letter 16
22 February 1920 (*one year, two months later*). Letter to Stina, Göteborg, from K.E. (*Karl Eriksson*), Edsbyn. *Stina became pregnant in November 1919. At the time of this letter, she was in Göteborg, Sweden's seaport on the southwest coast, preparing for her voyage to the United States.*

On the back of the envelope, below the return address of Oskar Nilsson, written diagonally in pencil are the words, "Send the letter to Karl if you think it is appropriate." I believe this implies that the letter can be returned to Karl Eriksson if there is assurance that its delivery can be secretly concealed. I also believe this was penciled by Karl himself. This letter has no postmark and was never mailed. It was probably handed to Stina. Karl Eriksson's name does not appear on the outside of the sealed envelope. He signs with his initials at the bottom of the last page of the letter.

Envelope: Fröken Stina Ohman

             c/o Johansson

             Oliverdalsgatan 3

             Göteborg

Envelope back: Oskar Nilsson

             Box 26

             Edsbyn

My very dear one!

If you leave Sweden now, it will be very difficult for me to also come. I think my father will stop me from going. Stina, you have asked me not to make trouble. If we are supposed to be together, no one can stop this. Father says he can see that I am in love, but I think he will stop me. I do not know if he can do that. So, would it be possible for you to stay in Sweden somewhere so that I can find you easily? Or else you will have to come back, which would be difficult for you.

If you go, I will do my utmost to follow you. If it will not be possible, you have to come back to **me**, if you so desire, which I think you want. If you should go and then turn back at once, just for show . . . But you know what is best to do. Just think if we should not meet again. Could you stand this? You know Hilding (*a male friend*). He now knows, but it will not go further between us here at home. You mentioned that we should keep it to ourselves, since other people might not know how it is. I think when this is past, I can agree with you.

You want me to stay so that I am well before I go. I can keep the color of my face for the people's sake. I hope my illness is soon over. You must write and answer me before you leave Sweden. Can you part from me forever? You are happy, as you have already made your decision to leave. So much to do before I can leave. If so, I will absolutely be yours. I still have my hope. I will never forget you. Please answer me with a thought.

Yours most truly.

The warmest heartfelt greetings from K.E.

This letter explains the complicated position Karl is in. Hilding knows that Stina is pregnant and that Karl is the father of her child.

Letter 17

22 February 1920. Letter to Carl Walhmark, Chicago, from Hildemar Widell, Edsbyn. *This letter has no postmark and was never mailed. It was probably handed to Stina to deliver to Carl Walhmark when she found him in Chicago. Since it was still in her possession, we can assume he never received it.*

Envelope: Mr. C. A. Walhmark

850 W 59th St.

Chicago, Ill. U.S.A.

Dear Karl!

I received no answer to my letter of November 1919. If you got it, do not answer to the address I mentioned in that letter. She has left and will probably be looking for you. If you could do something for my journey to America, I would be most grateful. Could you just send me a letter saying that you want me to come and that I could buy some land there? Please, then, recommend several places, not one in particular. Or, perhaps, I could start a business in some endeavor that would be possible during the first years. This would show I have an acquaintance in America and a reason to leave Sweden and be important. Please find suggestions before answering my letter. It will be much easier here in Sweden if I have a letter from a friend asking me to come. I have written to you before, but perhaps you have not received it. If you got the letter and do not want to deal with it, I will still be your friend. But please answer anyway, even if you do not want to handle this matter.

I am very concerned about my previous letter to you that was addressed to Stina Öhman, who will look you up. She travels from

Sweden on February 25, 1920. Her first address is Miss Stina
Öhman, c/o Mrs. H. Gustafsson, Star Route, Rhinelander,
Wisconsin, USA. Later it will be Stina Öhman, c/o Mrs. Anna
Blom, 3018 Pittsburg St, Spokane, Washington, USA. Please
excuse me for troubling you; I hope you do not mind that I ask this
favor of you.

I am well and hope you are the same.

Yours sincerely,
Hildemar Widell
Edsbyn (my address)
If you have received my last letter, please do not answer it, but
please tell me if you have received it.

*Hildemar Widell is a prospector looking for land to purchase or a
new business venture. He is eager to get to America.*

*It must be noted that this letter has the same date as Karl Eriksson's
letter to Stina. Both letters are written on identical stationery with
dark purple paper lined envelopes and identical handwriting script.*

Flowers were given to Stina in February 1920, prior to her leaving Edsbyn to travel to the seaport town of Göteborg where she boarded the ship Stockholm to travel to the United States.

The card within the bouquet read:

I bid you a tender farewell with these flowers.
As tender, as tender as no one else.
Sweet thoughts come from my heart,
hoping we will soon meet in the foreign country.
H.W.   K.E.

On March 3, 1920, Kristina Ohman set sail from Göteborg, Sweden, on the passenger ship Stockholm. The ship's voyage across the Atlantic Ocean took thirteen days. It must have been a grueling voyage for a young woman four months pregnant. Stina viewed the Statue of Liberty as she entered the USA through the New York Harbor Port of Arrival. We can only imagine her anticipation, fears, and emotions. No doubt standing in the massive line to be processed caused anxiety: "How will it be to be questioned by the authorities? Will I understand their directives? How can I prepare? Will I be accepted or detained? Will I pass the test?" Her processing took place on Ellis Island by the United States Immigration Service on March 16, 1920, the day she arrived. Her name appears in the Ledger Book, "LIST OR MANIFEST OF ALIEN PASSENGERS FOR THE UNITED STATES IMMIGRATION OFFICER AT PORT OF ARRIVAL," List 10, page 32, Line 30, dated March 16, 1920. She was alone, 26 years old, spoke no English, knew no one, and was pregnant. She was in good health and had US $170.00 in her pocket. Her sponsor was listed as Cousin Eric Ohman, and her final destination was Minneapolis, Minnesota.

Stina's father purchased her travel ticket to America. She was an embarrassment to her highly regarded family, as well as to the Hildemar Widell family. Carl Ohman did not want his daughter to continue her pregnancy in Edsbyn. It is said by family members that both Carl and Hildemar financed her start of a new life in the United States.

LIST OR MANIFEST OF ALIEN PASSENGERS
FOR THE UNITED STATES IMMIGRATION OFFICER
AT PORT OF ARRIVAL
Page 32 A
Left page of Ledger Book
(see book backgrounds of front cover and back cover)

QUESTIONS ASKED OF ALIEN:	ALIEN'S RESPONSES:
1. No. on List.	30
2. HEAD TAX STATUS	X
3. Family Name.	Ohman
Given Name.	Kristina
4. Age.	25 *(actually 26)*
5. Sex.	F
6. Married or Single.	S
7. Calling or Occupation.	Milliner
8. Read.	Yes
Language.	Swedish
Write.	Yes
9. Nationality.	Swedish
10. Race or People.	Swedish
11. Last permanent residence. Country.	Sweden
City or Town.	Edsbyn
12. The name and complete address of	
nearest relative or friend in country	Father: Carl Ohman
whence alien came.	Edsbyn

Ellis Island Questioning and Inspection Checklist

39

LIST OR MANIFEST OF ALIEN PASSENGERS
FOR THE UNITED STATES IMMIGRATION OFFICER
AT PORT OF ARRIVAL
Page 32 B
Right page of Ledger Book

QUESTIONS ASKED OF ALIEN: ALIEN'S RESPONSES:

13. Final Destination. State.   Minnesota
    City or town.   Minneapolis

14. No. on List.   30

15. Whether having a ticket to
    such final destination.   No

16. By whom was passage paid?   Self

17. Whether in possession of $50.
    and if less, how much?   170

18. Whether ever before In the United
    States; and if so, when and where?   No

19. Whether going to join a relative   Cousin Eric Ohman
    or friend; and if so, what relative   1439 S St.
    or friend, and his name and   Minneapolis, Minn.
    complete address.

20. Purpose of coming to the United States:
    Whether alien intends to return to
    country whence he came after engaging
    temporarily in laboring pursuits in the
    United States.   Yes
    Length of time alien will remain in
    United States.   3 yrs
    Whether alien intends to become
    a citizen of the United States.   No

LIST OR MANIFEST OF ALIEN PASSENGERS
FOR THE UNITED STATES IMMIGRATION OFFICER
AT PORT OF ARRIVAL
Page 32 B
Right page of Ledger Book (continued)

QUESTIONS ASKED OF ALIEN: ALIEN'S RESPONSES:

21. Whether ever been in prison,
charity almshouse, or insane asylum.   No

22. Whether a polygamist.   No

23. Whether an anarchist.   No

24. Whether a person who believes in or advocates the
overthrow by force or violence of the Government of the
United States or of all forms of law, or who disbelieves in or is
opposed to organized government, or who advocates the
assassination of public officials, or who advocates or teaches the
unlawful destruction of property, or is a member of or affiliated
with any organization entertaining and teaching disbelief in or
opposition to organized government, or who advocates or
teaches the duty, necessity or propriety of the unlawful
assaulting or killing of any officer or officers, either of specific
individuals or of officers generally, of the government of the
United States or of any other organized government because of
his or their official character.

    No

25. Whether coming to America to enter
the labor force.   No

26. Whether alien had been previously
deported.   No

27. Condition of health, mental and
physical.   Good

QUESTIONS ASKED OF ALIEN: ALIEN'S RESPONSES:

28. Deformed or crippled.
Nature, length of time, and cause.   No

29. Height. Feet. Inches.   6 -

30. Complexion.   Fair

31. Color of hair.   Brown
    Color of eyes.   Blue

32. Marks of Identification.   None

33. Place of Birth. Country.   Sweden
    City or town.   Edsbyn

Edmund A. Burke, Inspector/Processing Agent, signed and dated

(3/16/20) the bottom of the left ledger page 32A.

Stina wrote this promissory note. She arrived in Minneapolis and lived with her cousin, Erik Ohman and his wife, Berta. Stina lent Erik 550 Swedish Kronars (US $97.00) to help Erik and Berta in their permanent move back to Sweden. Erik wrote that he would send Stina the equivalent in U.S. dollars at the prevailing rate of exchange upon his arrival in Sweden. The note is dated April 19, 1920, and is signed by Erik Ohman.

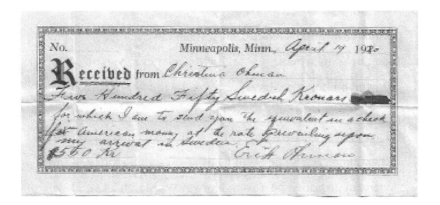

Letter 18

20 April 1920. Letter to Stina, Rhinelander, Wisconsin, from Karl Eriksson, Edsbyn.

Karl's name does not appear on the outside of the envelope. His signature and address c/o Oskar Nilsson, Edsbyn, Box 26, is at the bottom of the last page of the letter.

Envelope: Miss Stina Ohman

           c/o Mrs. Helga Gustafsson (*wife of Karl Gustafsson*)

           Robbins Route

           Rhinelander

           Wisconsin

           USA

Best Stina!

I have awaited a letter from you but have not received any, so I do not know where you are. I wrote a letter to you on March 20, which I hope you have received. I will be traveling on May 15 if nothing gets in the way. I am working on a passport, which I have sent to Gavle today. I will go to Stockholm on March 24 (?) and hope everything will be ok. I am writing today, so my letter can go with a boat from Norway on March 24 (?). I will arrange some other things when I go to Stockholm.

I will travel on the boat Drottningholm that leaves on May 15. I will then go directly to Gustafsson's in Rhinelander. If it is possible, perhaps you could meet me in New York, but only if you think it will be ok for you. Drottningholm is smaller than the

Stockholm, the ship you traveled on. The Stockholm will leave about June 1. I suppose you have read about the Stockholm when it sailed back to Sweden. I might wait and sail with the Stockholm, instead, but, you will have already received this letter, with the boat leaving on May 15.

When we meet, I will tell you everything. Now, I only want to tell you that your family is well. I have not spoken to them. My family is also well and will manage without me. I hope you are also well. I am forever true to you and hope you will not forget me. Soon we will meet again. What a meeting!

I will end now with many heartfelt greetings unto death, truly. Please do not give up on me.

Respectfully, Karl Eriksson.

Address: Oskar Nilsson

      Box 26

      Edsbyn

I will get your letter if you write directly to Oskar.

I question whether Stina actually went to Rhinelander, Wisconsin. I believe she traveled directly to Minneapolis, to her cousin, Erik Ohman's residence, which she stated as her final destination when processed at Ellis Island. Erik signed the promissory note in Stina's presence in Minneapolis on April 19, the day before this letter from Karl was written and mailed from Sweden. Stina would not have received this letter addressed to her in Rhinelander. I believe she received it some time later, and it was hand delivered by someone unknown to us.

Shortly after April 19, Erik Ohman and his family left Minneapolis and returned to Edsbyn. Stina then moved to the Eric and Signe Persson home.

Receipt

Minneapolis the 11 May 1920. *(Written by Stina.)*
Today Signe Persson acknowledges receipt of 60 dollars from Stina Ohman. This note verifies payment.

Mrs. Signe Persson

This receipt verified a rent payment to the Perssons. The Eric Persson family was originally from Edsbyn. Signe Persson was Stina's first cousin on her mother's side. Stina was six months pregnant.

Letter 19

15 May 1920. Letter to Stina, Minneapolis, from Karl Eriksson, Edsbyn.

Envelope: Miss Stina Ohman
              c/o Mr. E. Persson
              3250 6th St N
              Minneapolis
              Minnesota
              USA

Dear!

I have now done my part. I cannot come. Will you come home to Sweden? I have admitted to your father. If you stay in the U.S., I will find myself alone. I am at your disposal. Your father asked the question, and I said yes. I am divorced from the other. Now you have to choose. There might come a letter to you to try to break it up between you and me.

If you wish to come home, please stay somewhere where others will not know. I do not have any address right now, so you will have to ask where I am when you arrive. Please come soon. If you might write something, Oskar's address is c/o Dalkvist, Tundelgatan 1, Stockholm. If I do not hear anything from you during the next two months, I will understand that you are fine without me, and I will not arrange anything for you. If you still care for me, please send a very brief telegram with the following: Coming or Not Coming, Address, and send to Telegraph Station, Vallsta. You know the address (Eriksson, Söderhamn). Perhaps also Arbrå and Hälsingland. I have sent letters 2 and 3 to H. Gustafsson in America. Also, I sent you a telegram with an answer paid for, but have not heard back from you. I now have this address for you and hope you will receive this letter. I will try to figure out when a telegram could be sent from you and check with Vallsta to see if anything has come.

I think they are very concerned about you being in America and want you to come home. Please come home anyway. Do not bother about me. I shall not bring you any harm if you do not want to know me. But if you still care about me; that you should wait for 10-20 years, I am here. Please excuse my bad writing.

Many dear greetings. Good Bye.

Yours, Karl Eriksson

You can only reach me at Oskar Nilsson, c/o Dahlkvist, Tundelgatan 1, Stockholm.

Letter 20

30 November 1920 (midnight). Letter to Stina, Minneapolis, from Sven, Bollnäs.

This is a registered letter mailed from Edsbyn on 1 December 1920; received and stamped in New York, New York, on 20 December 1920; received and stamped in Minneapolis, Minnesota, on December 23; and again in Minneapolis, Minnesota, on December 24. Final stamp on envelope is Minneapolis, Minnesota, on January 10, 1921.

Envelope: Miss Stina Ohman

                 409 - 31st Ave North

                 Minneapolis

                 Minnesota

                 U.S.A.

Envelope back: Sender: Sven Bengtzon

                 Box 6

                 Bollnäs

                 Sweden

Only you, highly beloved!

Merry Christmas, my lovely girl wherever you are. I really hope you will receive this letter before Christmas, our greatest feast of the year. I hope you will have a nice day and not miss your dear ones too much. I want to give you a hot kiss on your little mouth. I try to be as close as possible to you on this day. I will kiss your photo warmly and dream that you are in my open arms. Can you understand how much I love you, my little dear one? It is not possible to show you my unbelievably deep feelings through a letter. It is very hard the way it is now. I can only dream, and I also now believe that my dream will come true that some day you are standing right in front of me. When you, on this day, let your thoughts fly over to your boy, Sven, here at home, please also think of our future, and what it will become, and what you have promised me, and what it all includes. I think you quite understand what I mean. Together with this letter I send you a little gift, very small but heartfelt. Only some Swedish Christmas magazines and a Swedish calendar for 1921, since you do not have that. I hope you will enjoy it. I have made some small notes on the calendar, and I hope you will make them come true, according to our agreement and your promises to me.

I want to thank you dearly for your letter that you dated as No. 13, although to me it is No. 11 (I suppose you have counted wrongly, little Stina). It is dated 6 November, and I got it the other day. How many letters do you have from me, including this one? Please tell me because I cannot count them any longer. I send you letters so often, but when my father died I did not write for a week. That must be forgiven. When you wrote your letter you did not know at all what had happened, but now you know. This is the way it is, little gold, when we are so far apart. I, myself, could die and would be buried without you knowing it. But let us hope it will not happen on either side of the sea. You said you had a dream with a flag at half-mast, and that actually was true. It was your own father-in-law *(Sven's father)* who died. You are now without both mother and father-in-law and will only get a brother-in-law. But why do you say that "I will put a bullet in your head?" I do not understand where you got this idea. I could never do that, but perhaps to both of us at the same time— if I were again terribly unhappy or if something went wrong with us again, and I could not find any way out.

One of the magazines I bought, *Home Home,* made me think of you and our home. Therefore, you must come home as we have agreed so that our little home can be ready for next Christmas if we are healthy, which I hope. Next Christmas, little Stina, we will spend our first Christmas in a sweet home, surrounded by warm family love. I have a very strong longing for this. Please let me not wait long in vain. You can understand how my Christmas is, without both Mother and Father, who have done all for their children to spread Christmas joy. I do not dare to compare old Christmases with this, since it will then be even worse. I am thinking of the joyful Christmases we have had in our beloved home that will never come back. How hard it is. But I hope I now own my little Stina completely, and that I can have you with me. You are now my only consolation—please come home soon to your lonely Sven. I do not think you can go against me. If you hurt me now, I cannot be healed, but I do not think you would want to do that. We should not talk about such terrible things. We must think such bad things cannot happen any longer. If I should hear something terrible about you after we have married, I would not know what to do. Why shall we talk about such things, but I still want to tell you how I feel. We must be counted as very lucky that we can have a clean conscience. It is madness to plant a thorn among such lovely red roses.

Are you now very, very happy to receive my letter? You said that nothing in the world makes you as happy as my letters. Are you now very happy with the boy, Sven, you have selected, my dear?

You should see the way I sit here, with a blanket around my legs and back. It is so very cold in my room. They are so stingy with the fires. I must be careful not to get a sore throat, which I so easily get. The clock is now 12:30 in the night, and everything is so silent. If (a big if) you were here with me, Stina, do you know what we would do? I think you are now laughing at me. Yes, then we would both go under the blanket to warm each other, tightly wrapped around each other. I dare not think such thoughts now, but they will return. I comfort myself. Is that not true?

Yesterday, I traveled to Voxna for a job, and then I slept in the same room as we once did after a ball (It was a sad remembrance. Do you remember?). We also stayed there another time (also not so nice for me). All these thoughts came up when I was there, and I started to long so intensely for you. Yes, we two have a lot in common, and it would be very hard if we could not marry soon. It is only with me that you have been so close, and why should I then not have you? I am the only one that has a right to have these thoughts. Is it not so?

You asked me once, and I am now willing to answer, regarding a business you would like to handle, a shop, when we get married. It is very nice of you to ask, and I think highly of you because of this. It is nice of you to help me with the income. But I want to ask you, do you think you would then still have time for our home as a good wife? I will of course do whatever I can. Anyhow, this is not something urgent. We can talk about it when you come home although I am not at all together negative. But I do not like that you start something where you are now, in the U.S., since you should be coming home to me soon. You could instead take the time, if you have it, to make things for our home, like you earlier talked about. Why do you not mention that now? Have you stopped preparing for us? We will see what you have had the time to do when you come home.

You still talk a lot about a certain pastor. That car ride, "a Friday night." I do not think you should have mentioned this to me. I should not worry about this since you now ought to know what you can and cannot do. I trust you now. If I should have mentioned something like that to you, I do not think you would have liked it.

Am I right? I have done nothing of the kind, I only meet people that are good for me and us. I am not interested in ladies here. Please do not mind my little-intentioned remark.

I agree with the wish in your letter that we will soon see each other and kiss each other for real and not via paper. We will have to work hard to achieve this goal.

Thousands of warm Christmas kisses from your own Sven. Greetings from your home. They are all well.

Tell me if the letter arrived safely. Were the magazines damaged? I did my best to make a good package. Did you receive the letter in time for Christmas?

Sven is not aware that Stina has a three-month-old son, Lennart, born August 15, 1920.

Letter 21

1 December 1920. Letter to Stina, Minneapolis, from her father, Carl E. Ohman, Edsbyn. *This is a registered, special-delivery letter; received and stamped in Saint Paul, Minnesota, and Minneapolis, Minnesota, on December 24, 1920.*

Envelope (*typed*):   Miss Stina Öhman
409-31 St Ave North

Minneapolis

Minnesota

U. S. A.

The postmaster crossed out the above address and the following
address was penciled on the front: 1044 – 20th Ave. S. E.

Dear Stina!

I do not know if you want any letter from me. You know my
weakness for you although I sometimes have been hard on you.
There has not been a day since you left that I have not been sad.
You were the sun of our home. Now you are not here anymore, but
you are shining in a far away country. Dear little Stina, this summer
I have been to several places in Skagen where you were with me as
a child. I especially was reminded of you at one place, and I sat
down and cried. There are so many things that remind me of you,
and just think of the great sorrow we have now over you. But
please, dear Stina, you must be happy and not sad. This was your
fate, and even if it seems very hard right now, it might be the best
and a salvation from what might have been much worse.

Right now I am sitting alone thinking of you and your Christmas
happiness and have to write to you, so you will receive my
Christmas greeting in time. Mother is lying down and does not feel
well. Nelly is at Emma's house weaving carpets. Åke is playing a
clarinet that the milk assistant owns (we now have a milk can here
that you perhaps do not know about). The others are out skating.
The clock is now half past 8:00 in the evening. Everything is as
usual, and we are healthy.

I have taken back the deposit I made to purchase two cars this summer, as I think you know since I did not have an answer from you. Please write something to me. It hurts me when I hear that others have received letters from you, but not I. Please forgive me, my Stina. I end with a dear Christmas greeting and my usual gift for you. We will also reserve a place for you at the Christmas dinner table in case we would have the joy that you should come. Oh, what a Christmas joy that would be, everything like before. It would be divine.

Good and happy and carefree Christmas!

Pappa

(2 Christmas presents)

P.S. Erjes' son, Lars, drowned last Saturday night as he went home from work at 4:00 PM. He was 29 years old. (*We can assume Lars was crossing a frozen stream and broke through thin ice.*)

Skagen is a popular vacation town in Denmark.

Letter 22

2 February 1921. Letter to Stina, Minneapolis, from cousin Erik Ohman, Edsbyn. *Letter is written on company letterhead: Erik Öhman, Metal Forge, Edsbyn. The letter indicated ten cents postage*

due and was postmarked in Edsbyn, New York City, and Minneapolis.

Envelope: Miss Stina Ohman

                  1044 – 20th Av S.E.

                  Minneapolis

                  Minnesota

                  U. S. A.

Return address: Erik Ohman

                  Smidesverkstad

                  Edsbyn

Best, dear cousin Stina!

I have now got your address, so I am able to write to you. We have received two letters from you, but you have not written any return address. Eric and Signe Persson have also moved, so I did not know their address either. I wrote Swanson some time ago, but he did not know your address. I used your money during the autumn since it was very hard here to get money from the bank, but now it is a little better. I am going to send your money around the 15th of this month. I will go to Bollnäs and arrange it from there, so nobody will know here. The dollar is sinking, so it is good for you that you have not yet received the money. I will check to see if it is cheaper to buy dollars at the post office. The exchange is now 4.50. But it has been over 5.00 since this summer. We have been thinking of you and felt very bad since you have not received the money, but we hope you have still been coping and have friends. I will send the money to this address and, at the same time, write Swanson in case you are not there. If I do not make the exchange in the post office, I will send a check with a loose letter, so you are sure to get it.

When writing this, I am thinking that it is a year since you were here in Edsbyn, and I was sick. So little you knew then what would happen. But I think it might still be good for you to prepare for the future and for eternity. It is for eternity that we must prepare. The time on earth is short. We have heard that you have not had a very good time in America. And who knows, if you had told us everything, we might have stayed in the U.S. because it would have been hard to leave you. We hope you are well and that everything will be good. In what you have failed, you have had to pay for, so we have compassion for you. So many times we have been glad that we brought you to God's house for the first time. I wanted so badly that you should go down on your knees. If you have not done that, please do before you return to Sweden, that is, if you do intend to return, but perhaps it is as good in America. I do not want to say this, but, at first, I thought it would be better to stay in the U.S. because it would feel so strange to come home to Sweden. It is not the way you think it is. But I know I have been so busy that I have not had the time to think about it. It might be possible to earn money here, too, in Sweden, but the money is not enough. There is a price fall right now, so many people are having a very hard time, and I think it will be even worse. My greetings to Mr. E. Persson. We are all well. Berta will also write a few lines to you.

Dear Stina!
I often think of you and wonder how you are. I hope you are well and are healthy with a good spirit. You should have had full

confidence in us so that perhaps we could have helped you in any way. And Stina, if you wish for something or you feel you want to say something, you can say it to us. We want to be your friends, if you will. I would have liked to ask you so many things but there is no paper left. Have you met Mrs. Ving? And how is she? I do not take the time to write. I feel so good at home here in Edsbyn, and I have no longing for America, not even for one hour. Yes, it is very expensive here, but prices are going down, so I hope it will be better and better. Now Erik says stop. Please, send me a letter. My greetings to those that I know. Your friend, Berta

Letter 23

25 February 1921. Letter to Stina from cousin Erik Ohman, Edsbyn.

Envelope: Miss Stina Ohman
              1044 – 20th Av S.E
              Minneapolis
              Minnesota
              U. S. A.

Best cousin Stina,

Tomorrow, I will go to Bollnäs and send the money, which I hope you will receive safely. Please write at once, so we will learn if you received it. We are all well. We have been healthy all winter, and now it is such lovely weather, real spring weather. It really is lovely here in Sweden.

However, it is a difficult time right now, as many do not have work, but still, not in the worst way here in Edsbyn. The factories have almost nothing to do. The prices are going down, so the ones that have stocks are losing a lot of money. Many in Sweden are now bankrupt. I think it is going backwards, also, for the Widells. It has been too expensive here, so it is a good thing that the prices are going down.

I do not have any other news that would interest you. We will write more another time.

Many greetings to you from all of us.

Sincerely, your cousin Erik

I have now got the check and put it in the mail. I hope you will get it: 570 kroner minus 20 kroner for processing, is 550 kroner (*US $126.50*).

The lower the exchange rate, the higher the Swedish kroner in US dollars. Erik borrowed the money from Stina on 19 April 1920. He returned the money on 25 February 1921.

It is interesting that Erik would specifically mention the Widell family as having financial difficulties.

Letter 24

20 March 1921. Letter to Stina, Minneapolis, from Sven, Bollnäs. (*This letter had no envelope.*)

Beloved girl!

Warm thanks for your two letters (No. 14 and 15). One dated February 10, arriving on March 3. The other dated March 6, arriving on Good Friday. I am sitting alone here with my warm feelings for you. I really feel sorry for you, little Stina. You ask for compassion, but that is not needed. When you have a good and honest heart, it comes on its own. You know how many times my heart has been bleeding, and been torn, and been healed through naive fantasies. It will probably not be healed forever through happiness, truthfulness, and love. You know, through my good fate, I should not imagine something like that.

I am happy to learn that you are alive and that you are healthy, and also that my little but well meant Christmas gift has arrived without being broken. On the other hand, I am not happy to hear that you are sad and, as I understand, unable to function due to worry and grief over my recent absence and me. I also do not like to hear a lot of other things that I will tell you more in detail. I hope you will respect what I have to say. There were many warm letters from me earlier. You say you have not received any letters lately, but you received my last letter between Christmas and New Year, and you, yourself, have not written to me since February 10. So, for over a month you have not written to the one, as you have said many times, who is "the most dear to you on earth". The least I want to do is make you sad or make you believe that my feelings have faded away, or that I should have done something without telling you. I think you can understand that it is not only your little mistake that has made my thoughts wander in uncertainty and put me in a bad mood. As you know, when Sven is not happy, I am not worth much. Your silence has made me despair over what I have been hoping for, for so many years. I think we can agree that the silence this time has been from us both from different sides of the Atlantic, whatever the reasons might be. We will see what the future will bring and if we survive, and if Emma's good words are really true. As I see it right now, I will not destroy anything. What you have told me, I hope, are your own words of your innocent heart.

Time flies. It is now a year since you left Sweden and turned your back on me. I can still not understand how you could do this to me. Soon we will have a wonderful blooming summer. But I have not heard any serious word from you that you are coming back to "the one that your heart has selected." We discussed many things not long ago, and I believed you were truthful. Now it seems there will be another long dark winter before we see each other for fidelity and happiness forever. I will not speak any more of this right now. I will not ask you for anything that you do not want to give. But please understand how I feel if I have to wait mercilessly for so long. I am more than ever in need of a peaceful and happy home with a loving wife. I cannot help that I am lonely, getting old, and serious. I now look at life from a happy and practical side. I feel love was taken from me at a young age, as well as my heart, faith, and happiness. I ask you to read the poems that I wrote and gave you together with the pink carnations, as a last token of my love before you left. All the work I have done, together with my anxious heart. I simply cannot understand you. I should not say this, but I think I see life more and more from the dark side. Sometimes I wish I could join my dear parents and have an innocent sleep without any troubles.

My beloved whom I miss so much, I wish you were here with me and that we could talk so that you understand me. It is so difficult to write about everything. It is easy to be sadly misunderstood. I guess I will just have to wait until you come home. I have been thinking of you so very much lately and thought perhaps I would have a message that you had come home.

One night it was worse than usual, and I lay in my bed crying for you. Before I fell asleep I thought that what I dreamt that night might be true. But then, I dreamt something very awful, which if it were true, I do not know what I would do. I do not know where you live. As you know, dreams can be very confusing. I dreamt that I came to you, and you were lying in bed and had given birth to a child. Your mother/dear Aunt met me crying, just as she had done when she thought we had broken our engagement. She asked me to have mercy. She said, "Poor Sven and poor Stina. The child's father is a married man. Why could it not have been you?" This was the worst dream I could ever have! I do not, so much, believe in such things. I still must say, however, that I am now even more worried that there will not be a future together for us. I have thought that if this dream is actually true, it would explain why you left without telling me anything and that you wanted to keep a secret from me. Had we still been engaged and I should hear this news, I would again be in hell.

You know this is only a fantasy. Could what is true be on the other side of the water? No, dear Stina, come home to me. Please let me be the father of your first-born child. Am I not, in your eyes, the only one who should have that right? I am longing very much for that day when you become a mother and I a father. As we speak of this, I want to tell you that if everything goes well, my nephew who is married and living in Voxna, will soon be a father. And I will then be an uncle. If you would have agreed, and I, of course, too, we could have been married two years now, and perhaps also have had a boy (that, I would prefer) or a girl. He should have the name Sven Lennart as we have often talked about.

How will this summer be? I hope you remember what we have both dreamt about, to be alone together at a wonderful cottage, where we could enjoy life and rest (you . . . after your return journey home). But now you only talk about traveling on to another place. So do you not mean what you are saying to me? Such things make me wonder if I am really the only one for you, as you have said, "The most dear on the earth." You once talked about a ring you should send, but I have not seen it. Do not send it. Please come home instead. We will engage where we meet. We will be married when we have found an apartment, just as we were talking of some time ago. I think you should not wait too long. I have, of course, many temptations here at home, and I say this without any hesitance. No one knows what a too-long longing can do. Times are strange now, and I want to tell you, without bragging, that I have had many proposals from girls. However, I have not found anyone with the good characteristics that I once, in my youth, found in you.

You talk as if you need to keep our correspondence secret, but from my side that is not at all necessary. You should and ought to be mine as you have been before, no need to change for any reason.

I do not like that you have not written to your home. Your mother and father and your siblings mean too much to you to forget. Remember, they are the link to our family. For my sake, if you listen to this, you should not act this way.

I am sorry, but this letter to you was delayed because I have had a severe cold and have been in bed. I am now better, although, I still have a bad cough, especially during the night.

Soon we will have summer. It has been a very lovely spring, and no snow is left now. Shortly, everything will be green. You never know what will happen this summer. Will it bring my Stina to me with her silent, serious smile on her lips? Or shall I go alone and perhaps do something stupid? Fate will show its strong hand that saves us from all evil.

I send you a picture that has been taken here in my room on a Sunday. What do you think? I will send some more in another letter. Thank you for sending the lock of hair—that I often kiss. I send one to you, too, taken from the front of my head.

With a hearty greeting and many warm kisses from your forever, own, Sven.

Emma is Stina's older sister by five years.

Letter 25

25 September 1921. Letter to Stina, Minneapolis, from Sven, Bollnäs.

Envelope: Miss Stina Ohman

　　　　　3911 Dupont Ave North

　　　　　Minneapolis

　　　　　Minnesota

　　　　　U. S. A.

The postmaster crossed out the above address and the following address was written on the front of the envelope:

　　　　　2844 – 44 Ave So

Return Address:　Sven Bengtzon

　　　　　Box 16

　　　　　Bollnäs

　　　　　Sweden

Dearest little Stina!

A wave of warm gratefulness seeks its way to you for the gift you honored me with on my 26th birthday. The welcomed package gave me such joy. Still, I have to mention that I was a bit surprised, as the package did not arrive until the 19th. The package has traveled over huge foaming waves and was packed with great care by the girl I warmly loved and still do. Did she pack the things she wanted to give to her former boy to show him what her heart silently speaks of? Your poems and the beautiful ring, however too small for the finger you meant it to go on—the same finger where I earlier had a heavy gold ring with the inscription, Stina 12 August 1917. So, despite the joy of your gifts, I started to think of what might have been if the sun had wanted to shine on Sven and his Stina. My deepest thoughts I cannot tell you in a letter, but perhaps I can tell you sometime when we are eye to eye if we ever meet again. The photo with the frame was sweet, but why was it cut? As if something that I should not see had been in your lap. Considering your poem, I feel entitled to ask, even if it is none of my business. I have never wanted to be hard on you or force you into anything, but I have always thought highly of honesty and fidelity, and I still do.

Time changes all beings, and also me. I am no more the rash young boy who four years ago swore to be true to the girl I loved. The love is gratefully kept in the depth of my heart. Perhaps the happy flame can once more be lit, but for that, absolute honesty is needed. Do you understand me? However strong love might be, unforeseen forces in the life of a woman cause her to end a relationship. What do you think is the best and happiest: Secret— marriage—truthfulness, or perhaps, disclosure—divorce—scandal and thereafter a broken relationship? I would like to talk to you about this. A full heart speaks through the mouth, but I am unable to write these things. If God wants, perhaps, we will meet one day, but that day seems to be very far away or will never come. You know what I really want. Please do not linger too long. It might be too late. I am still a free young man who thinks often of his Stina in spite of it all. Do you honestly still really love me and believe my words would bring you comfort and joy?

I do not want to be more than I am and would not like to give you any false hopes. Please receive my inner good, my little girl, in exchange for all that you have given me!

The summer is now gone. Autumn is approaching and then the long winter again. During my vacation for twenty days, I traveled around visiting friends and relatives. I went to Göteborg, Skövde, Mariestad, and Gullspång. I also visited the archipelago of Söderhamn and did some bathing. I went to Edsbyn once to visit your family during "Persmässan," but I was shocked by the behavior of your brother-in-law, Karl Klang *(Emma's husband)* who was drunk. It should be forgiven, but still, he should have known what he said. It was just trivial. Once when the train stopped in Runemo, he said I had not greeted him and taken his hand. I was on one of my missions, so I guess I was occupied by other things. I dismissed it, but apparently, he was very offended by this. I do not care for his friendship and do not want to say any more.

Not much more to tell this time, so I will finish with warmest greetings from your affectionate Sven

Here are some beautiful words for Stina that have remained in my memory after reading the book, *In the Eleventh Hour.*

You had me, dear. Just now I would have laid all that I had at your feet. I would have sacrificed all the world for your heart, for your hugs, for your kiss. The love that we shared was happy till it faded away because of our faults and failures. What we are able to forget, remove from your memory. Today our love is a sad dream, tomorrow only a memory from our youth.

Bollnäs, Easter Monday, 1921, Sven

Persmässan is a holiday when the old settlers are remembered. Handcrafts of old are demonstrated. People dress in clothing from the past and herd goats and cows through the streets.

Reflections

Letters 1 – 25

The content of the first 25 letters shocked my inner soul and profoundly altered my perspective. The negativity I felt toward my family in Sweden ended. The letters told a different side of the story, one my father and I never knew.

My Father, Lennart (Leonard) G. Ohman (1920-2010)

My father (and therefore, I) surmised that Stina had been disowned and chastised by her family after disclosing to her parents that she was pregnant. We knew early in her pregnancy that she was sent away, not to another village in Sweden to wait out her pregnancy, but to a new continent an ocean away, to a place where she would not be known, nor the family scrutinized. My father went to the grave knowing this, as he internalized his mother's (and his own) disgrace. His knowledge of his family ended there. This was all he knew for certain.

My father, Leonard, did not know who his father was. When I was young, I asked him to tell me about his father, my grandfather. He said that his mother told him his father died in a train accident shortly after he was born. She said his father was employed by the railroad. This demise saddened me. I accepted it, but as I grew older, I sensed my father was not completely satisfied with this explanation. It was, however, an easy out for him when others asked the question. My father did not want to talk about his father, nor did he want me to ask my grandmother, Stina, about his father, as it was too painful. So, I never did. When I was tall enough to see the top of my father's dresser, I noticed a very small portrait in a very small frame. It was a photo of a man. He was smiling. I asked my father who this person was. He said this man and his mother were close friends. I now realize this was a photograph of Sven.

My father had an inferiority complex that manifested in an outward show of arrogance and distrust. He trusted no one, not even his immediate family, not me, nor my brother, nor my mother. Life threatened him.

I felt my father's heartache and anguish, as living with him in our home, it was evident he held these thoughts and feelings. I felt sorry for him. He referred to himself as a bastard. He was schizophrenic, as he believed everywhere he went people "knew" he had no father, i.e., his job, his friends, my mother's family, the church. He feared others considered him a bastard. He was possessed and disturbed by this complex, truly, unto death. My father was a victim of circumstance.

My Great Grandfather, Carl E. Ohman (1866-1947)
The first time Carl Ohman wrote to his daughter, Stina, was after her immigration, in December 1920. Lennart was then four months old. I was apprehensive when Eva began to translate and share the content of Carl's letter. I feared his reprimand of my grandmother, and I did not want to hear it. Internally, I put up a defensive barrier, and prepared for disdain. Eva sensed my anguish. Slowly, she began to translate my great grandfather's letter, and as she read, I, literally, collapsed in disbelief. Carl **loved** his daughter, Stina. She was loved and missed by her family. I was shocked by Eva's words. I fell to my knees and burst into tears. I left the room and wept

uncontrollably for my father's sake, as he never knew of this blessing of love for himself and his mother.

In his letter of 1 December 1920, Carl shows compassion and unconditional love for his daughter. Carl pleads, "Please forgive me, my Stina." He tells Stina she is missed and that he wants her to return to Sweden. The family saves a chair for her at the Christmas dinner table should she surprisingly appear. They loved her! Carl's love for Stina was an unbelievable and utterly remarkable revelation! My father believed his entire life that his mother was an embarrassment, ostracized, and banished by her family, and I believed this as well.

Hildemar Widell / Karl Eriksson (1884-1932)
In reexamining the letters written by Karl Eriksson and Hildemar Widell, I believe Karl and Hildemar were one and the same person. The name Karl Eriksson is a very common name in Sweden. There are thousands of Karl Erikssons. I believe Hildemar wrote letters under the disguise of Karl Eriksson to protect his name and family, should the very personal content of any of his letters be intercepted. He did not want others to know Stina was pregnant nor that he was the father of Stina's child. Hildemar was a family man, well known, and highly respected in Edsbyn. The town's people would talk. In 1919, when Hildemar and Stina were together, Hildemar was married with three living children born in 1909, 1911 (this child died of tuberculosis in 1915), 1914, and 1916. Another child was born to Hildemar and his wife in February 1920. My father was born six months later, in August.

Hildemar wrote a letter to Carl Walhmark, Chicago, on 22 February 1920 (ten days before Stina left Sweden for the U.S.) asking Carl to send him suggestions for land and business opportunities in the United States. I believe Hildemar gave Stina this letter to deliver to Carl when she saw him in Chicago. Since it was still in Stina's possession, I believe Carl never received it. If Stina did visit Chicago, it was simply to transfer trains as she continued on to Minneapolis. The letter confirms Hildemar's intent to leave his family and join Stina in the U.S. to begin a new life and a new business venture. Hildemar hoped to have the help of Carl Walhmark.

Hildemar's double identity as Karl Eriksson became evident as I pondered why two sets of initials appeared on the card enclosed with the gift of flowers given to Stina just prior to her leaving Edsbyn. Why would two suitors give a single gift to a young woman? It was inexplicable. The only logical conclusion was that Karl and Hildemar were one and the same person. It became evident when comparing the handwriting of the two letters written on 22 February 1920. One letter was given to Stina with very personal content and signed by Karl Eriksson. The other letter was also given to Stina to deliver to Carl Walhmark in Chicago. This letter asked Carl for help in finding a prospective business opportunity in the U.S. and was signed by Hildemar Widell. When examining the two letters, the cursive script of individual uppercase letters is unmistakably the same. Both letters are written on identical stationery and both envelopes are lined with dark purple tissue paper. Neither letter had a stamp and neither had a postmark. Stina's personal letter was sealed. Carl Walhmark's was not. I believe

Hildemar discussed his fictitious identity with Stina and she agreed with this deception. Hildemar gave both of the letters to Stina. One was for her to keep and the other was for her to deliver in Chicago.

Hildemar writes in his letters of 20 April and 15 May 1920 that he has left his wife and has made preparations to join Stina in the U.S. He awaits a telegram or a letter of assurance from her as he plans to leave on the ship Drottningholm. Stina must not have wanted to reunite with Hildemar, nor did she favor him as a lasting companion or she would have accepted his proposal, welcomed him as a permanent partner, and acknowledged him as the father of her child. It appears she did not respond to Hildemar.

My Grandmother, Kristina (Stina) E. Ohman (1894-1984)
The letters were revealing. I was shocked by my grandmother's blatant infidelity. Sven introduced a new dimension of her character previously unknown to me. In his letter to Kerstin (Stina's mother) he writes, "She has no morals," (letter of 28 November 1918). "She is out every night . . . with different men," all while wearing her engagement ring. "I cannot get the ring back; she is still wearing it," (letter of 28 November 1918). Stina did not take Sven's demand of fidelity and commitment in a betrothed engagement seriously. By Sven's accounts, Stina was a loose woman. We have proof of Stina's intimate relationships with several men by the myriad of love letters she kept.

As distraught as Sven was by Stina's behavior, I found it heartbreaking that he would resort to contacting Stina's mother. Sven felt it imperative to inform Kerstin of her daughter's questionable conduct. Sven turned to Kerstin and implored her help in curtailing Stina's careless and dangerous activities. Sven urged Kerstin to "punish her," (letter of 1 December 1918), however he begged innocence in the disclosure. His actions certainly weakened Stina's confidence and trust in Sven's judgement. Stina "tormented" Sven; she abused him. Yet Stina relied on Sven and regarded him her loyal friend and caregiver.

The Stina I knew was a very private person. She rarely talked about her homeland. She was hardened. The only time I saw emotion from her was when she received word that her sister, Anna, had died. She naturally, was distressed, and my father, mother, and I went immediately to be with her.

Had Stina remained in her homeland throughout her pregnancy, my father would have been born in Sweden and very likely, my children and I would be citizens of Sweden perhaps living in Orsa, Edsbyn, or Stockholm.

Sven Bengtzon/Bengtsson/Bengtzzon (1895-1969)

Sven was a romantic. He was also excessively loquacious. He wrote descriptive and poetic letters of prose. Assuredly, his letters were welcomed by Stina and read and reread.

There are no words to adequately explain Sven's intense love for Stina. His "unnatural love" for her is mentioned several times. He longs for her life-long commitment, yet both Sven and Stina find fidelity difficult as suggested by Mohlen in his letter of defense in February 1918 just six months after Sven and Stina's engagement. Both Sven and Stina must accept guilt. Sven finds himself again and again with a "torn and bleeding heart" (letter of 20 March 1921). Sven threatened rash actions.

Sven was patient with Stina. He waited for her to disclose the birth of her child. However, Stina was not ready to reveal her secret. In his letter of 20 March 1921, Sven tried to open the conversation by telling Stina of his dream of her giving birth to a child. Still, Stina was not able to admit the truth to Sven, even though it was obvious by Sven's description of his dream, that he was aware of her child's birth. In this same letter, Sven pleads with Stina, "Please let me be the father of your first born child."

Sven invited Stina, again, to be truthful, in his letter of 25 September 1921. He asked why the photo she sent of herself had been cut off, as if there was something on her lap that she did not want him to see. This, again, verified his knowledge of her child (*Lennart is one year old*) and her inability to be forthright. This behavior was puzzling and unfortunate, and foreign to Sven.

Stina named her baby boy, Lennart, as she and Sven had often discussed naming their firstborn son. He should be named Lennart, after Sven's given name, Sven Lennart (Sven's letter of 20 March 1921).

"Dearest Little Stina!"

Part Two

Letters 26 - 50

5 June 1922 — 27 May 1926

Enterprise

Courtship

Edsbyn's Bow-Saw Frame Factory

The Inventor of the Bow-Saw is Dead

Reflections

Letter 26

5 June 1922. Letter to Stina, Minneapolis, from Carl E. Ohman
(Stina's father) in Edsbyn.
(*This letter had no envelope.*)

My little Stina,

Forgive me for not writing to you. I know how it is to wait for a
letter when you have questions and your thoughts are of dear
memories. I really feel sorry for you since you do not know the big
changes that are happening in your hometown. Almost without
exception, even the wealthiest are without money. I will soon write
you a long letter and tell you about everything; this is only a few
hasty lines since my heart is full of thanks to you for the gift you
sent, a curl of your hair. This was the best gift you could send. I
have never received a gift that has been more meaningful or has
affected me so deeply. It made my thoughts deepen and reflect on a
father's responsibility. Thank you, my little Stina. I do not know
what I can send you that would be of equal value. I now believe that
you are beginning to understand the love and joy of caring for a
child. Nothing can be better than to receive a curl of hair from the
one whom you have seen in your home so many times, the toddler
whom you have held in your arms. And now that we are so far
apart, I wonder how your future will be. My little Stina, we know
you have a good heart, a big soul, and a great love for us, and you
are good in all ways. You must not believe that what has happened
to you has diminished your dignity in our eyes. We truly believe
that it was your way to happiness. We, and also you, see the truth in

the words we know so well, but I still want to remind you of the following: "Do not judge the misguided with contempt, proud brother. You did not bear the burdens that fate brought to her shoulders. You did not meet the battles that fate brought to her. You did not feel the pain her heart endured."

Yes, this is the way it is in life, my little Stina. Short are the moments of happiness, long is the day of sorrow. The law of fate crushes what you dreamt of in moments of hope.

Life is often gloomy and heavy when you only see others' happiness. To me, the creation has given me regret and sorrow.

Yes, my little Stina, this is how the world is. The good person has not met the best. I am surprised by your clarity and wisdom, and you are so capable in everything you do. I am sure you will soon find happiness.

I like your suggestion about a fur business and also that you journey home with cars. You only have to telegraph, and I will send you money. Come soon, but be careful. As an example, I want to mention that a Ford in Denmark now costs 2,700 kroner.

We found something this winter that would truly suit the Dollar Land (*USA*)! Oh, the lady who should wear this fur! You cannot think of anything more beautiful. Göthe and the girls brought the furs to the market in Uppsala. When they showed them, all the people in the market went after them. Experts have now advised us to go and hide our furs. Can you imagine, thousands of furs are shown in Uppsala each year, but no one had seen furs like ours. They are two silver fox furs or a cross between a silver and another fox, bigger than a usual fox. We do not dare to sell them in case there is a fortune in them.

I will soon write again, little Kristina. You can keep the furs I sent. I cannot think of anything else. I am longing for you. We now have Whit Monday (Pentecost).

Pappa

Letter 27

13 August 1922. Letter to Stina, Minneapolis, from Sven, Bollnäs.

Envelope: Miss Stina Ohman

           1419 – 8th St. South

           Minneapolis, Minn.

           U. S. A.

Envelope back: Sender: Bengtzon

                                 Box 16

                                 Bollnäs

                                 Sweden

Dear you Stina!

It has been a very long time now since I've written a long letter to you. It has also been a long time since I have written several letters in frequent succession, as I used to do before. To me it is natural that I have been silent, but from your side it might be understood in a different way. You have encouraged me several times with gifts and letters for which I now want to thank you warmly! Thank you Stina! Please do not think badly of me since I have waited so long. I have intended to write several times, and I even have two letters laying here that have never been sent. Something has interrupted me each time, a thorough reflection that brings me to my senses or puts me in a different mood than when I began the letter. This is my explanation. I have wanted so dearly to write, but have not had the right spirit.

I have received a photo of your son, a collar protector, and a wallet, all in good shape. I had to pay customs an additional four crowns for the wallet. I have enjoyed all this, but you should not send too many things to me. The last thing was very nice, so thank you very much. I was glad for your letter since it was now in a friendly tone, as it should be, don't you think? After all that has happened, I hope you will understand that there can be nothing else but friendship between us now, and I ask you to comply with this. I now have an idea about what happened and perhaps you have also understood this from my letters. I am not surprised that you had difficulty telling me, but I cannot understand how you could let something like this happen with a married man. I think you ought to describe to me what happened. It must have been love in some way? You must have known all this when you left Sweden. I have left the painting of the boy in Edsbyn for they all wanted it. I think that is where it belongs. I paid a visit there three months ago. I have not mentioned that you intend to come home soon, and I will not mention it, as you have wished. Of course you can come and see me, although I am not the same anymore, surely not. Times change, and we do also. You get older and, at the same time, more sensible. The past fades and seems like a vague memory, and I like that. Not until now, have I felt good, like a human being again, and could show a happy face. If only it wasn't for the bad times here in Sweden. If I had the money, I could have a good life. But, sadly enough, this is not so. I have so many debts that I do not know what to do. It is not possible to borrow money or sell something. Apart from all this, I want to tell you that I am now happy. What I have longed for, for so long, I finally have. There really was a girl left for me, who understands me, and who truly loves me. Not for a single little moment do I doubt her love. She is giving me the most affectionate and warm love, just as I have been longing for. I will tell you who she is in the future. I pray God will save our love.

Recently, the two of us, her brother, and some other friends have had a vacation together on an island by the sea. I have never before had such a lovely time. We are healthy and suntanned, and are all now back to work, each one at his own job. We all look like negroes. Her brother calls us the "negro and negress." Otherwise, everything is much the same here in Bollnäs, and I will remain here with my sweet girl, who is now my everything and my little sunshine.

I have not seen your family lately; I seldom travel that way nowadays.

I do not have much more to say, but I want to thank you warmly once more for what you have sent me and also for your nice thoughts in your letters. I also want to wish you all the best for the future.

Hello, greetings!

Sven

Lennart is 2 years old.

Letter 28

9 October 1922. Letter to Stina, Minneapolis, from Sven, Bollnäs.

Envelope: Miss Stina Ohman

                1419 – 8th St South

                Minneapolis

                Minnesota

Envelope back: Sender: Sven Bengtzon

                            Box 16

                            Bollnäs

                            Sweden

Dear you little Stina!

Thank you, sweet you, for the letter that arrived on 7 October. You do not seem to forget your little Sven! I must say that I long for your letters, and they bring me joy, especially the way you write nowadays. You are feeling well. You are healthy and joyous. So it is, even for me, although every day is hard. Often, I am not in a good mood, but so far, I have succeeded to manage everything that has come my way. We will see what my future will bring, but I hope, so hope, that happiness and calmness will come. Do you not hope so, for me too, little Stina? It is so good to know that I have a heartfelt, good friend behind me who is far away, who has good thoughts for me, whom I can trust with difficult things, and best of all, who understands me.

Now the summer has totally left us, and we await the arrival of the long, dark, and snowy winter. The summer has been boring with only rain and more rain. But the autumn has been enormously beautiful, and I like it very much: sunny days, warm and lovely, and cold nights. You should see everything that I enjoy. You cannot imagine how beautiful our Norrland is now with all its colors: red, brown, and yellow, like spots in the endless woods. Yes, I have now become a real nature lover, and I often wander in God's free nature. Yesterday, Sunday, I was out all day. I was up on the Bolle-berget, and from there everything was even more beautiful. Yesterday, we also had a competition between cars. About 30 cars started, and among them was your sister, Nelly, who got compliments from the newspaper for her impressive showing among the men competing with her. I do not know if she got any prize. This news can serve as a greeting to you from your loved ones and your home. I have not met them for some long time now; they may all have forgotten me.

Thank you for your good thought of sending something to me for my 27th birthday. Sure, you can send something if you want to, but how can I give something back to you for all the things you have given me? I really would like to, but as things are now, I am unable to, dear Stina. You can have my best friendship, sincerely from the depth of my heart if you can be happy with this. I enclose a picture from our vacation in July by the sea, and I think you will recognize me, don't you? Some other time, I might be able to send more photos that I have been in, although I do not have a camera of my own. My girlfriend, whom I mentioned in my last letter, has a camera, and we often take pictures. She has taken this picture from the front of the motorboat. Now my dinner break is over, so good-bye; I will continue later.

Later this day at 9:00 PM: So this day is over, and I can settle down to write again "before I go to bed," as you say nowadays; it is your country's expression. Also, I think I have so much to talk to you about, but I come to the paper, and it remains blank. As you say, I would also like to talk to you a lot when you come to Sweden. As you say, we will arrange a meeting "unnoticed" in Göteborg. I will go there to meet you. Sven really wants to do this – don't you think it will be fun? I hope I will have the time and money to be with you there for a couple of days. We could agree to stay at the same hotel so we can really be together all the time. Do you think the same? Nothing must stop this. If, by <u>then</u>, I would be engaged, you must promise not to tell anyone so that I will not have any new troubles. You know that our Swedish friends often misunderstand everything. When we meet, we do not need to be intimate, but just be able to talk. This no one can begrudge us. I trust you and you can calmly trust me. I must tell you that I will be engaged early in 1923 if I live and am healthy. Do you not think that it is nice that your little Sven has finally found "the one" and is feeling happy? Within me, I am hoping the same luck for you, that you will meet a boy to your liking that can make you happy <u>forever.</u>

Regarding your father and money, I dare not to ask him for help, and I do not think that he would lend it, either. Of course, he would be my best option. If he would agree to loan me 8000 crowns, I would then be free from everything that now is a burden to me. I have some value in the house, but I cannot reclaim the amount if I were to sell. I am just waiting to win something on the lottery or a premium bond, but so far I have had no luck. But it is still good to have the hope, you know? You see, Stina, I am behind with debts since I studied in Stockholm. My schooling was expensive. I no longer have my father whom I could ask for help and forgiveness. I am really, really alone. Just think if I had a wealthy uncle somewhere that would remember me, but I don't even have that. I am nowadays really not the same, Stina. I think about a lot of things, and not having enough money is hard on me. Also, I have sorrow over the loss of you. We were together since 1917. This has worn on the boy, Sven, more than you can imagine. I must admit that after you left, I self-indulged and did not take care of my body. But, for the past year, to my luck and because of having better friends, I have had better thoughts and ways. Can you imagine, Stina, I have almost totally stopped drinking! My body cannot take it anymore. For her, I no longer binge or carouse. I do not find it fun anymore. You must understand that things have changed for me because I am really happy.

I would like to explain how much I have suffered during my years of lost love and infidelity with you, but I cannot do it here and now, perhaps when we meet.

I now feel I cannot write anymore this time, some melancholy has come over me. I do not understand what it is. This happens sometimes nowadays, but I hide everything and keep it to myself.

Good night. Sleep well where you are this night and every other night. You know that I am glad to hear from you, so please write again soon.

Warm greetings! Sven

Enclosing a clip from the paper today regarding Nelly's car race. I am sending you a picture of when I was swimming during my vacation. So now you have two photos of me.

You have not changed much, and I do recognize you.

Nelly is Stina's younger sister by nine years.

Letter 29

14 March 1923. Letter to Stina, Minneapolis, from her father, Carl E. Ohman, Edsbyn.

(This letter had no envelope.)

My kind Stina, away from our home,

We send you a copy of a motor paper from your homeland, so you can read about the popular Swedish motor lady, Nelly. In another paper, it has been written that she was the first female participant in a speed race for motorcars within the country, and many motormen respect her abilities. She has achieved notoriety. It is captain Heren in Stockholm who writes about her. Look at the pages 169-170 and you can see what the Swedish motor clubs are saying.

When you come, we will meet you in Göteborg, at the exhibition.

Many greetings

Pappa and Mamma

I am sorry we do not write very often. I can understand that you are hoping and longing for a letter, and you mostly have to be disappointed, as nothing comes from the post office.

Father

Letter 30

12 July 1923. Letter to Stina, Minneapolis, from her father, Carl E. Ohman, Edsbyn.

(This letter had no envelope.)

My little Stina

Thank you for your letter. But just think, we will not see you this summer. From your letters during the winter, we have trusted you would come this summer, but now this happiness is gone. If we live, we will have patience also for next summer, but I cannot forget my wish to see you once more before I die. If I could be sure that you would have a happier future here, I would do everything to get you home, but I dare not give you any advice. But, it seems to me that it would be the right time for you and your sisters to start a shop in your area of interest. I could help you to begin with at least 10,000 kroner, but I must leave this to your own choice.

I can see that you did not like it that Nelly was working at Signe Persson's clothing store. Also, I was much against it. It is of course, a good opportunity for her, but having her work makes it appear to others that we need money. You must know that everything is declining here. Both income and reputation are almost finished, and the fortune is declining. We will perhaps be able to live on it for four to five more years, unless the economy turns around.

I must tell you, it was very unfortunate for us when Erik Ohman returned to Edsbyn from the USA. He has built a big workshop beside the warehouse made out of stone and a big house beneath it. Last year, he and Delander took the dealership of selling Ford cars from me. You know that I sold the first Ford here and have been working for Ford for the past 14 years. Now, we have lost the only business we had. The bow-saw business is also gone, and the workshop is empty. You cannot imagine how decimated we have been by this family. One day Erik called me and was very rude. It is not nice to put this into writing, but he said that if he would remain the way I had raised him to be, he would be a "no good." We cannot remember doing any harm to him at all. I have not even said a bad word about them taking the Ford dealership away from me. Probably it is because I continue to sell some, but they have sold twenty, and I only five. He is in cahoots with Delanders and Widells and all the religious people. One night he is with them, and the next night he is out drinking with the others. Berta and Erik accompanied Delander's daughter to Göteborg this summer, and you should know, they felt they were better than us. When they passed us, they made fun of us. That is our thanks for caring for them, and now they are more prosperous than we. So now you know that all eight of you children are "no good" because I raised you. I will soon write more and send Christmas gifts. Just think, we are getting old and things don't get done.

Merry Christmas Greetings
Pappa and Mamma
Little Stina, please come home soon.

You can see when I started the letter (12 July), and now it is 6 December.

Carl makes reference to the bow-saw business. Carl was an inventor and metal smith.

Note the following two articles after Letter 50, this section:
Harry Pettersson, "Edsbyns Bow-Saw Frame Factory," NÄR
INDUSTRIN KOM TILL BYN (When the Industry Came to the
Village), 1995, p. 38.
"The Inventor of the Bow Saw is Dead," Organization of
Blacksmith, Forging, and Mechanical Foundry. January 31, 1947,
p. 43.

Letter 31
18 April 1924. Letter to Stina, Minneapolis, from her father, Carl E. Ohman, Edsbyn.

Envelope: Miss Stina Ohman
              1906 Park Ave
              Minneapolis
              Minnesota U.S.A.
Return address: Carl E. Ohman, Edsbyn
My little Stina,

   Thank you for the card, I got it yesterday, Good Friday. You have not forgotten us, our little child, and we really have not forgotten you, although it could look like that since we do not write.

I gather you would like to hear something from your home each day. We do not intend to be hard on you, not to let you know continuously about everyday life here at home, but let's hope we will be better and write more often.

Yes, it is now 1:00 PM on Good Friday and here we are sitting, Mother and I, old and with white hair, listening to our youngest children, Åke, Nelly, and Jussi, making beautiful music. We have humble thoughts of you who have already left our home. We wonder how Gustaf, Emma, Anna, and Göthe are. We are feeling blessed since you are all healthy and good people, and not one of you eight has been hurt. Just think, that we today can sit and listen to the beautiful music of our youngest. I believe that when you, Little Stina, hear your youngest brother and sister play, you will be brought to tears. Åke has now joined the big violin orchestra here. They will tour this summer. Here in Edsbyn the Hälsinge Music Festival will be in June. If you, Stina, are wishing to see us, as much as we are wishing to see you, we would like you to come on June 1. I will pay for the tickets, also the return tickets, for both you and Lennart. I do not know if it is possible for you. But if it is, I am sure you would like to come. It would fit in so well since Göthe's semester in Göteborg will be over, and Anna will finish in Stockholm. Then we could all gather in our home again once more. Please remember there is not one day that we don't cherish your little child, Lennart.

We have made a good invention again, so, not to mention too much in this letter, we will probably win some contracts on it. Those who know what it is all about say we might make a million on it, but we are grateful for less. A German, Alex Veltin, has entered our firm as a sales representative. He has been contracted for the sales in Sweden, Norway, Finland, Poland, Estonia, and Canada. He will go to America to promote our business in magazines, and then he will surely look you up. He is a big, splendid man. He has also been in America for a Finnish firm. He will visit you in the USA if you are not here at home, <u>which we hope you will be.</u> I suppose you will soon see my application for the patent in the American newspapers. As soon as you have received this, you will have to prepare for the journey. If you do not have money for the journey, you must send me a telegraph at my expense. We hope you will be in Göteborg on June 1 (I am serious).

Pappa and Momma
Jussi has been sick for two weeks with the Spanish flu.
We still have one meter of snow here.

Stina, like her siblings, was a gifted musician. She played the piano by ear. I watched her sit at our piano for hours robustly playing and singing Swedish folk songs. It was obvious that with each melody a certain memory was brought to the surface. Her private performance always ended with a vibrant smile and tearful eyes.

The invention that Carl refers to in this letter is an apparatus on the bow-saw. It is a mechanism (latch) that can be released so that a dull blade can be removed and replaced with a new saw blade. I am holding one of Carl's original OHMAN saws in the photo. Göthe (Eva's father) gave us this saw during our first visit to Edsbyn in 1974.

The newer G-MAN saw (photo, lower saw) was initially made by Edsbyns Industri (EIA) manufacturing company and later by the Sandvik company using Carl's specifications. The angle of the bow was changed and a handle was added. Carl is mentioned on the G-MAN website which can be translated into English by clicking on the British flag. URL: g-mantools.se
ABOUT G-MAN; History; Nordic Saw Makers; paragraph 6.

Letter 32

28 July 1924. Letter to Stina, Minneapolis, from Sven, Voxna.

Envelope: Miss Stina Ohman

              1906 Park Ave (Apt 12)

              Minneapolis

              Minnesota

              U.S.A

Dear friend Stina!

Thank you for your last letter of May 21. Also, thank you for all the other letters although I have not answered them!

Yes, you are right. Many, long years have now passed since you turned your back on your homeland. I really did not think you would stay this long but that you would be homesick. It seems you have not suffered from this illness at all?

I have heard that you have met a Swedish aviator, and I know him. But isn't the name wrong? Isn't his name Fallin (not Falen)? What he has mentioned to you, that I have left Bollnäs, is, however, wrong. I will probably stay and live here. There has been a change within the railway that should be to my advantage, although not yet decided. Olle Andersson, my old colleague, is now the stationmaster in Alfta after stationmaster Pehrsson. Perhaps you knew him, the vigorous, well-known Alfta stationmaster, known for his cheerful nature. He died in autumn last year after all his suffering.

Yes, this is the way it is now. The position of stationmaster in Bollnäs should be mine, although I have not yet had any confirmation from the railway about this. I only do my same job as best I can. It would affect my workload if the Bollnäs position was added, but I would have nothing to gain from the extra work that I would have to do. I am still the stationmaster in Edsbyn, as I was promoted from being an office assistant in July 1918, when you were here. It was because of this promotion that I began to think of marriage plans that we had already started but did not happen, as "fate" changed its course in another direction. My wish might still be to leave Bollnäs if other, long-awaited, more favorable opportunities become available.

Quite suddenly, I had an urge for America this spring and I intended to go, but since my financial situation is still bad, I cannot go. I must stay in this place. Perhaps you get tired of listening to me lament about my finances. This was not my intention.

It must be a good thing for you to be able to communicate with someone from your own home village. Such coincidences, I suppose, do not happen every day in America. I have not met or visited your family for a very long time, and I think it will still be some time before I do. Still, I might be visiting Emma and Kalle, since they have asked me many times, but I have not yet decided if I will go. I now have a vacation from June 12 to 30, and before this vacation is over, I might decide to visit your family in Edsbyn.

I have been in Stockholm for four days at a convention for our office staff organization. It was a gathering of 60 officials from all over Sweden and an honor to be selected as a representative from our area. Of course, there was also some partying going on during the evenings, whether we were tired or not. And as you know, your former fiancé has nothing against being with friends, especially nowadays when nothing remains but my feelings of desire and loneliness. Regretfully, I should add, but this is the way it is, at least for me.

I am now with my brother in Voxna until I go back to work again. It is very nice to be free and do whatever I like.

I heard yesterday evening when I was in Alfta that your little sister Nelly has a fiancé. Did you know this? Perhaps Uncle Ohman will soon have a <u>real</u> son-in-law, who knows? And you would have a nice brother-in-law sometime in a couple of years when you might happen to visit. I have heard what people say about us, that I should wait for you and that we should get married when you arrive back in Sweden. I only say, playfully, "Who knows?" It is mostly the women who speculate. Just let them. They say you should be so much in love with me now that you realize how wrongly you treated me, and between us, there should be a secret stream of love. If we compare this with reality, we both know how it is, and in what direction it is going, do we not? As for me, I dare not with conviction mention what decision I would make <u>now,</u> if Stina <u>now,</u> would be the woman I once <u>thought</u> she was.

Thank you for the photos. They were very good and one of them very beautiful. I might send some of the vacation pictures in this letter or in some other letter. I now have a camera of my own and take many, many pictures. It is such gloomy weather here. This will be the third rainy and cold summer if nothing changes soon.

When I was in Stockholm I met Oskar Nilsson. I showed him your photos, and he asked me to send his greetings the next time I wrote. He seems rather as before, but, of course, a little older as also I am. We young guys also get older.

Nothing much more to say. Magnussons are all well. I visit them sometimes. I like them very much. They are so kind and sweet. Alva and Sven are two beautiful and dangerous youngsters with whom you could easily fall in love. Sven seems already to be hard on the girls, but I hope that will change. Alva is so very sweet. If I was not so old and had not had a past, I might have asked her to marry me, but, of course, this is totally ridiculous.

I think you are now tired of me. I have much more to say but have to stop for this time so that you will be able to read it without getting tired.

Let's see if I will hear something more from you. You have not told me if you are married or not, but I have understood that you are not. Am I right? You once said that you were in love and thought that you should soon be married, or was it just a thought?
Live well and have a good time!

Heartfelt greetings from your true friend, Sven

P.S. I have now been in Edsbyn. I had a good time with Emma and Kalle. They are the same, and their son, Lennart, is now a big boy. They all send greetings to you. Anna was home from Stockholm, and I met her at Klang's. She is so joyful and zippy. I really like her. I popped in to your home on the way to the train. I met Aunt, but Uncle was not at home. The old woman was also much like before, I think. As always, she was very happy and also surprised to see me. It was as nice as it had been in the past, and it was over two years since I last paid them a visit. Emma and I had not seen one another for five years, so you can imagine.

Yesterday, on 30 June, Anna was in Bollnäs (I am home in Bollnäs now). She called, and we met for a while. She, Göthe, and I went by car to my apartment, and they stayed for about an hour. I have a lovely apartment here with three rooms and a built-on veranda. You would like it if you saw it. D.S.

D.S. (Deinde Scriptum) at the end of a letter means "in place of a signature," "the same" (the same signature as written above).

Letter 33

21 August 1924. Letter to Stina, Minneapolis, from Sven, Bollnäs.

Envelope: Miss Stina Ohman

               1906 Park Ave (Apt 12)

               Minneapolis

               Minnesota

               U.S.A.

Envelope back: Sender: Sven Bengtzon

                     Box 16

                     Bollnäs

(side margin reads: Greetings! from Alva)

Dear friend Stina!

It has been quite some time between letters. Even so, it is between your country and my own beloved Sweden with its high mountains, blue heaven, and mirror-like lakes.

Were you so very surprised over my letter? This I can understand, since it was very long ago that you received something from "your former fiancé" as you name me. Although you should not wonder, Stina-friend, as you reflect, maybe "he" might be more remarkable than any other. I suppose our earlier relationship is something that will still be present in our lives. Perhaps it is difficult to totally forget old things although they are now past. There are many things and happenings still in my memory. For instance, at the secret cottage and its "rooster." That was no other than me, a frisky steed who had no idea of what was to come over so many long years. I have decided to forget all these places and memories and draw a thick line through them. Although when the memories come back, I can again sense the feelings that I had, like a "kitten's" immaculate heart.

The book you are talking about, I am sure I can read. Have you forgotten that I studied both German and English at school, although mostly German? I have also been interested ever since and tried to get better. I am sure I would find it interesting, too.

The picture that I found, so beautiful, was a view of the full moon. I love these types of views of the beauty of nature. I have always loved them, but now even more!

The only thing that is really true is the enormously beautiful creation of nature and, for sure, it is the only thing worth giving your love to. I, therefore, say, please try to get as much sun and natural life as you can get.

Days go by so quickly. Soon another summer is ending; its visit was too short. It will now turn its back on us, and the long, cold, autumn nights are coming. We can find the calmness and comfort by the magical fire and dream about the summer and its sweet memories. I love where I live now and spend my free time. I have never had it this good and have everything that I need. Still, it feels as if something is missing. I cannot understand what it is. I do not think I have described my home to you and hope you will like that I do. In the picture that was taken this summer, you can see the small house situated beside the "Dala-bureau." The upper floor has three nice, small, rooms where I and another boy are living. There is also a fireplace. Outside is a garden area where I have planted nasturtium, sweet peas, and red geraniums. It is so very cozy here. I feel so happy when I can quietly sit and dream about all the fun I had during my youth, days that will never come back. I sit by the fire in the hall during the cold winter nights. On the first floor, there is a café, so we will never be without coffee. But we also have dinnerware and an electric cooker. Now you know how it is at my house. It is really something different than the "Hansson guest house."

Yes, Stina, I must admit that I have a great longing for America. I would like to see something else before I get too old and before happiness is gone forever. As you know, my 30 year birthday is not so far away. I will be 29 on the Moses-day. I do not think anyone else but you knows this, and perhaps soon I cannot even count on you? Since my dear parents died, there is seldom any acknowledgment on my birthdays, especially on that day. I miss all that.

Today, I have made a little of this and a little of that. I have been cleaning a wardrobe, and yesterday I was cleaning socks that today I have mended. Do not get too surprised. As the saying goes, "a good man can handle it himself." There is not much help for washing clothes here, and I cannot afford to buy new socks very often. Sometimes, I do not want to do the female tasks, but sometimes I have to.

Now is the time for crayfish, so sometimes we go out. I will probably have a little party on my birthday, and I will invite Anna. I have promised her an invitation, and I think she will be happy for that. Anna is so mischievous and zippy, so she is more than welcome. Please, you also come, but since this is not possible, think of us that night. I promise to write you a card on that night so that you can feel the party mood. I will arrange it as nicely as I can, perhaps with colored lanterns and other lights. It is nice to have something to look forward to.

I now send greetings from the Magnussons and especially sweet little Alva, who is so much waiting for a letter from you. She has written to you. Why do you not answer? I will now scold you a bit, so perhaps you will send her a letter.

I will now go to bed since it is 11:00. If you were here, I think I would give you a real "kiss of friendship" on your mouth. Watch out, for here it comes ------ ------ !

Heartfelt greetings and have a good life!
Sven

Letter 34

30 September 1924. Letter to Stina, Minneapolis, from Sven, Bollnäs.

Envelope: Miss Stina Ohman

1906 Park Ave (Apt 12)

Minneapolis

Minnesota

U.S.A.

Dear Stina!

Tonight, to my big surprise, I had another letter from you. Thank you for your letters of September 10 and 15. You are so caring that I do not quite recognize you, little Stina, but poor you who has to wait so long for my letters. I should not have any excuse, but I have to work so much for the Dala-trail, and I am so tired when I get home. I am still satisfied, since I am moving "forward." The only things I want are hope, patience, and advancement.

I intended to write a long letter, but I send this one first, since I want to send it tonight. I am invited to a family birthday party, so I cannot write that much. I also send a picture of me in my new uniform, one you have never seen, Stina. What do you think? Do you recognize me? I think I look thinner. Recently, I called tel. No 10 and talked to Justina with greetings from you. My tel. No is 503. Many greetings to you from them. They sent a letter 28 September that you should get before my letter. Yesterday evening, I saw Alva and forwarded your greetings.

I will speak about your journey home in my next letter in a day or so. Sure, I think it will be nice, very nice. Paris, yes, if we could meet there in spring or early summer. I do not think it would be impossible for me. Thank you, kind Stina, for your question regarding whether you should buy me socks, pajamas, and other things. You should not buy things for me. But is it much cheaper over there? I could send you the money.

As I said, you will have another letter soon, little Stina, and good night with heartfelt greetings from "a good boy."

Good night! X x x x x

Letter 35

16 December 1924. Letter to Stina, Minneapolis, from Sven, Bollnäs.

Envelope: Miss Stina Ohman
              1906 Park Ave (Apt 12)
              Minneapolis
              Minnesota
              U.S.A.

Envelope back: Sender: Sven Bengtzon
                            Box 16
                            Bollnäs
                            Sweden

Dear Stina!

Many thanks for the letter and my most unspeakably hearty thanks for the charming "pajamas" and the stockings, you, with a kind heart, have sent me! (*This sentence was written in English!*)

Everything has arrived safely, and I am now sleeping so well in my new nightdress, something I have never before had on my body. It is so very stylish—but what should I buy for you? If I were rich, or at least had more money than I do, I would find something, but unfortunately, I have not. Happiness and sorrow never come alone as they say. When I received the package from you, I was promoted to first office printer. This was on 2 December. I have been longing for this advancement ever since my education, 1918-1919. I had many congratulations with flowers and telephone calls on my name day, 5 December. I also had a small party for about 20 people with some dancing. Everyone was so happy and pleased. The Sven-boy was very happy.

I finally have a more solid ground for my future, perhaps a dear home of my own and for my future bride.

Perhaps it is too hasty, since despite my age, I have not yet understood what it is like to be happy, but we will see. It seems, nowadays, I have more girls to choose from, but I will not be hasty.

Soon we have Christmas again, although we have no snow and no real winter cold. What will Christmas be like here in the north without snow, the jingle of harness bells, the silvery moon, and the glittering from thousands of snow crystals?

What do you think about my English? Do you understand it? I think I could manage to write a letter all in English, but it would take too long, and soon it is night again. I will now go to bed in my lovely pajamas. I will have a good night's sleep and see what I will dream of.

On Christmas Eve, I will go to my brother and sister-in-law's home in Voxna and will stay for Christmas day. I will have to go to work again the day after Christmas. In the evening, I am invited to visit a family where I know I am very welcome. Then it will soon be the New Year again.

I wish you a Merry Christmas and a Happy New Year!

Good night! I will now go to bed.

Heartwarming greetings from the boy,

Sven

Letter 36

24 December 1924. Letter to Stina, Minneapolis, from her father, Carl E. Ohman, Edsbyn.

Envelope: Froken Stina Ohman

                    1906 Park Ave

                    Minneapolis

                    U.S.A.

Return address: Carl E. Ohman

                    Edsbyn

My little Stina and my Lennart,

It is 11:00AM.

We are now home from the church. The seven of us all got up on Christmas day and got into the car, our small Citroen, and intended to go to church. But the load was too heavy so a tire blew out right in front of Ole's. So from there we walked, Mother, Jussi, Anna, Nelly, and I. The boys stayed to change the tire. We have talked a lot about you both on Christmas Eve (last night) and today, as we always do, especially when we light the Christmas tree. We are then reminded that it was you who used to light the tree when you were home. We are sure you feel most lonely when Christmas comes, since Christmas is the family holiday. Thank God, next Christmas you will be home. There is no winter here yet. Today is + 6 degrees C (*43 degrees F*), and it has been like this for several weeks. On the 14th, Mother and I went to Skagen, and it was the same weather, +6. We carved the date on a cliff in the woods just to remember. We have warmer weather here than on the Riviera. It is blooming. The trees have buds, and all is green. We will let the cows out today. Our cow "Beautiful" has a daughter that is two years old and is soon going to have a calf. She is milking extremely well, just as "Beautiful" did. The boys have bought seven hens that they care for. They had their first two eggs yesterday on Christmas Eve. As you can imagine, they are very happy. I'm sending you a clip from the paper, so you can see what an unusual year we have had. We have not had such a winter since 1780. The sun is shining beautifully today (*Christmas day*), and everything is green.

Jussi and I have been busy from early morning till late in the evening for four days buying furs from local trappers. I sort, and she writes and handles the money. The house and especially the hall and the office have been full of people every day. Sometimes we have not had the time to eat. We have already bought 2,000 furs. You know we are now established in the business, so the revenue increases for us each year. You must continue this business after me and combine it with a nice fur and fashion shop, which I hope you will own and oversee together with your capable sisters and brothers.

On New Year's Eve we will go to the Temperance Hall and listen to Åke and Fingal. They are hired to play as we count down to midnight. You know how good he is to play the most difficult pieces like Donauwellen, Hammarforsens brus, Destiny, and more. For him, it is very easy and with the most beautiful sounds. If you could hear Göthe on the second part, Åke on the first, and the girls accompanying on the piano, playing the installation march of the German Queen, I am sure you would need a handkerchief, my goodhearted, Stina.

Anna and the boys went to Bollnäs yesterday and bought a few things for Christmas. The boys bought two grey Persian caps that are beautiful and Åke also bought an Ulster (*a camel coat*). The caps were 75 crowns each. You know, now that a higher class of patrons are hiring them, they must look good. Nelly worked in Signe Persson's shop yesterday when Signe went away. Nelly always works there when Signe goes away. Why should you not have a shop of your own?

At last I would like to wish you a Happy New Year, but above all, good health, happiness, peace, and a happy journey home. Pappa

We are all healthy and well. We get along well with one another and have a blessed peace. We have not said a single harsh word to each other for several months and years. It shows we have a very good and understanding relationship among us. I guess it helps that my anger and impatience has been better during the years. You older children had to suffer from this many times, and for that, I really want your forgiveness. You have already forgiven me as you have said in your letters many years ago. You said it was forgotten long ago and forever. Thank you little Stina.

Pappa

Thank you for all the letters, for the nice Christmas card, and for the photo. I have kissed the little gold nugget and his noble mother. Please be patient with Lennart and greet him from his grandfather.

Letter 37

26 December 1924. Letter to Stina, Minneapolis, from Carl E. Ohman, Edsbyn.

Envelope: Miss Stina Ohman
              1906 Park Ave
              Minneapolis
              Minnesota
              U.S.A.

My little Stina and Lennart,

Thank you for your letters. We can see that you are not healthy, and it worries us. You should think of yourself. It is easy to believe that you do not get the proper care. Please be careful so that we can see each other once more in life. On the other hand, perhaps you should not come if it is necessary to stay in the U.S. in order to live and take care of your little boy. But, for me, I should value it very much to see you once more. As I promised you when you left, I would like to contribute to your journey home. You have now been gone from us four Christmases. We believe you when you say this is the last Christmas you will be away from us. Next Christmas you will be here, and perhaps even sooner. Thank you, God. We are all healthy and well, but we have had some trouble with the patents for the inventions. Tomorrow night at 8:00, we will all go to Bethlehemskyrkan (*The Church of Bethlehem*) and listen to Åke. They will do a charity concert for the poor people for Christmas. It is the first time he will perform in public. There are fourteen in the orchestra, and they asked Åke to play with them after ironmonger Bergstrand died. As you perhaps know, he died in Jerusalem this summer. I am sure you would like to listen to Åke; he is such a good musician.

I am sending you a little Christmas present. Please let us know as soon as you are healthy again. Everyone is home except Gustaf, Emma, and you. Anna is in the factory with Åke, Göthe, and Lindkvist working on the new bowsaw. You should come home and start a shop somewhere so that your siblings could have something to do. I am really sorry for them. You could have one together, and I will help you get started. Emma and Klang will start with a hardware and sport shop. They intend to buy it from Frid. There you could also have a shop together, or maybe you would like to start a shop at some other place. If you cannot come, we are seriously thinking that the girls could try a fashion shop and something else, perhaps shoes, in one of the ends of the Frid's house. If it should not work out well, we could sell the house. Please let us know about your thoughts.

From our heart we wish you a happy and good Christmas.

Pappa

This is our business card:

CARL ÖHMANS SÄGBÅGSFABRIK
FIRMAN GRUNDAD 1890
EDSBYN, SCWEDEN

Representant: ALEX VELTIN

Carl Öhmans Sawbow Factory
Established in 1890

This is an order form from our catalogue that our salesman uses:

Edsbyn Sawbow Factory – Carl Öhman.

Established in 1890.

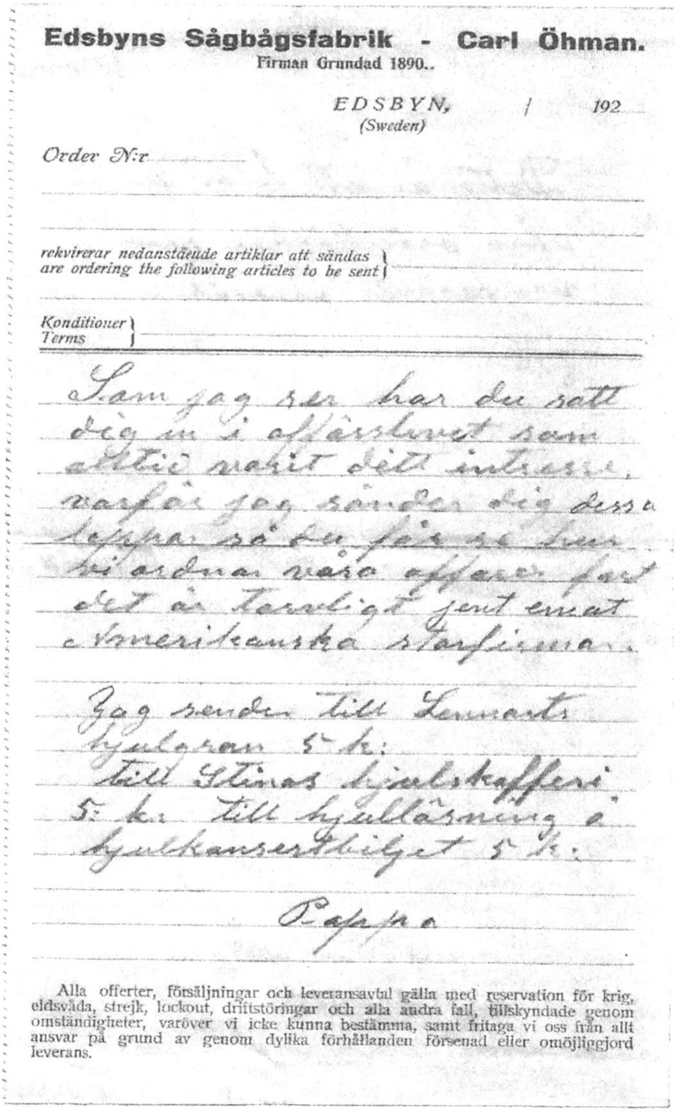

Edsbyns Sågbågsfabrik - Carl Öhman.
Firman Grundad 1890..

E D S B Y N, / 192
(Sweden)

Order N:r

rekvirerar nedanstående artiklar att sändas }
are ordering the following articles to be sent }

Konditioner }
Terms }

[handwritten letter in Swedish]

110

(Carl's handwritten note on the front of the order form)
Since we can see that you understand business, you should have
your own shop. Business has always been your interest. I, therefore,
send you these notes so you can see how we arrange our offers,
although this of course, is very simple compared to the big
American companies.

I am sending 5 crowns for Lennart's Christmas tree and for Stina's
Christmas food and 5 crowns for some reading and a Christmas
concert.

Pappa

(Printed at the bottom of the order form)
All offers, sales and contracts are valid, except in the case of
war, fire, strike, lockout, disruption in production, or any other
situation that is beyond our level of control. In which case, we
cannot be responsible for delivery, as case shipments may be
delayed and shipment orders may be cancelled.

Postcard to inform patrons of representative's upcoming visit:

```
                    Edsbyn, poststämpelns datum.

        S. H. T.

        Härmed beder jag få meddela, att min repre-
        sentant Herr ALEX VELTIN omkring den...............
        skall hava nöjet göra Eder sin uppvaktning.
        I hopp om att Ni åt honom reserverar Edra
        värderade order har jag äran teckna

                        Med all högaktning
                    Edsbyns Sågbågsfabrik
                        CARL ÖHMAN.
```

Edsbyn. postmark date.

I hereby ask to inform you that my representative,

Mr. ALEX VELTIN, will be around the *(enter day, month)*

and will have the pleasure to visit with you.

I hope you will reserve your highly appreciated order with him.

Yours sincerely,

Edsbyns Sawbow Factory

CARL ÖHMAN.

Letter 38

1 February 1925. Letter to Stina, Minneapolis, from Carl, her father, Edsbyn.

The opened envelope was sealed, but there is no name, stamp, or address on the envelope. "Our dear children are not at home" is penciled on the front. The entire letter is written in pencil. It is unclear how Stina received this letter; perhaps it was enclosed in a package.

Dear Stina!

Thank you for the letter. It is so comforting to know that you are well again and in a good mood although life is hard. Now we have something to be happy about and to wait for, since it seems you are seriously thinking of coming home to see your family. It might be a tough journey for you, but how could we think of not being able to see each other again? You have to decide now; you know that we cannot come to you. I will keep my promise, as you know me, and I will cover the expense for you to come. You will never know what fate has in store for you, and we do not want to have any influence on your decision. We are so happy and will meet you somewhere south. We will take two cars, so the whole family can come.

We have not made any business deal yet with Signe. We have offered 7,000 crowns but she asks for 8,600. If we cannot make a deal with her, we have decided to go for Frid's instead. We have come to an agreement with them: 25,000 for the stock of shoes and 35,000 for the house. We can have it at once if we want it. Then we will keep the shoe shop and will prepare a fashion shop in the same building. The girls can handle both shops, but they want your help to begin with.

Yes, little Stina, this is the way it is with me. I started to write over a month ago, but then I stopped since I could not finish it in one sitting. Now I intend to continue since we are alone.

Anna, Nelly, Göthe, and Åke have gone by car to Mora/Dalarna this morning for the Vasaloppet. Just think of it, such an unnecessary trip, 10 miles of driving without a profit. But they are too old now for us to say anything. We do not want them to be mad at us. Only Jussi, Mother, and I are at home. Gustaf has not been here since February of last year. Signe Persson did not move, so we cannot buy her shop. We have not finished the deal completely with Frid's, although we have only to decide, yes or no. It is, of course, a risk; the girls are rather lazy and not so competent. The best would be if you were at home. It seems from your last letter that you are unsure again. The decision must be yours since we do not know what such a journey will bring for your future. You must not strain yourself. To me, it should be good for your future if you had your own shop here, but I do not want to give you any advice. Still I would be glad to help you.

Tomorrow, Göthe will go into the military, and on Friday, Mother will be 60.

If you have now decided to come home you must inform us soon, so we can send the money. If you should want to go before the money has come, please telegraph, and I can arrange to pay for the journey here with the agency. They can inform their office in America, and you can go as soon as you want, i.e., within a few days. I have arranged that it will not be deducted from your inheritance (if there is anything left). It will be a totally independent common contribution for your trip that will not be counted on, about 2,000 crowns. I hope you will understand this correctly.

Thank you, I have now received two letters from you before I had this one ready to mail.

Can you imagine, it is so strange in Sweden this year. I can mention that the people from Stockholm who usually go to their houses in Rattvik and Leksand (*cities in Dalarna*) to dance around the Christmas tree, have danced around the Maypole instead this year. We have had almost no winter at all, and the ones selling firewood in Stockholm have had a bad business. Next month, our traveling sales representative will start to travel again.

Just think my dear little one, my highest wish is that I could have you here with a nice shop somewhere in Sweden, so we could visit each other. Do you not think that we should try to make this happen while we are all alive and before it is too late?

Dear greetings from the heart of your Mamma and Pappa

Just imagine if you do not want to be here in Edsbyn anymore and if you'd like us to move, that would be possible for us. We do not have much to keep us here.

The Vasaloppet is an annual, long distance cross-country ski race inspired by King Gustav Vasa who fled from foreign soldiers during the winter of 1520. (Wikipedia: online resource.)

We can infer that Carl and Kerstin would consider moving to another town in Sweden, not to the United States.

Letter 39

18 February 1925. Letter to Stina, Minneapolis, from Sven, Bollnäs.

Envelope: Miss Stina Ohman

1906 Park Ave (Apt 12)

Minneapolis, Minn.

U.S.A.

Dear Stina, little friend!

I have a concern deep in my heart, and I do not really know why? There has been something strange in the air all this so-called winter. One day like summer, and the next day like winter, but mostly as if it were spring. In spring, so many things are brought to life again, and great wonders happen. Then you believe it is finally here, the most wonderful season of them all, just to find that it was only a tease of nature. All falls into the land of deep dreams and dormancy to again be awakened when the final spring arrives. Stina, you cannot imagine the strange winter we have had in the land of the north; not yet, has there been any snow. However, tonight a little snow has been falling, making many happy and satisfied. They are putting ice in the railway cars and transporting it to Stockholm, Göteborg, and Malmo. This has never happened before, and there is a threat that the lumber workers in the woods may lose their jobs. But let's hope that everything will be OK again.

Thank you for your long sweet letter or rather for both of them. I have received two letters from you since I wrote to you last. You are scolding me for not writing to you, and you always wonder why I cannot send letters more often. This question, I cannot answer myself, since I do not know why. Many times I think I will write, but then, something is missing or something prevents me from writing. <u>You</u>, in your last letter, told me how much you love me, and what I <u>once</u> was for you. What I, then, wanted to be. All this makes me happy to hear although it is the result of what I have given. Now that I have reached a mature age, I realize that this is true. Things like this, of course, give me a renewed hope and safe ground to imagine our life together again, and I can let down my guard. However, "A burnt child dreads the fire." Stina, have you ever thought about how many years have gone by since our engagement was broken and what this might mean? I, as well as You, have had the opportunity to evaluate others for marriage, but as I sit at this table, I do not know who "she" will be. Fate is so fickle and unpredictable; one never knows when "the true one" will be found. There are a lot of <u>sweet</u> girls here who like me, I know that. Some care a lot for me. I can tell you this openly without being egotistical, but when I contemplate a new relationship, there is something missing. I have some unrest. You say that I am not satisfied. You give me advice, or, what should I call that which you give me? Your advice cannot help me, as I am who I am. I have become what I am through the hardships in my life. That is, I cannot help who I am! Sometimes I feel that I am fond of you, or should I rather say, I again feel the warmth when I think of you. But other times, I have no true feelings for you, not the kind of feelings I had in my youth. I've always wanted to be honest with you, and that is why I am telling you this now. Perhaps this is an explanation of why I don't write that often. Many times, especially when reading your letters, something warm and affectionate comes over me, and in these moments, my answer to your question, would be, "yes."

After a while, however, I, again, come to my senses. This is what I feel right <u>now</u>: Stina, it is a good thing that you are so far away. This distance is good for the happiness of us both. Don't you agree?

When you once again come home, we will meet and see how we both feel toward one another. Are you happy with what I suggest, and can you also see the seriousness of what we then decide? Until then, I promise, I will not become serious with another, and when I see you, fate will decide.

You must not feel this has broken our secret relationship. On the other hand, it is a strong link in the entwined chain of our lives that could once again be strengthened! Please do not understand my words to be a promise. When we see each other, I will tell you all about my life since 1920. Of course, I am longing for a home of my own, and I would have had this home two years ago had it not been for my debts. But this is not the only reason. Perhaps I will never have a wife of my own to love. Perhaps I can never save the money to purchase a home. Knowing this, makes me worried and sometimes depressed.

The Magnussons are all well, and I give you greetings from them.

It is now midnight, and I will have a new working day in a few hours. I must leave you now and go to bed. I will keep you close to my side, little Stina. I give you a long and warm goodnight kiss. Many many greetings! Live well!   Sven

You are so sweet in your costume. The photo is a little dark. It is too bad.

Do you have handsome neckties in the USA? Please send me one that you like, to make your Swedish boy look good. Please do not be angry with me for asking a favor of you.

Letter 40

12 June 1925. Letter to Stina, Minneapolis, from Sven, Bollnäs.

Envelope: Miss Stina Ohman

             1906 Park Ave (Apt12)

             Minneapolis, Minnesota

             U.S.A.

Envelope back: Sender: Sven Bengtzon

                        Box 16

                        Bollnäs

Dearest Little Stina,

Thank you, sweet Stina, for both of your letters. They are always so welcomed and longed for. The kisses you are sending me, I received. They are so dear and warm, although they are not real kisses. It feels so wonderful in my heart, also hard, since the distance and time will not make it possible for real feelings. And when once we meet again, life may be exactly as it once was. Perhaps it feels even greater, apart, because the distance keeps the great feelings stronger.

Almost every time and especially the last time, when I read your sweet and affectionate letters, I get sad. I wish to be alone with my thoughts, and too often I want to cry. The desire to cry and then hold it back shuts my throat and makes me choke. At this time, my whole life seems to have no meaning, and it seems totally wasted. But then, it is over. It has to be so, and the usual life goes on. The days come and go, almost always the same. We, humans, can so easily get accustomed to the simple things in life. Those things that are really valuable seem to stay away and may never come back. You may take a new step in life, but before this can be realized, so many things must be considered.

I have just come home from a little trip and just received your letter. I am sitting in my little apartment all alone. The sun is shining through a cloudy heaven like threads of silk beyond the veranda door behind me. Since I have been sleeping well, I feel refreshed. I sit down to write to you as you have asked me to do so many times before. I have been down to Alingsas, close to Göteborg, to visit an old roommate in his parents' house, where he is spending his vacation. We have had a nice time sunning and swimming at the beach. You may think I look like a negro; you should see my black face. I have now used some of my vacation for this year. I still have fourteen days left. I have not decided when I shall apply for these days. Of course, I would like to have the rest of my vacation in July or August during the summer months, and I'm sure you will not be home until after this? I would like to spend my vacation with you as you have suggested, but you know, little Stina, I don't think I can wait because it seems you have not yet made up your mind to travel here. Perhaps it will not happen. This may be all words and no action, like in the past. Anyway, I do not think you will be home before August. What do you think? Perhaps you will be here in time for my 30th birthday on 4 September? I had hoped to be married before this birthday, but it will not happen.

Of course, I would like to go to Germany with you, but I cannot afford that. It is still as sad as before and difficult for me to get rid of the heavy burden of debt. It will follow me to the grave. Because of this, I suppose, I will surely live alone, unless I happen to win the lottery. I have been playing the lottery a lot during the past years. I will say no more of this as you may be bored.

Thank you for considering to purchase the tie. I am confident it will be a very nice tie knowing your good taste.

Emma is writing to me saying how good-looking I am. I don't think I have ever been stylish. I am sure I have not changed much from looking at me, but I'm sure I am different on the inside.

Not long ago I made a business trip to Edsbyn on the trolley. I went there in the evening and visited the Ohman house. They were all very nice to me. I got a meal and stayed the night there. I stayed in the small room beside the kitchen. The last time I was in that room was during the night when Emma's Lennart was born, and I believe that you, Stina, were there with me a great part of the night. This memory made me sad. Gustaf was also home for a visit, but left for Stockholm in the night. Everyone is well, and they are waiting for your arrival. Your mother is still so nice to me. Åke has a motorcycle that I am driving a lot. I will probably buy it from him, but then again, I lack the money. This always interferes with my plans.

We are having a very warm summer; it is too bad the summer is so short. You will have to hurry if you want some summer in Sweden. If you decide to come to Sweden, please inform me as soon as possible, and I will meet you at the boat in Göteborg. You are <u>so</u> welcomed home and <u>also</u> welcomed by me.

Many warm and dear greetings, a thousand kisses, and a great hug from your old boy, Sven

Letter 41

21 June 1925 (Mid-summer). Letter to Stina, Minneapolis, from Carl E. Ohman, Edsbyn.

Envelope: Miss Stina Ohman

1906 Park Ave. (Apt 12)

Minneapolis

MINN U.S.A.

Dear Little Stina,

Mother and I are sitting alone in our summer cottage. Nelly and Anna are on the second floor. Jussie is with Emma at their house. Göthe and Åke are seldom at home on Sundays. Åke is so busy, he is never with us. He is playing three times a week at the café and every Saturday and Sunday at The Dance. In between, he plays at the hotel. And so it is, at home in the garden, we seldom have any music.

We are now sitting and thinking of you. We had arranged to have two cars so that the whole family could come to meet you and be comfortable. We were so sure you were coming. But now we can see that you cannot come for various reasons, which we are not surprised over. We have now left everything to fate to see if we will ever see one another again in this life and be able to hug one another.

You see, we are longing so enormously for you both. If we had something to offer you for the future, we would force you to come home. But since we do not have that, it is better that we leave the decision with you, and we will still have the hope that fate will bring us together for an unspeakably happy reunion. We remember you as a young child at the table with us, you, on your mother's knee, where without problem you took your first little handful of bread.

We are now waiting for Gustav who will come home from Stockholm later tonight. He is bringing home the third car in three weeks for us to sell. It is a passenger car, larger than the others. We will keep this ourselves until you come home. He will stay over through mid-summer, so now you are the only one who is not at home.

We intend to go out in the lovely green of nature during the days and go home during the evenings to make it easy for Mother. We want to live in a simple way to just enjoy the beautiful season, the best of all seasons. I'm sending you a leaf from the birch that you planted near the gate. It is now higher than the barn. This birch is the first to bud in the spring and the last to lose its leaves in the fall. It also has the most beautiful leaves.

Have you suffered much from the heat wave, the storm, and the natural disasters that we are reading about in the U.S.?

When you come home, bring a good car.

From Momma and Pappa

Göthe is going to begin his military service commitment in October. He will serve as a fortress engineer.

Stina, age 31, and my father, Lennart, age 5,
returned to Edsbyn during the late summer of 1925.
My father enjoyed the companionship of his cousins,
as he spoke fluent Swedish.
His cousin Lennart Klang (Stina's sister, Emma's son)
became a dear friend.

I remember my father speaking of Lennart Klang. He said he played with Lennart when he was in Sweden as a small child. My father loved his cousin Lennart. When my husband, Jerry, and I returned from our first visit to Sweden in 1974, my father asked if we had seen Lennart Klang. We hadn't. My father often wondered if Lennart was still alive. He hoped to see Lennart Klang again, but unfortunately, this never occurred.

Letter 42

20 October 1925. Letter to Stina, Edsbyn, from Sven, Bollnäs.

Envelope: Froken Stina Ohman

                        Edsbyn

My own little Stina,

I recently talked to you on the phone. I'm happy you are not
cross with me. You must forgive your little boy's stupidities, but if I
had been able to see you, since I had waited in the cold two hours
for you, it would never have happened as it did. But this is OK now.
Don't you think? After all, this is our first disagreement (and it
surely won't be the last) since you've come home.

Would you please give the enclosed installment check to Uncle
so that I can put this burden aside for a month or so? It is a pity and
perhaps unkind of me to let my little fiancé handle my financial
affairs. But still, it may be all right since we were born to help one
another. At least, I see it this way more and more. The only thing in
life that I want is to have you at my side as it once was meant to be.
However, I don't need any return for us as long as we are able to be
satisfied in life. At least that is the way I think right now. I
understand more and more each day that you are here with me
again. And what is your innermost wish (as you said to me last
Saturday when we met at my house)?

When we were together in Sundsvall, or to say it more correctly,
when we met, I intended to ask you about something that I need to
know right now. It didn't seem the right time, then, especially since
I had been drinking too much. But now I still want to ask you, and
hope you will understand me the way you always do, and answer

me without being sad. If you would not like the question, we will just forget about it. Here it is: Can you, little Stina, without reservation, lend your unfortunate little boy, for a short time, 150 crowns? I have to get this money quickly to sort out some business. You, and no one else, know so well that I have difficulties with money. I think I can turn to you, although it is hard for me. You must know this. Also, you must <u>not tell anyone else about this</u>. Do you understand me? Yes?

You, my little girl, must forgive me in many ways. In God's will, everything will settle in spite of it all.

Sleep well. I will call you tomorrow as usual.
Kisses and kisses from your Sven

Letter 43

5 January 1926. Letter to Stina, Edsbyn, from ??, Alfta. *Alfta is a small village 15 minutes southeast of Edsbyn. This letter is written on Swedish Motor Club stationery.*

Envelope: Froken Stina Ohman
                    Edsbyn

Beloved!

It was a pity that we couldn't meet last Saturday evening. I was very disappointed about this, since I had been looking forward to it. But I can see that it was difficult for you to travel.

I think our telephone call of today was rather weird, and there is a lot of it I do not understand.

I hope it will be as we have decided before! That nothing in this case will stop it. I will be able to see you. Do you understand this? How could it be any other way, my dear beloved, Stina?

I therefore think when you know how much I love you, nobody, and nothing must come between us, and everything shall be clear.

During the near future, I might suggest a trip again, and hope this time it will come out better, so that we can talk about many things.

From today's telephone call, you understand that it will be difficult for me to go to the U.S. And for what reason, you ask? It should not be more difficult than it is for others who go, both married and unmarried. What will be more difficult is to make a living when I am there in case there are no jobs, but I hope this will be fine. I will manage.

I have been to the cinema and have seen *Captain Blood*. Nice picture with many thrilling scenes, American. I will now try to find some beautiful music on the radio. That is the only fun you have here.

I wish each evening that I could be in Edsbyn and could see you. That is the only thing I am longing for. And why should it be so difficult? I hope the day will come when we can be together forever.

Your, ??

This admirer signs his initials at the end of the letter. The script is unintelligible.

Letter 44

12 January 1926. Letter to Stina, Edsbyn, from ??, Alfta. *This letter is written on Swedish Motor Club stationery.*

Envelope: Froken Stina Ohman

Edsbyn

Beloved!

Since I do not have you here, nor can talk to you in any other way, I write. I think that it is not good to say too much over the phone. Yes, here I am, all alone, thinking only of you and wishing you were here, so we could really talk.

You apparently do not understand how much I love you. Neither do you understand that I want you to be my own, and no one else can come between us. I have told you this before, but it doesn't seem that you understand how I feel, when I, by chance, hear that you have been out for a walk with someone else. Please do not get angry when I repeat this to you, but try to understand my feelings for you!

I am sitting here because I have no peace or quiet in my home, neither early nor late. The worries don't leave me. If it isn't one thing, it is another (my marriage or my business). I am destroyed, tired, and nervous about all this turmoil. How many times have I not thought about earlier times? Why did we not, then, understand each other? Stina, a life together, you and me with love and happiness would be much more lovely than all of this.

I am not able to write everything about my thoughts in this matter. But I will explain all of this when we meet.

I have another thing I would like to ask you about! On several occasions you have told me you know many men (lovely and beautiful) in America that you like a lot. Is it only here in Sweden that you are thinking of me? How will it be if I come to America? Will you forget me there when you meet all your other acquaintances?

Are you really sure in this case, Stina, that you are not acting too hastily? I hope it is the way you have told me; that makes me happy.

You sweet thing, how is everything with you and your cold? I hope you are taking care of yourself so that you will not get sicker. You see, I must see you soon. My last visit up there was so short. You didn't have much time, and my chauffer didn't have much time either. Better luck next time, I hope.

Last time, you asked me about a curling iron for your hair. But, I have not been able to find the price. I will tell you as soon as I have found it.

You, and always you, are always in my mind.
Your, ??

Please excuse me for this short letter.

Letter 45

16 January 1926. Letter to Stina, Edsbyn, from ??, Alfta. *This letter is written on Swedish Motor Club stationery.*

Envelope: Froken Stina Ohman

          Edsbyn

My beloved!

It is so difficult to convince you that some things are absolutely safe, that you could actually write and explain some things to me in a letter. First, I have a post box of my own. Secondly, I usually get the mail myself, and if I knew that you had written to me, I would, of course, get the mail myself.

You said over the phone that I was very impulsive and erratic when I was younger, but I would not say this is true. I, myself, had to find out how it was to be in love, not knowing whom, or where my beloved would be found.

You knew that I loved you already years ago. That made no difference to you, although I told you this many times. If you had not been so erratic yourself, everything would have been very different. Your way towards me has not changed. It is still the same. That is why I do not trust you and why I have so many questioning thoughts.

I will call you today, and then, I will know if I can see you. It is such a long time since we've seen one another, and I long for you so terribly much.

I have been thinking a lot about how I will proceed from this point. But I would like to talk to you about this and hope that it will soon be possible to meet!

I have been to the cinema and saw a Danish film with Danish film stars filmed in Rome. As usual, it was a happy ending after many adversities.

From what I hear, you will be going to the cinema. I hope the movie you see will be as good as the one I saw.

If real life were like the authors of these films suggest, the sorrow in life would always be replaced with double the happiness. If this were true, then I couldn't wait!

Yes, my beloved, Stina, I must stop now. I hope my writing is readable. I will call you as usual. I will not fool you this time, as you usually say.

Greetings from your, ??

Letter 46

20 January 1926. Letter to Stina, Edsbyn, from ??, Alfta. *Letter is written on Swedish Motor Club stationery.*

Envelope: Froken Stina Ohman
              Edsbyn

Beloved!

Since I could not talk to you over the phone today because you were not well and had gone to bed, I am now writing to ask how you are? Do you have a cold? Are you not taking care of yourself when you take your walks? I hope it will soon be over, and you will be feeling well again. I intended to go to Edsbyn today, but when I heard that you were sick, and I could not see you, I changed my mind. But, still, I wanted to write to see how you are. Please give me a call when you are better so that I may talk to you.

Have you done what I told you over the phone to do? If not, do it now, and do care for yourself. This, your ??, is asking you to do so.

Letter 47

2 February 1926. Letter to Stina, Edsbyn, from ??, Alfta. *Letter is written on Swedish Motor Club stationery.*

Envelope: Froken Stina Ohman
              Edsbyn

My True Beloved,

I am sorry that I have caused you some trouble since some people now know my feelings for you. You must understand, Stina, it is difficult for me not to tell friends about my feelings for you, especially when I get to see you so seldom. And then it happened that I have been a little careless when talking on the phone. If I could only talk to you again, I would be more careful about what I say. Do you still love me as you earlier said you did? I think I have noticed some change in you, or is it only that I am imagining this? I hope it is all in my mind, or else you will make me very unhappy.

You said you had so many things to say to me and that you should write. Well, I think you should write, too, so I can see how things are going. I want to see you, and have to do so soon. I am longing so much for you. I have tried not to call you and not to see you, but I am longing so, indescribably, for you. I'm convinced that this is nothing else but <u>love</u> for you—pure, true, love.

How I wish it was the same for you, too, Stina. That you were loving me so tenderly and that there was no one else for you. We would live happily together. However, I want to see you soon, and talk to you, and just be happy with you for a little while. Our last meeting was so short. I wish I could write all that I feel for you or that I could tell you in words, but I cannot. I become speechless. That is why it has been declared so little, both in the beginning and towards the end.

Now, I will call you and talk to you for only a moment. YES! I have just spoken to my beloved over the phone. I am now crazy, crazy, extremely crazy about you. Stina, ich liebe dich (*"I love you" in German*). I want you. You must be my little wife.

Please write to me just once, and please decide when I can pay you a visit. Today, when I called on your father's business, he said, "Welcome to Edsbyn." I, then, wished this had been many years ago. I could have traveled there often, mostly to be able to see you.

I hope it is the way I wish, and that my wish may come true. I end with greetings from your ??

Letter 48

27 April 1926. Letter to Stina, Edsbyn, from ??, Alfta.

Envelope: Froken Stina Ohman

               Edsbyn

Darling!

Call me at 6:00 PM today. I really would like to talk to You. It has been such a long time since we have spoken to each other. I was hoping to see you last Sunday, but I suppose you did not go as far as Alfta. I called You long distance yesterday. Is your line still broken? I then called on the local line, but You seemed not to be home.

I hope you will call me at the time I have mentioned above.

??

Letter 49

19 May 1926. Letter to Stina, Edsbyn, from ??, Alfta.

Envelope: Froken Stina Ohman

               Edsbyn

Beloved!

I am now enclosing the photo of you that you have asked for. I hope I will have it back as soon as possible. It is the only one I have that I can look at when I cannot see you.

134

I am longing for our next meeting. I now know that the only thing for me is to own you by myself. Dare I hope it is the same way for you? Until then, I will not be happy.

As I said, I do want to meet you, but we will have to decide a date over the phone. Tomorrow, I will probably go to Edsbyn together with my new business partner. We will probably also visit Erik at the car dealership. I, then, hope to see a little glimpse of you, my dear Stina.

I hope these hasty lines please you.

Your ??

P.S. You must not forget to return the picture. D.S.

Letter 50

27 May 1926. Letter to Stina, Edsbyn, from ??, Alfta.

Envelope: Froken Stina Ohman

          Edsbyn

Beloved!

I should not write to You. You were so mean to me over the phone! Why were You angry? You can be sure I will go to Edsbyn tomorrow and see You. I will call you as usual at 6:00 tonight and will then tell you the place and time to meet. I would suggest the same place as last time at 10:30 PM at the railway crossing when it is getting dark. This would be the safest place.

I hope you will then tell me why you were so angry. I hope that nothing has changed. I hope that it is, like it was before, and that you are still mein liebchen (*"my beloved"*).

??

NÄR INDUSTRIN KOM TILL BYN

Harry Pettersson

WHEN THE INDUSTRY CAME TO THE VILLAGE

Harry Pettersson

Edsbyns Sagbagsfabrik

Edsbyn's Bow-Saw Frame Factory; Karl Ohman

Translated by Nisse Nilsson

Utgiven av Ovanåkers Hembygdsförening 1995

Edited by Ovanåkers Homestead Properties

INNEHÅLL

Sid

138

Edsbyns Sagbagfabrik (Edsbyns Bow-Saw Frame Factory)

Karl Ohman

A dynamic craftsman came walking to Edsbyn in the beginning of the 1890s. It was Karl Ohman, a smith from the nearby parish, Alfta. He had known that in Edsbyn and Ovanaker they were calling for skillful people. He, like so many others, came from another parish, settled down at Borgen in North Edsbyn, and built his first smithy.

In order to be closer to the market place and the railroad, he soon moved to the south of Edsbyn where he built a new house and a new smithy nearby the house. There he invented a bow-saw frame of steel tubes, which was adjustable to fit the length of different blades. The frame was constructed with ingenuity and had a lever to tighten and stretch the saw blade. He applied for a patent in many countries during 1901-1902. The demand for the bow-saw frame was great in the forests, as it was so easy to handle. Even common people were looking for the frame, and changed their old clumsy wooden saws to this new saw frame to use when they cut their own firewood.

Sales

The bow-saw was sold all over Sweden, and sales spread to neighbouring countries. It was even exported in large volumes to far away countries like Canada and many more.

All the time Karl was working on frame improvements. The frame was made with the help of a template. In the beginning the steel tube had to be filled with fine ground sand in order to keep the shape when bended. That was a time consuming and expensive step in the production, and caused much angst and trouble shooting. Finally, he solved the problem with a new genius construction of a bending tool. This proved that even big problems are small when they are once solved.

Unfortunately, Karl did not apply for the patent on the new bending tool. However visitors to the smithy saw the tool and observed how remarkably it worked. They were amazed. They then reproduced the idea and applied for the patent. They utilized Karl's invention for personal gain.

Operations

The activities were at high level in the factory. Karl Ohman taught and trained his four sons in the factory work, and instructed them in technical learning and experiences. Now they were working together with employees—sometimes in shifts, busy to produce and deliver the bow-saw frames, which became highly in demand. The factory was built of wood, in two levels, and every space had to be utilized to its maximum.

Despite the recession at the time, the sales increased and the orders were streaming in, putting the factory at full production for many years.

Any desire to enlarge the building for expanded operations was not considered. The farming field close by was perhaps tempting to use, and it was probably discussed between the brothers. However, no decision was made, and they were satisfied for the time being.

Changes

During the 1920s there were many changes. Karl Ohman's old patents began to run out. He did not look after and renew them—just as he had neglectd to apply for the patent for the genius blue print of the new bending tool. This was his biggest mistake, because it meant that other factories could start the same production without changing anything in the design of the tool. Other factories became more efficient in their production, had larger production facilities, and larger sales organizations with better marketing.

Probably that was the reason why Karl Ohman's oldest son, Gustaf, moved to Stockholm in 1921 and started his own workshop. The rest of the brothers stayed in the factory at home, inventing new solutions to make the bow-saw frame even better, in order to meet the sharper and sharper competition.

They succeeded by bending one end of the frame considerably longer than the other. That change made the sawing much easier—especially where it was narrow or difficult to access. At the same time they invented a new, safer and easier device for the blade. This construction remains.

Karl Ohman

Karl Ohman was obviously a very enterprising and technically skilled person. His ingenious bow-saw frame is proof. It places him among those, who, like Olof Abergs axe factory and Edsbyns Ski factory, who at the same time made Edsbyn well known, far outside the border of Sweden. The bow-saw frames must have been a profitable product. It made it possible for Karl to build a large, magnificent house in Edsbyn, Ojollasbacken, where he planted a garden with trees and bushes, and laid out a showy flower garden. All of this surrounded by a high, thick hedge.

Karl was approaching the age of 70. He was still vital and took part in the work at the factory whenever he wanted to. Certainly, he had been thinking about who of the sons would be best suited to continue the business. His choice was Gote. He was the second youngest among the brothers, just over 30. He had been in the factory since childhood and knew almost everything about what was going on there.

The Year 1936

The factory was transferred to Gote Ohman in 1936. His brothers were still there for a while, but soon they went on to other business interests. Gote Ohman was working with a few employees, and presumably sometimes when they were busy, Karl Ohman assisted in the factory when he was needed. In this way the company was carried on, with no desire to enlarge and expand. Karl Ohman passed away in 1947 at age 81.

Gote Ohman continued in this location until the middle 1970s when the growing town was closing in on his old worn out factory. He saw no other option other than to move away. He found a property in Ullungsfors, just outside Edsbyn. On this property he built both a home and a shop. He continued with his business at that place until 1981 when he suddenly passed away, 75 years old.

Ake Ohman

Ake Ohman was the younger brother of Gote. When the factory was transferred to Gote, Ake started on his own. He bought a bike shop, Nystroms bicycle shop, on the main street in Edsbyn, where he also started a mechanical shop. He employed two brothers, William and Martin Viklund, who later on became his partners in the tire shop. Ake was lucky, because the two brothers were musicians. William played the piano and accordian while Martin was playing the drums and percusssion instruments.

Ake Ohmans dance band that had been shattered during the war, could now be re-established. Presumably, all three of them had escaped from being drafted into the army, because repairing and vulcanising old tires was essential for the war effort.

Ake Ohman rented a big space in "Rosa" Holger Tornqvists newly built premises, well suited for industrial operations. There he made farm trailers and surreys. The wheels were taken from old scrapped automobiles and in this way, could be refurbished. This was a great novelty not only for the farmers, but also for the horses. The horse no longer had to drag the old heavy surrey wheels.

The great flames of music

All of Karl Ohmans family were musically gifted. It is uncertain from whom the children inherited their abilities, Karl or his wife, Kerstin. Karl encouraged them by buying a table piano made of walnut, at which time, daughter, Nelly, proved she had a great talent. Each of the children could choose the instrument they wished to play. Presumably, there were many people who would stop by to listen when the Ohman family practiced their music.

Ake, the youngest, was the first who really wanted to start a dance band. He was just 20 when jazz, and then foxtrot, became popular in Sweden at the end of the 1920s. The old Swedish folk dances of hambo, polska, and schottis were soon forgotten. Despite the bad times, there was a great demand for simple ballroom dancing.

Ake put together a band with himself playing the violin and saxofon, Gote playing klarinett and saxofon, and Nelly at the piano. Brass players and and drummers were also found. Wherever his band was playing, big crowds gathered. Akes dance band toured all over Helsingland until the war started in 1939, when the armys drafting made it impossible to continue.

Ake Ohman passed away in 1959, too young, at 51 years old.

Sågrörbågens uppfinnare död

Smidesfabr. Carl Öhman med den berömda sågbågen.

Den 2 januari avled fabrikören *Carl E. Öhman*, Edsbyn. Han var född den 31 maj 1866 i Ovanåker.

Den bortgångne härstammade från en vallonsläkt och fick därför i unga år lära sig smidesyrket av sin fader, Erik Olov Ulrik Lizederius, vilken som knekt fick tillnamnet Öhman.

Redan som liten flyttade han med sina föräldrar till Grängsbo och fick där sin uppväxttid. I tjugoårsåldern flyttade han med sina föräldrar till Bollnäs, där han emellertid stannade endast ett år för att i stället flytta till Edsbyn och öppna egen smidesrörelse.

Genom intresserat och ihärdigt arbete kröntes hans ansträngningar snart med framgång. Hans klara blick och goda omdömesförmåga satte honom i stånd att komma med den ena uppfinningen efter den andra, och stora äro de tjänster, han på så sätt gjort såväl industrin som skogsbruket. Den mest kända av Öhmans uppfinningar är rörsågbågen, genom vilken han gjorde sitt namn känt över hela landet. Senaste patentet är en maskin för filning av sågblad.

Intresserad av allt som var nytt blev han ägare av den första bilen i Ovanåker och därmed även innehavare av det första trafiktillståndet i socknen.

Ett av Öhmans största intressen vid sidan av arbetet var jakten, och då han därtill hade stort intresse för vapen, sökte sig de flesta av jägarna till honom, då deras vapen behövde repareras. Under ett 40-tal år var han uppköpare av viltskinn.

Den bortgångne var en idérik och skicklig yrkesman och länge kommer han att minnas av sina vänner.

Yrket har gått i arv till sönerna, av vilka en fortsätter smidesrörelsen i Edsbyn, en annan innehar Öhmans Smidesverkstad, Karlberg, Stockholm.

Journal of the Organization of Blacksmith, Forging, and Mechanical Foundry
(Translated by Eva Johansson)
31 January 1947
Page 43

The Inventor of the Bow Saw is Dead

The forging manufacturer Carl Ohman shows his famous bow saw.
(caption under photograph)

On January 2 the inventor and manufacturer Carl E. Ohman, Edsbyn, passed away. He was born on 31 May 1866 in Ovanaker.

Carl descended from a family of French speaking Walloon ironworkers who migrated from Belgium to the Swedish iron mines. His grandfather, Carl Ulrik Diziderius-Ohman, took the surname Ohman while in the army. Carl learned metal forging from his grandfather, as well as his father, Erik Olsson Ohman, who died when Carl was 30 years old. Both men were a great influence in Carl's interest in metallurgy.

When Carl was a young boy he moved to Grangsbo with his parents, where he was raised. When he was about 20, he moved with his family to Bollnas. He only stayed there for one year, and then moved to Edsbyn to start his own forging business.

Because of his great interest and hard work, he soon was very successful. He saw what was needed and had a good mind for design, and made inventions and improvements continuously. His inventions have revolutionized industry and forestry. The most well known invention of his, is the bow saw. This made him known all over the country. His latest patent is for a machine that files saw blades.

Since he was interested in everything that was new, he was the first owner of a driver's license in the Ovanaker parish.

One of his biggest interests, apart from the business, was hunting. He was also very interested in weapons. He repaired many weapons for hunters. For forty years he was a trapper and dealer of wild skins.

He was a creative and skilled craftsman, who will long be remembered by his friends.

His sons have inherited the factory. Gothe took over the home business in Edsbyn, Gustav owns the Ohman Forging Factory at Karlberg, Stockholm, and Ake opened a second metal forging factory in Edsbyn.

Reflections

Letters 26 – 50

Carl Ohman (Stina's father and my great-grandfather)

Carl was an inventor in metal forging. His father, Erik Ohman
(1833 – 1896) was also a metal smith and founded the factory of
forging furnaces, machines, hammers, and dies in 1890. Access to
raw materials was in place when Carl inherited the shop. One of
Carl's first inventions was a method to bend a metal pipe ¾ inch in
diameter to form a handle for a saw blade. Up until this time, metal
would pinch or break when bended, and most saw handles were
made of wood. Carl patented this bowsaw made of metal tubing in
1901.

The German army used an invention of Carl's in World War I. It
was a metal ammunition box. A leather belt strap was threaded
through the box. A soldier could throw the strap over his shoulder
and carry his ammunition. These were used on military treks. The
ammunition boxes were sold throughout Europe, but were primarily
used by the German troops. My father, Leonard, had one of these
boxes that his grandfather had crafted. I saw it when I was young. I
thought it was heavy, too heavy to carry, especially if it was filled
with ammunition.

Carl's later invention is noted in his letter to Stina on 18 April
1924. It was an apparatus attached to the handle of the bowsaw that
when released, loosened the blade for removal, i.e., blade
replacement or blade sharpening.

I remember my grandmother Stina criticizing her father for
failing to renew the patent on the bowsaw and neglecting to apply
for a patent for the tool used to bend the pipe for the upper bowsaw

handle. Carl also forgot to apply for a patent on the new lever release that would allow the blade to be removed from the bowsaw. My grandmother said her father was lazy and did not want to work hard in the factory. She said he liked to take walks and daydream in the woods, leaving the factory work to her brothers. Carl was an outdoorsman and especially liked to hunt moose. Grandpa Carl (morfar; Mother's father) took young Lennart moose hunting several times during Stina and Lennart's visit to Edsbyn (1925-1928).

Carl opened a Ford automobile dealership in Edsbyn in 1909. He purchased a Model T for himself and also sold his first car as a dealer that same year. He was the sole proprietor of Fords in his community for thirteen years. A family feud emerged in 1922 when Erik Ohman, Carl's nephew, and others, formed a partnership and opened a second Ford dealership taking business away from Carl (letter of 12 July 1923). This is the same Erik Ohman (with his wife, Berta) whom Stina lived with when she first arrived in Minneapolis in 1920. Stina lent Erik money when he and Berta permanently returned to Edsbyn shortly after Stina's arrival.

A post-war economic recession affected all of Europe after World War I (1914-1918). Sweden, also, experienced financial strain. Carl writes to Stina in his letter of 5 June 1922, " . . . without exception, even the wealthiest are without money." In early 1922, in a letter to her father, Stina suggested that the family consider a venture in selling wholesale furs. Her brothers had trapped and sold wild pelts for years. Stina also suggested that she select and purchase new cars for Carl's dealership and accompany their transport to Sweden. Carl would send Stina the start-up

146

money. Carl liked both of these ideas. Two new ventures would help alleviate the financial burden during the economic recession due to the shut down of the foundry. The letter of 24 December 1924 mentions that Carl and daughter, Jussi, worked for four days at the villa buying fur pelts from local trappers. These furs were then sold at the fur market in Uppsala.

Carl missed his daughter immensely. He often mentioned in his letters his desire for Stina to return to Edsbyn and establish a fur and fashion business with her siblings while he was still living. The family prepared several times for Stina's return to Edsbyn. Each time they were disappointed. Stina questioned her return to Sweden all along, as she had acclimated well to the U.S. The family and Sven learned to take her mention of returning to Sweden with skepticism.

On our first trip to Sweden in 1974, my husband, Jerry, and I met Eva and her parents: Göthe (Eva's father and Stina's younger brother) and Singa (Eva's mother) in Edsbyn. Göthe and Singa did not speak English, and we did not speak Swedish. Eva, who is one year younger than me, was our interpreter; she had learned English in school. All of us did a lot of smiling, head nodding, and "Ya" ing to assure one another's acceptance. We found body language worked well, and also facial expression. Göthe and I could stand next to each other and feel the warmth of family. There was no need for words. Our commonality, as family, was present.

Göthe proudly showed us his forging shop and gave us an "Ohman" bowsaw. We still have it. The label on the saw handle reads:

ÖHMAN

EDSBYNS SAGBAGSFABRIK

LANDETS ALDSTA TILLVERKARE

OHMAN

EDSBYN'S BOWSAW FACTORY

THE OLDEST MANUFACTURER IN THE COUNTRY

The bowsaw hung on the wall in our home as a conversation piece for many years. Now, since we live in the woods, the saw has been used numerous times for sawing wood, and the word OHMAN has worn off.

Göthe inherited the metal forging factory after Carl's death and owned the 1901 patent papers on the original bowsaw. He later moved the factory to his own property and homesite. The factory was near a cold, freshwater creek fed by the runoff of mountain snowmelt. During the tour of the factory and surrounding property, Jerry and I noticed an animal cage in the stream and asked Göthe what was in the cage. Eva translated our question to Göthe, and with a large grin, he answered in Swedish, which Eva translated to English, "Eels, . . . we eat them."

My Great Grandmother, Kerstin Ersdotter Ohman (1865 – 1952)
We know very little about Kerstin, Stina's mother. We have no evidence that Kerstin ever wrote a letter to Stina. However, five of the nine letters sent from Carl to Stina are signed, "Pappa and Mamma." I'm sure, living in a new country among strangers, Stina

had many questions throughout her pregnancy and also at the time of Lennart's birth for which a mother of eight children could have offered much reassurance and guidance. The enormous distance between mother and daughter fostered the barrier. Stina relied on the Swedish community of Minneapolis to aid her during her pregnancy and through the adjustment to a new country and way of life. Stina's circle of friends helped her acquire a job, provided childcare, and supplied her with food, clothing, and lodging. Carl and Kerstin believed Stina's situation was of her own doing. It was fate that landed her in this predicament, and likewise, it was she who must strive to overcome her own adversity.

I believe a personal note of encouragement, good luck, and love from Kerstin might have encouraged Stina and would have been welcomed as Stina prepared for the birth of her first (and only) child. Perhaps Kerstin did write to her daughter, but we have no evidence of this in the letters Stina saved.

Sven appreciated Kerstin, as she was an advocate and treated him well each time he visited the family. Kerstin cried when Sven told her that he and Stina had broken their engagement in 1918. Sven wrote four letters to Kerstin asking for her support in dealing with Stina's infidelity.

Sven
Early letters in this section reveal that Sven and Stina's relationship has cooled a bit, yet both appreciate their long-standing friendship. Sven calls her "Stina-friend." Sven has now found love elsewhere and is happy and willing to distance himself from Stina. He mentions his approaching engagement in early 1923 and refers

to his new love as "the one" (letter of 9 October 1922). With this in mind, I was bothered by Sven's nonchalant agreement to meet Stina in a hotel upon her arrival in Göteborg when she and Lennart returned to Sweden. While they planned to be in the same hotel for several days, Sven adds in his letter, "We do not need to be intimate, but just be able to talk." (Really? I question his intent and integrity.) Sven writes that if he is engaged at the time, their meeting must remain a secret so as not to cause him "any new troubles." It appears infidelity to a betrothed was a common characteristic of both Stina and Sven. My impression of Sven and his deep devotion to one and one alone is diminished by his indifference. Unfortunately for Sven, his engagement never occurred. In her letters, Stina continues to tease Sven with her mention of love and memories of years past. She sends him gifts, such as photos, socks, pajamas, a tie. Stina unfairly manipulates Sven's emotions and affection.

Once Stina arrived back in Sweden, Sven continued his love and faithfulness should they have a change of heart and decide to marry. Sven truly loved Stina deeply. He would welcome her as his wife and her child as his son. He believed they could pick up where they left off five years earlier, committed to one another. Sven referred to her once again as his fiancé. He is caring, loyal, and loving, everything Stina would want in a husband, but he had one serious and notable imperfection: Sven cannot manage money. He had outstanding debts from years past. He borrowed money from Stina's father and was paying his loan back to Carl in monthly installments. Within a few weeks of Stina's return to Edsbyn, Sven asked Stina for a 150 kroner loan. The Carl Ohman family was financially comfortable during the 1920s and Sven's shortcoming, more than likely, did not set well with Stina nor her parents.

No doubt Stina had difficulty making ends meet while living in the U.S. Being an unwed mother with a young child complicated matters further. Now that she had returned to her home in Edsbyn, she was pleasantly reminded of how comfortable life could be among family. On the other hand, life with Sven would be financially stressful. Also mentioned in various letters was Sven's occasional heavy drinking and weakness for lottery gambling. These indulgences were also reason for concern.

?? (Mystery Man) from Alfta

A new admirer enters the picture in January 1926. Who is this guy? He wrote letters to Stina on Swedish Motor Club stationery. This gentleman had a beautiful handwriting script, yet his initials at the end of his letters are indiscernible. He writes abruptly and to the point (a marked difference from Sven's prose). He is persistent and domineering . . . a 'take charge' kind of guy. ?? speaks both Swedish and German.

Stina and ?? have known one another since their youth. She mentioned that he was impulsive and errratic years ago. He counters by explaining that he had to experiment to find out how it was to be in love, not knowing whom would be his beloved. ?? told Stina years earlier that he loved her, and he now wished the two of them had become closer and had married at that time. He believed they could have flourished in a happy life together. ?? recognized, however, that Stina had not changed since their earlier years. She did not take his love seriously, neither then, nor now, and therefore, he did not trust her devotion. Stina asked ?? to return to the U.S. with her. His main concern, however, was the availability of jobs (letter of 12 January 1926).

?? is bothered by the turmoil of his marriage and business. He is not a native of Alfta, and he is disappointed with the social offerings of this small community. Listening to music and cinema movies occupy his spare time. He writes, "This is the only fun you have here" (letter of 5 January 1926). Alfta is located midway between Edsbyn and Bollnäs, fifteen minutes from each.

?? had an office in Alfta with a few office workers. Stina's father, Carl, welcomed him to Edsbyn when ?? called on Carl's dealership. ?? appeared to be a sales representative of metal works: automobile parts? miscellaneous sundries? curling irons? (letter of 12 January 1926).

?? was intense. He wrote a letter to Stina each week in January 1926. This frequency in letter writing was unchallenged by any other suitor. Stina did not appear to be charmed by this Mystery Man from Alfta.

Stina / Lennart

Stina, age 31, and Lennart, age 5, returned to Sweden in the late summer of 1925. Stina regarded her visit to Sweden as temporary and planned to return to the U.S. at some point in the future. Her father was hopeful that her return to Edsbyn was permanent, as he prepared to open a Fur and Fashion shop operated by his daughters and managed by Stina (Carl's letter of 24 December 1924). Carl continued to negotiate and explore private enterprise options throughout his life. Stina remained independent and unfaithful to

Sven (even with Sven in Bollnäs, a half hour drive from Edsbyn). More than likely, my father met Sven and spent time with him while Lennart and Stina were in Sweden.

Carl Ohman, Stina's father, had a mistress and another family on the north side of Edsbyn. His wife, Kerstin, the children, and probably others in the small town of Edsbyn were aware of this. Carl supported two families.

"Dearest Little Stina!"

Part Three

Letters 51 - 78

31 May 1926 — 6 August 1954

Courtship

Flight

Reflections

Photos

Letter 51

31 May 1926. Letter to Stina, Edsbyn, from ??, Alfta.

Envelope: Froken Stina Ohman
           Edsbyn

My Beloved!

As you can see, I am keeping my word as always, especially to You.

After our call today, I decided to go to Edsbyn to look at the football match and possibly see a glimpse of you, but, unfortunately, the match did not happen, and I did not go to Edsbyn.

How shall we be able to meet? It sounds so difficult to You. Couldn't we meet a little north of Edsbyn? Here it would not be dangerous in regard to the traffic. You could walk towards the road to Woxna, and we could meet there. This is only a suggestion from me, which I hope You will accept.

In regards to my business, as I mentioned before, I will arrange to form a limited liability company and keep my part in the business, which would be good for the future. If I do not establish this before I leave, I will have to sell the shop. This would not be good, since I would have to accept whatever they want to pay for it. Once this is in place, I will still have my shares, until the time comes when I will have to replace certain persons. By then, I will have skilled men who are interested in the shop and are able to handle it. I, therefore, think that this is the best option and hope that You think so too. I have explained this only to You but will inform the others in the business when I have finished my term obligation here in Alfta.

I will then go to South America to try to get a job within my business, for which I have put time, effort, and money. Here in Sweden this type of business, the machine industry, is totally dead.

I have been thinking of the above from both sides and found that this would be the best.

If I go to South America, I hope You understand that I want you to come with me. We can live happily together there.

I hope that You, as You have said, love me, and that nothing or no one must come between us. I must own you, my beloved Stina.

Asking for this is your ??

P.S. I will call you as usual. Or would it be better if you call me around 6:00 PM on Monday in case it is difficult for you to be alone when talking to me (because of the 60th birthday party)?

This suitor spells Voxna with a "W." There is no town in Sweden by the name, "Woxna." His intent was Voxna. The letters and sounds of "V" and "W" are often interchanged in the Swedish and German languages.

The family is celebrating Carl's 60th birthday.

Letter 52

6 June 1926. Wedding invitation to Stina, Edsbyn, from Mimmie
Johansson, Stockholm.

Envelope: Froken Stina Ohman

              Edsbyn

Miss Stina Ohman

IS HEREBY INVITED TO THE WEDDING BETWEEN

OSCAR NILSON

AND MY DAUGHTER

MARTA

AND ALSO TO THE WEDDING DINNER

FOLLOWING THE CEREMONY

At The Stallmastaregarden, Stockholm

Midsummers Eve, 21 June 1926, at 7:00 PM

MIMMIE JOHANSSON

Grateful for a reply by June 15.

Letter 53

15 June 1926. Letter to Stina, Edsbyn, from ??, Alfta.

Envelope: Froken Stina Ohman

     Edsbyn

Beloved Stina!

I hope You are not angry with me any longer, as You said You were when I called You yesterday.

I do want to see You again. When and where could this be? If You only knew how much I care for You and how much I love You, I am sure You would then promise me a meeting!

I will cover the car better, so there will be no risk, and we can be utterly safe. We can meet at the bridge at Walls, and we can travel to Vangsbo along the new road that crosses the country road at the bakery. On this road we can be totally safe, especially if I cover the car with the sidepieces. But let us change the time to eleven o'clock, so we do not need to hurry.

It went well last time we were out driving although You were so worried. I do understand this. You must understand that I do not want to put you into any trouble because of me. Therefore, I must be as careful as possible, but I <u>must</u> see you. I cannot wait longer.

Beloved Stina! Please do whatever you can, so I can meet you soon. Your ??

Letter 54

28 June 1926. Letter to Stina, Edsbyn, from ?? Alfta.

Envelope: Froken Stina Ohman

            Edsbyn

My most beloved!

I must write You again. I was happy to be able to meet You in person, but since this did not happen, I have to communicate in another way. I would be so happy if I could go to Edsbyn to meet you every evening as I did in earlier years, but fate (the cruel fate), has made it different. Fate cannot be that cruel that you should not be able to own the one you have <u>always</u> loved and still do.

You have doubted that I have always loved You, and I can understand that, but now You should not doubt this, Stina. I have always been fond of you as long as I can remember. Later, my feeling grew into love, but perhaps it was too late. I did tell You about my feelings and asked for Your love—I then thought nothing of your love was left for me and <u>tried</u> to forget You. I started to amuse myself with other girls, something that I deeply regret. But I was still thinking of You, Stina. I could not forget You, not even during the years You were in the USA. I was so very happy when G.P. told me that you had come home, and I called you immediately. This is the way it has been over the years, and I do not want You to doubt this. I do hope fate has not turned its back on us.

I suppose you are tired of me talking of the past, but I cannot help remembering. When I read this letter, I can see the language is not too good, but I hope You can still understand what I mean.

What will happen tonight? Can I see you? You know that I am longing to see you. Time and place can be decided over the phone. The side plates have been mounted, so there is no risk.

I could pick you up at the Karlsson turn, but you can decide time and place.

Your ??

Letter 55

3 July 1926. Letter to Stina, Edsbyn, from ?? Alfta.

Envelope: Froken Stina Ohman
                   Edsbyn

Beloved!

I now would like to talk to You in person about many things. I am worried, and there are some things I cannot understand when we speak over the phone. There is always something that I do not understand. Why can't You be sincere, trust me, and explain yourself regarding Your return to the USA and your relationships there? You have not told me about these before. What did You mean by this?

When I called You earlier, You said that You have to go to Stockholm to meet a man there. Is it really necessary to go? Do You have to do this? Could we not meet instead? We so seldom meet. I am awfully jealous. Do You think it is funny to make me jealous?

Please remember how much I love You. Perhaps it is now as it was before, that my love is not worth much and will be thrown away again because of <u>others.</u> I am irritated and can no more think of this but have to stop for this time.

Yours ??

P.S. I will call You as usual. D.S.

Letter 56

13 July 1926. Letter to Stina, Edsbyn, from cousin Oscar Nilson, Stockholm.

Envelope: Froken Stina Ohman

                 Edsbyn

Dear little cousin S ----

   Thank you for your letter that I have just received, and I will give you an answer directly. When I read your letter, I was sad for you, for everything that has been, and especially for your unlucky situation today. Please forgive me, dear Stina, for being angry with you when you said you were not coming. No one can imagine my feelings when I heard you were not coming. I was so disappointed and said that it was typical; you should never trust an "Ohman." I had been looking so forward to your presence at my wedding that you can never imagine. But now I understand how everything is. Poor little Stina, I feel so sorry for you. I am so happy and content with my life, and I wish it will always stay this way. From all of my heart, I wish you could also be happy, and not like this. Please try to make some changes, so you can stay at home, or else it will only be worse for you. That I really believe. I just had a letter from Adil, and she is wondering if you came to my wedding. She is really homesick now, and I feel so very sorry for her.

You think, and I believe, you could have a good income here in Stockholm. It is a good place to live. Oh, if you could just come and try working and living here in Stockholm. My wife sends her heartfelt greetings and welcomes you to our dear home whenever you like. I hope you will come soon. Now, I will arrange some food for my brother-in-law and the bridesmaid who are here. They like it here so much, that we are almost never alone.

Please write again soon. When you have troubles, please write to me, and I will answer you.

Warm greetings from Oscar,

I think I can never forgive your father for being so narrow minded.

Letter 57

29 July 1926. Stina is in Edsbyn. She sends a letter of application, two letters of recommendation, and a letter she received from a former employer to:

The Fashion House Regent

Regeringsgat. 37

Stockholm

With reference to your advertisement, I would like to apply for employment. Some time ago, I returned to Sweden from the USA for a visit, but I have now decided to stay in Sweden if I can find good employment. Because of this, I am not able to provide a recommendation from my last work at Connoy Hat Shop in Chicago, but instead enclose a letter from this company. I also enclose recommendations from two other persons.

I gratefully await your highly important reply.

Respectfully,

Stina Ohman

Recommendation Letter 1:

I hereby confirm and acknowledge that Miss Stina Ohman, who has learned the art of fashion from me, is very willing and hard working. I would recommend her as one of the best.

Stockholm April 1, 1916

Beda Tapper

This is confirmed and witnessed by:

Herman Lindquist

Emma Klang

Recommendation Letter 2:

Minneapolis, Minnesota

May 10, 1923

To Whom It May Concern:

I am pleased to recommend Miss Stina Ohman, who was in my employ as a copyist and second trimmer while I was manager of the Millinery Department in the Rhea Shop at 904 Nicollet Avenue, Minneapolis, Minnesota.

Stina is an excellent copyist and gets your ideas quickly and correctly. Her work is far above the average in neatness, and she is also very rapid and not a time-waster. Anyone employing her will be entirely satisfied.

> Yours very truly,
> Margaret M. Carthy

Letter 3:

Minneapolis, Minnesota

January 23, 1924

Miss Steena Ohman

Chicago, Illinois

Dear Miss Ohman,

Just a line tonight as we have been talking matters over and think we would like to have you back and ready for work Monday the 28th. Mrs. Connoy is very eager for some "Ohman-hats," so she says, but I think she is eager to have Miss Ohman herself. Am inclined to think she has missed you quite a little. Hope you can come conveniently on such short notice.

Sincerely,
Connoy Hat Shop
By Bell Williams

P.S. Mrs. Connoy wrote to your home address, but thought there might be a possibility of your not having received it. D.S

This must be a copy of the originl letter sent by Stina to The Fashion House Regent, women's wear clothing store, Stockholm.

Stina writes in her letter of application that she has worked at the Connoy Hat Shop in Chicago. In Letter #3, Bell Williams writes from the Connoy Hat Shop, Minneapolis, Minnesota, to "Steena Ohman, Chicago, Illinois." There is no indication Stina ever lived or worked in Chicago. The two recommendations may be authentic, but I question the legitimacy of the reference to Chicago.

Letter 58

8 August 1926. Letter to Stina, Edsbyn, from ??, Alfta.

Envelope:　Froken Stina Ohman

　　　　　　Edsbyn

Beloved!!

I will start the letter while waiting to get through on the phone to Edsbyn. I have to call You a second time today, despite our last call. Perhaps You will think it is too often?

You must know that I was disappointed yesterday when I could not see you. I waited and thought You would be coming, but when it got so late, I understood that something had come up for you. Oh, now the telephone is ringing. I will now get to talk to my darling!

I have now been talking to you, but, we were, of course, interrupted by a long distance call. I can never talk to You without interruptions, but I will call you again.

I have been thinking a lot about the possibility of seeing You at least once more before I see You in Stockholm.

We could meet along the Woxna-road, or, to be precise, just after Mortens in the north of Edsbyn, or, to be even more precise, 200 meters after Eklund's shop along the Woxna road. We could meet a little earlier and continue towards Woxna and then on to Dalfors. Here we will not meet anyone whom we know. If you take a walk there by 9:00PM, there will be no risk, since not many people are out at this time of the day. If we put the hood up and also the side panels on the front seat windows, no one will see who is in the car. Isn't this a very good idea? Then, we can go to Woxna or continue on towards Lobonas. We will have more time together if we can meet earlier at the place mentioned above.

Now I have called you again. I think I should probably only call you once a day.

I hope the above suggestion will be acceptable to You, my darling.
Xxx
Your ??

Letter 59
12 August 1926. Letter to Fashion House Regent, Stockholm, from Stina, Edsbyn.

In reference to my earlier application for a milliner's job at your shop together with my recommendation letters, I now enclose pictures of me as you requested over the phone.
Respectfully,
Stina Ohman

Enclosure: 2 photos

Perhaps one of the photos Stina sent was the photo she requested ?? return to her.

Letter 60

24 September 1926. Letter to Stina, Edsbyn from ??, Alfta.

Envelope: Froken Stina Ohman

Edsbyn

Since the last time, it has been almost impossible to talk to You over the phone. You have had so much to do, and, therefore, I take the liberty to write. I am not able to see you often enough. There is too much time in between our visits. I would like to see you every day, but I suppose this is not possible for still some time. I hope this time is not too far away!

I have again written to South America, but I suppose the answer will not come for some time. I have also been writing to the United States.

Yesterday, a Swedish American went back to America from Alfta. I have never before had such a great longing to go with him, but, I suppose, my time will also come. Then, I will come directly to you. I do not care what you might want. My plan is made up, and it is not possible to change.

I have a sense that unavoidable fate will play a trick on me. Perhaps, by then you will have married and will have forgotten everything between you and me. I hope this will not happen. I hope it will be me who shall own you as my wife, my beloved Stina.

I have not written for a while because I thought I would be able to see you tonight. Since this has been postponed several days, I send you this letter, together with a prayer to be able to see you soon. You must not think that I write and go to Edsbyn, as you have stated, just for the fun of it. I go because I love you. I love you more than you can ever understand. You say that I do not mean what I have said to you. What I say to you is that I love you and will always love you. You <u>must</u> understand and believe that.

I'm hoping to see you soon.

Your, H.?.

This letter is signed with a legible first initial. It is an "H."

Letter 61

7 October 1926. Letter to Stina, Edsbyn, from H.?, Alfta.

Envelope: Froken Stina Ohman

               Edsbyn

Beloved Stina,

Since we could not decide anything today over the phone, I have to write to you and, with humbleness, ask for a meeting as soon as possible. You see, I long <u>so very much</u> to see you again.

On Thursday, I'm sorry, but I do not have the time. I have a meeting. I could call you, or better yet, you could call me around six o'clock if it suits you so that you can be alone. I, then, will await your call and will answer it myself.

If I can see you, we might perhaps choose a different place if by chance someone has seen us from the last time we met. A suitable place would be where we met earlier, at the railroad crossing. You know, close to the house on the hill. I don't know its name, but it is crossing number two between Alfta and Ovanäker. Number one is at the coal bridge. Do you understand which one I mean? If not, I will go straight to the big stairs *(the villa, Stina's parents' home, where she and Lennart are staying)*, go in, and get You. I now remember when we were sitting in the garden, and I, as usual, asked you to be mine. Your father was close by, and I wanted to talk to him, but that was absolutely forbidden by you. I very much regret that I was so compliant to you. I have asked you the same thing many times before, and you always give the same answer, "NO." And still, I love you. Please do not forget to call me. I will be waiting.

Yours, forever, affectionately, H.?.

Letter 62

19 November 1926. Letter to Stina, c/o Karl Klang, Edsbyn, from H.?, Alfta.

Envelope: Froken Stina Ohman
                  Address: Forester Karl Klang
                  Edsbyn

172

Today I had a sad message over the phone, and I don't know from whom it has come, but probably from someone who has overheard our telephone conversation. It is sad if you have some problems because of me. Still, we have to arrange to see each other. For your sake, I shall now be more careful.

I still have so much to tell you. That's why I have to see you as soon as possible. My earlier messages and explanations are totally true, which I hope you believe. I also hope what you have told me is not only because of what has happened but because there is some meaning to it. This time, there must not be any misunderstandings between us as there have been before.

I have now seriously thought about it. I will also write to some acquaintances to see if there are any jobs available. There may be some possibilities here in Sweden, but then, you would need to stay here in Sweden.

When can I see you? As soon as possible!!

H.?

Stina is staying with her sister, Emma, and brother-in-law, Kalle (Karl) Klang.

Letter 63

24 November 1926. To Stina, Edsbyn, from H.?, Alfta.

Envelope: Froken Stina Ohman

              Box 41

              Edsbyn

Mein Liebchen! *("My Beloved!")*

    During the past days, I have been thinking of our last meeting. You were so different from what You usually are. I have been worried. I wonder about what You had said to me earlier, if it should not be true, but I do not want to believe that. I really hope that You feel as you have said before, and that I can trust those words.

    There are so many things I would like to say. I hope I will soon meet You, and then I can tell You everything. Of course, I have said these things to you many times before, and I want You to believe that I am truly sincere.

    Our telephone conversation today was very short—and good! Has something happened to You? You seemed so sad. In that case, I hope everything will be fine again so that You do not go back to the USA soon, as you mentioned.

    I really want to see you. There is too much time between our meetings, especially since I am longing for You so much. The saying "Ready any time," I still hold on to. I hope our courtship as it presently is will not linger too long.

    If You do not think it is too often, I will call You at the usual time. Then you can tell me when we can meet.

Yours H.?.

Letter 64

7 January 1927. Letter to Stina, Edsbyn, from H.?, Alfta

Envelope: Froken Stina Ohman

Edsbyn

Stina,

There are not many opportunities to speak to You about the usual subject, which you might think is beginning to be boring. We have discussed this several times, but I still think it is not clear.

To begin with, I would like to tell You that my feelings for You do not leave. As long as I can remember, I have felt the same for You. This is no hasty thing. That is why I am so afraid that You will reject me again. You will accept my love for some time, and then, you will reject it.

I do not have any right to make demands of you yet. As you know, my wish would be that you would not see other men. But you do not comply with my wish!

Edsbyn has just now come through on the phone. I had the opportunity to talk to You a little while, "mein liebchen." I am in a better mood now. I was a little sad earlier since I had not been able to talk to you over the phone the past few days. Because of that, I have been thinking a lot and also have been imagining things. These thoughts are now gone after our telephone conversation. I hope I am your only love. You are "mein liebe" (*my love*). H.?.

Letter 65

12 June 1927. Letter to Stina, Edsbyn, from Sven, Orsa (*a town in Dalarna County*).

Envelope: Froken Stina Ohman

              Edsbyn

Dearest little Stina,

You might be surprised now to open this letter. You have the right to be. It's from an old, old boy—who was once called your fiancé!

Stina, I cannot help sending You some lines, but also telling You what You might not know. I have been transferred to Orsa and have left Bollnäs surely forever. On May 1, I was transferred from our old station where I had been struggling so much and where I had experienced <u>so</u> many things, for instance all of our story. The Bollnäs station has been closed down, and even the office is gone. I would never have thought that I would work in Orsa where I had been raised as a child without any sorrows and problems. The only happiness for me here is that I can take care of the graves of my beloved mother and father, whom I miss so much. You know the place yourself, and I have now made it so nice with many blooming flowers.

I do not have much to do, and I feel rather lonely here. My thoughts ponder away as through a labyrinth of the long gone. Still, it feels good to remember many old things. I have also been thinking of you. Before You go, and if You really want to go, please think about us <u>one more time</u>, and please do not make any serious decisions. Despite it all, I am here, and I feel it would be important to meet You!! Is this possible? When and where? You can come here discretely.

You are welcome here, perhaps forever, if You would feel like that. I suppose I will get a letter first?

I hope I am not damned by <u>You</u>.

Greetings, Sven

Letter 66

21 June 1927. Letter to Stina, Edsbyn, from Sven, Orsa.

Envelope: Froken Stina Ohman

             Edsbyn

Dear Stina!

Thank you for your lines that you agree to a meeting. This meeting is important. Still, you do not understand my purpose for this meeting. I will not write too much about this now, but I will speak to you when we meet.

I see that it would possible for you to meet during midsummer, and that would also be possible for me. I do not know where we should meet. Perhaps it should be where we would not be recognized. I think it would be best here in Orsa. We could also go to Rattvik or Leksand, but there will be many people there during midsummer and surely people we know. Also, it will be expensive. Here in Orsa, there will not be so many people. You're welcome here on Midsummer's Eve or Midsummer's Day. I would be grateful for your decision and for information on what train you will arrive. I will arrange it nicely for us two.

I suppose you have no other suggestions? You could buy a ticket from Edsbyn to Mora, just to deceive the stationmaster in Edsbyn, if you wish. However, I would not care if the whole world would knew we met.

Heartfelt greetings from Sven

Letter 67

3 July 1927. Letter to Stina, Edsbyn, from Sven, Orsa.

Envelope: Froken Stina Ohman
                     Edsbyn

Stina!

I suppose it was fate that we did not meet. At least we can say that it is. It must be something.

You are so calm and reserved. I do not recognize you in your letter. You speak so naturally sweet. You are your mother's caregiver, just as it should be. I think she is so happy and glad with her Stina. When I think of this, I remember a telegram sent many years ago from your mother, saying, "May the sun shine on you and your Stina."

You say, "Youth is flying away." Yes, I know that, but couldn't we still be counted among the young ones?

My old heart and I have been deeply tested. We are happy that you still want to meet. We await better weather and hope this will happen soon. I will await you in Orsa as we agreed earlier, perhaps on Saturday, July 9, at 7:10 AM? The train originates in Edsbyn at 5:02 AM. I will welcome you! Don't you think this will be best? We will then be able to talk and plan some things.

I should have a vacation at the end of July or beginning of August. Perhaps at this time, you could make a little trip to Orsa as well. I will probably stay for some time in Voxna and the surrounding area. You can plan and give suggestions for when we can meet. After our first meeting, we can make a serious decision as to whether we meet again or not. I hope you will agree that a meeting together is reasonable if not totally natural? Please write a few lines to let me know if you will come here.

Well! Good-bye, until next time!

Many greetings, Sven

Letter 68

16 July 1927. Letter to Stina, Edsbyn, from Sven, Orsa.

Envelope: Froken Stina Ohman

               Edsbyn

Dear You!

Thank you for yesterday's letter!

Yes, I was surely awaiting You. I also went down to the train "to receive" my guest. So, apparently, it was a "no thank you" to my invitation. I do not begrudge you for this, I mean, that you did not come.

Tomorrow, on Sunday, I will be in Voxna all day. I will go to Edsbyn in the afternoon and will be there at 3:15 PM. If You will not be at Klang's home after that time, I will call You to see how we can meet. I will probably ride my bike, and we will see how the weather is. I intend to pay a visit to the stationmaster.

Are You sure we will now meet? A hasty letter during my lunch break.

Greetings, Sven

Letter 69

2 August 1927. Letter to Stina, Edsbyn, from Sven, Orsa.

Envelope: Froken Stina Ohman

              Edsbyn

Dear Stina!

When I came home yesterday from a short trip, I had your letter, for which I thank You warmly. Thank you, also, for our nice meeting last time during my short trip to Edsbyn.

The journey home on my bike was really wet. It poured down, and by the time I got home, water was flowing from my whole body. But this does not bother me because I had the opportunity to meet You. Although I felt warm and in love, as before, I also was a little disappointed. I did not earlier understand the love You have for your new country. I would have thought once you were home that you would like to stay and that Your motherland should be the most dear to You. The meeting did not end the way I had hoped. Your last letter also confirms this. It is like a knife in my heart. I still feel your tenderness toward me under the circumstances, and this is much appreciated. I had hoped we might be a couple again and you might stay with me here in Orsa. As it turns out, one of us may cry from regret. If nothing unforeseen happens, one of us will suffer and be unhappy. Perhaps, both of us will suffer. I must ask, though, why does it have to be this way?

With what you now have and what you will have, we could be more than happy in our own nice home anywhere on the earth. I would be your very true husband and your own, sweet little boy's father. I think we are already married from birth, and perhaps your friends in the USA have heard of me and seen photos of me. I have been good to you, Stina. You must decide if you are making a big mistake, or even committing a crime, by not staying here with me.

Love is the gold you are searching for, this richness you have here, and you can get it from me anytime.

What will I then be called, when I am now called a "poor homeless boy?" I dare to, my dear Stina, tell you my innermost secret: that I am at my end. The only thing that can bring happiness to me is You, only You. If you stay, you will see how good it will be.

They say that my good friend, Sven Hellander, in the USA is dead. He has killed himself. If he had stayed here at home, his friends' compassion might have saved him.

It is bad that I only have one day free, apart from Sundays, this month. I am happy that I can go away for a couple of days to Bracke where I have been swimming and have had a very good time. We also went to Åre and Sollefteå, so I got to see something else besides Orsa and Voxna. When you become my little wife, we will often go on trips in our country. That will be easy for us as we will both have railway passes.

I'm happy for you that the beautiful wall hanging you have made is now completed. Thank you for your good thought, but I don't have any place for it if you do not stay with me.

I hope you will be happy to get my letter. You have had to wait a while for it because of my journey.

Greetings to Emma and Kalle, but more so to You and Your little Lennart.

Warm greetings, from the seriously determined, Sven

Stina's Hälsinge-bock (*goat*) wall hanging.

The bock is the symbol for the Swedish landscape of Hälsingland. Edsbyn is in Hälsingland. Stina designed the pattern and wove the long pile wool. It hung in Kerstin and Carl's home for many years. It also hung in my parents' home. Sven refers to it in the letters of 2 August 1927 and also 27 September 1927. It measures 3 feet x 7 feet.

Stina was also a gifted weaver of rugs. As the letters indicate, all of the Ohman sisters wove rugs. During my grandmother's visit to Sweden in 1954, she acquired a 4-harness, full sized, fully functioning floor loom. It was large: 5' 2" long x 3' 4" deep x 5' 4" high. It was either owned by the Ohman family, or she purchased it. Stina dismantled the loom in Sweden and had it shipped to the USA. It was delivered to our house because it was too large for her apartment.

She tirelessly worked many hours for many days to reassemble her precisioned machine. She re-strung the loom with warp. It was a tedious job. Once the loom was work-ready, she prepared the weft by cutting slightly wider than one-inch wide strips of wool fabric. She sewed the ends together and rolled the fabric lengths into balls. Wool suits and wool blankets were purchased from the Salvation Army to cut into weft.

I enjoyed watching my grandmother weave. Stina began by removing her shoes; she wove stocking foot or wore hand knit slippers. The removable stool she sat on was securely hooked to the loom base. She rhythmically worked the pedals to lift the warp and slide (toss) the shuttle that held the length of wool weft through the open warp strings. Then she would push the other set of pedals with her feet and return the shuttle the opposite direction through different warp strings. The pedals controlled which warp strings were raised or lowered. After every couple of shuttle tosses she pulled the beater forward, slamming it several times toward her to pack the weft evenly into place.

Stina was happy and young when she was weaving. She sang Swedish folk songs and wove until the balls of wool weft came to an end. Her rugs were colorful. I have six of her rugs and dearly treasure each. One is a hallway runner, three feet wide by fourteen feet long. Her floor loom stands in our sunroom still cradling an unfinished partial rug. Stina left the rug unfinished probably because she ran out of the color of wool needed to complete it. She surely looked for more wool fabric, but apparently, was unable to find the matching color.

Letter 70
9 August 1927. Letter to Stina, Edsbyn, from Sven, Orsa.

Envelope: Froken Stina Ohman
                    Edsbyn
Dearest little Stina!

Thank you for your letter, today. I hurry to send you an answer.

I am so enormously happy that you have come to realize the seriousness of your decision, and it seems that your thoughts are warmer and more affectionate towards me and also for us. I think that a new separation would be fatal for both of us. I dare to say there is an unnaturally warm thread that binds us to each other. If you were to return to the USA, I believe you would find you have made a very unfortunate decision and have a great longing for the one you left behind. As You can see, I really can sense Your serious feelings for me.

I can't make it without you. I will be lonely. A good woman like you, with your caring hand, would change my life. I would like to spend my life with you. Please understand the importance of what I am telling you. If you will fail me now, I will do something rash. I will get another woman, but not for love. It will not be the intense love that I have had for you these past ten years. Wouldn't it be nice to prepare a home for us here in Orsa until we can find something better? You are welcome here.

I met Anna yesterday. I suppose she will be home the end of this week. If you will not come here on Saturday, I will go to Voxna in the afternoon to go fishing and will return here on Sunday afternoon. If it would happen as my dear friends in Voxna say, if it would be determined between us, that is, a true engagement, you would be welcome to join us on the fishing trip! Without an engagement, they feel you should not come, for our own sake, because of those who will gossip.

You can understand that I would really like to come to Edsbyn, but I won't for the same reason as mentioned above. I wish we could fly away somewhere. Still, the most important thing is that we come to a conclusion and meet in Voxna, where you will meet all of your new relatives, my family.

186

I do not want my little fiancé to be nervous. It is enough that I am nervous. I want you to work with me in serious thoughts and to work to achieve what both our hearts are striving for before we get old.

My long distance telephone number at my office is 235 between 9:00 AM-3:00 PM, but it would be better to call the Railway Hotel during my dinner, between 5:00 and 6:00 PM each day.

Heartfelt greetings to my little Stina. Sven

Letter 71

15 September 1927. Letter to Stina, Edsbyn, from Sven, Orsa.

Envelope: Froken Stina Ohman

Edsbyn

My Beloved Little Wife!

Thank you for the letter with the unforgettable, more determined words. So, it will <u>finally</u> be a home for Sven and Stina, giving so much longed-for sunshine to life. I think you have made the right decision! We now have to arrange for the move. The apartment has been available since Sept 1. I intend to move into one of the rooms as of October 1 and begin living as a bachelor. And you, on your behalf, will arrange for whatever is needed. You know what is needed to begin with, and then we can complete as needed. I intend to buy some things here or in another place, but it would be necessary that you be present. I will not have any free time this month, and this Sunday, I will also be at work. We might be able to meet one another on Sept 25. The engagement, yes! Right now, I do not have the money for a ring. It must be arranged later. We must meet soon! I will call you tomorrow at 8:00 AM, so we can talk for a while. I didn't get your letter until yesterday evening. I have been on a fishing trip, and I am now working. You have to be satisfied with these lines for this time.

Dear Greetings, from Your Husband, Sven

Letter 72
27 September 1927. Letter to Stina, Edsbyn, from Sven, Orsa.

My dear girl!

Thank you for allowing me to visit you at Emma and Kalle's. Give my greetings to Kalle and Emma and to little Lennart. It is Lennart's name day tomorrow.

It was so lovely to be with you, and even more lovely to know that soon we will have only days of sunshine in our little home, where you have promised to be my loving sun and will arrange our home for two lovebirds. I hope I do not wish for too much.

I didn't have the time yesterday, but today I paid a visit to our furniture store, and I looked into the windows during my usual evening walk. I fell asleep already at 10:00 PM having lots of thoughts as to how to furnish our home. You should be here to help me think. Please come soon. I send you some photos of the furniture I have seen. Please return them: 1) buffet, 2) kitchen table, 3) four chairs, and possibly a corner cupboard for the living room, together with the sofas, and possibly a smoking table. The table can be lengthened. I like this furniture very much. I'm sure it will fit together nicely with your wall hanging. Also, we need a big warm floor carpet, solid and cozy. What do you think, my fiancé-wife?

	Price:
Furniture:	300 crowns
Carpet 2 ½ meters X 3 ½ meters:	143 crowns
Possibly a cheaper one:	120 crowns
Total around	450 crowns

You remember, we decided we need a buffet. The carpets are very classy and nice. There are many of these in town, so perhaps we do not need to go to Stockholm to buy one. If we buy many things from him here, I am sure we will get a discount. We can get a smoking table for around 45-50 crowns. This is in addition to the items above.

The bedroom furniture is available for 600-725 crowns in birch if you would like birch. We could get pine for much less. The set in the photo is very stylish and is in a brown/reddish color, which is what I like. Look at this, my little girl, and please return the photos to me, or bring them when you return here.

The journey to America that you have spoken about makes me nervous and almost dizzy. As you can understand, this is not possible. It is insane, don't you think? People, both here and there, anticipate our engagement and question our plans when you talk of the USA. I need you here and your income, or else things will go bad, I'm afraid.

Can you come this Saturday so that you can have a look at the furniture I have been looking at? Have you arranged for your registration to be moved from Edsbyn to Orsa? I think everything now seems so safe and serious, so I will not be talking about how much I love you. You can read between the lines.

Good night, dear. Warm greetings with hugs full of kisses,
From your Sven

P.S. I will call you tomorrow at Klang's. Go there between 7:30 and 8:00 PM.

Stina and Lennart returned to Minneapolis in 1928.

They lived in Edsbyn over three years,

and often during that time, Stina considered and reconsidered

living permanently in Sweden.

Lennart began school in Minneapolis in the fall of 1928

at the age of eight.

He knew little English and found school difficult.

His teachers thought he was learning disabled.

Lennart missed his cousins in Edsbyn and the Swedish language.

He wanted to return to Sweden.

Letter 73

22 April 1929. Letter to Stina, Minneapolis, from Sven, Orsa.

Envelope: Miss Stina Ohman

1906 Park Ave Apt 12

Minneapolis, Minnesota

U. S. A.

Little Stina!

Thank you for everything that you have sent to me since you went back to the USA. This has made me happy, but at the same time, I cannot send you anything back. You must forgive me for not writing to thank you until now. I intended to write earlier, but it did not happen. I have not been in a good mood lately, and I think you know why. Also, I have been sick with a gastric ulcer. All this affects my mood. They say I am too young to have this condition.

I don't want to blame you in any way, but if you would have stayed with me, as I sincerely thought you would, life would be different for me, I think. Or am I just imagining this?

Life is better for me now because someone is caring for me, and she appreciates the good in me that might still be there.

I will marry this summer. My first Sunday to the church will be on April 28. My little girl is good and sweet to me, just the way I want her to be. She is 24 years old and daughter to the postmaster in Falun. She has already given me a sweet little daughter on April 1. Little Sven is a happy father. I hope always to be, forever, for my sweet girls. Stina, I am so happy and proud. I do not regret my decision. I so needed a good wife and a sweet home of my own as I am now preparing.

I hope you will not forget Sven totally. I thank you for all that you have meant to me all of these years. I wish you happiness in life.

Heartfelt greetings,

Sven

P.S. Do you know about Mard's wife, Maria's tragic ending? She died quite suddenly last autumn because of an accident. She got a piece of metal in a bowl of cabbage soup. She swallowed it, and it got stuck in her throat. I feel sorry for her poor children.

Letter 74

7 July 1929. Letter to Stina, Minneapolis, from Sven, Orsa.

Envelope: Miss Stina Ohman

               1906 Park Ave.

               Minneapolis, Minnesota

               U. S. A.

Dear Friend!

I will always call you that. But, I must not do that anymore.

I, alone, am not the reason for your unhappiness—I think you, yourself, have a lot to blame yourself for, my dear friend, especially now when fate has made its last move. There is nothing to regret, especially now when it is too late. You talk so much about your happiness and that your beloved must and should have been me. <u>Not only once</u> did you have this love and total happiness in your hands. You could have acted differently so that you could have kept your happiness. Isn't this so, Stina? You were thinking too much for too long and <u>against</u> my inner wishes. You fooled me yet another time when I believed in you. You left me damaged permanently. I then threw myself into an irreversible decision that could not be taken back. And now, I am and will remain no one else's but hers. I have promised to be true to my good and sacrificing fiancé and soon to be my little wife. She is living totally for me and for my very best. It is not right for you to interfere with my real happiness with your belief that I am "reckless and stupid." You should not be saying something like this since you know me and have owned me. Is that not so? I am sure if someone had said something like this to you, you would not have liked it. Isn't this so?

You can remain my friend, and I want you to be, but you cannot have any other claims on me. I like to receive your letters, and I thank you for your last letter! I thank you for all the gifts. I shall try to give you something, too, that you wish for. It is not necessary for me to send the ring. I suppose it would be an expensive customs duty for it. Wouldn't it be better that I return it to you when we meet next time in Sweden? You might be home again in Sweden some time. I do not have what you mentioned in your last letter. Perhaps they have not sent it according to your wishes. It would be very welcomed, dear you, especially now that my fiancé and I are preparing our home and all is very expensive. (*I surmise Stina requested a larger item from her parents' home in Edsbyn be given to Sven for safekeeping. Stina cherished keepsakes from her childhood home and with seven siblings, items she valued disappeared from the home between her visits to Edsbyn. It appears her family had not yet complied with her wishes to give Sven the item Stina requested. We can assume that Stina plans to get this item from Sven when she next visits Sweden.)*

I will be married in Falun on 15 September this year. I have a newly decorated, very nice apartment of two rooms and a kitchen where I can receive my bride—I am now very happy and content, Stina, and I regret nothing.

I would like to explain to You why I decided so hastily to get married. This will help You better understand. However, you must not tell this in any letter to the mother country. You know there is so much gossip. This is still my little secret. I have gotten as far as You earlier had, now forgotten and hidden in the mouths of people! On April 1, my little fiancé gave me a sweet baby girl, all from our love and to be admired. This is not the proper way of doing it, I admit. But, I am proud of my little daughter, and I feel the great and strong responsibility for her future happiness and prosperity. My girls are my whole life now, and only death can make me part from my beloved two!!

When we met, our attraction to one another resulted in a child. I will now make the best of my life! Now, you can better understand, and perhaps, You also know how she would have felt had I left her.

You and I have had a long life together, Stina. I have been strongly committed in my love for You and my belief in You, but there have been many things that have made me doubt us. The years have been extremely long, and I do not want them back. I have suffered much for Your sake, more than You can imagine. But, I do not blame You now when I am leaving you!

Please leave my happiness alone. Appreciate what You have been in my life, and remain my good friend forever. This is my wish.

Greetings / Sven

Sven, age 34, married Kerstin Danils, age 24, on September 15, 1929, in Falun. His romantic involvement with Stina lasted eleven years. This was Sven's final letter to Stina.

There were many disturbing worldwide events that occurred during the ten-year period between Sven's letter of 1929 and Stina's sister, Nelly's letter of 1939. A month after Sven and Kerstin's wedding the American stock market crashed in October 1929. The Great Depression closed businesses, factories, and banks. Jobs were lost and farms were auctioned off for mere dollars an acre. The economy of the United States as well as the entire Western world was affected. Franklin Roosevelt became President in 1933. That same winter Adolf Hitler rose to power in Germany. In the Soviet Union, Joseph Stalin crushed the hopes of the Russian revolution. The stronger powers of Europe invaded the smaller, weaker countries. The United States remained neutral as it still suffered the aftereffects of World War I and chose (for the time being) not to enter another European war. In 1938 Hitler invaded Austria. Jews in German-occupied countries were persecuted. In 1939 Germany invaded Poland, and the Soviet Union invaded Finland. In 1940 Hitler invaded Denmark and Norway. It was an uncertain and frightful time for the developed world. (Jennings & Brewster, pp. 65-97.)

Letter 75

26 November 1939. Letter to Stina, Minneapolis, from Nelly and
Bror, North Edsbyn.

Envelope: Miss Stina Ohman

1806 3rd Ave S. #27

Minneapolis, Minn.

USA

Dear Sister!

You can be happy to be in the USA. Here we have terrible times.
Any day now old Sweden might be at war. There is a mobilization
every day. Twice a day we must listen to the radio to find out if they
want us to be ready the next day. They announce different cohorts
every day. It is terrible. You see men in uniforms wherever you go
in this little village. Not to think of how it must be in larger towns.
Many people from the big cities have rented places here in Edsbyn
since they think it is safer to be in the countryside.

So far, Bror, and also Göthe, and Åke are at home. My brother-
in-law, Gunnar, is in Göteborg for six weeks. Every second son has
been called to enlist. Lennart Klang is also in the military service;
his duty has been extended several times. He is in the Life Guards
in Stockholm. We are all waiting for America to come and end the
war. We have food ration cards, and we have not been allowed to
drive a car for two months. However, now it is allowed again. All
church bells ring once a day, and also the whistles blow from the
fabric factories.

We have heard that there are good times in the USA. I guess
because you are delivering such large amounts of heavy munitions

for Europe. Finland is having a very hard time now. Just think of those who are volunteering for Finland.

I send you some photos from this summer when Jussie was at home. Such a very sweet child she has, but he is being spoiled. As you can see from the photo, Jussie has become very thin, but Emma is growing thicker. You always seem to stay the same way as you were before.

I have greetings to you from Uncle Pelle. He often comes to shop in our food store. Now that the new road from Falun is ready, it is easier for him to go to Edsbyn than to Alfta. Perhaps you do not know that we now have a big, broad road to Falun through the woods. It starts at Plita's farmhouse; goes past our grandmother's, between the house and the lake; and then continues onward passing Anders' farm. There are buses between Edsbyn and Falun many times a day.

Perhaps you know that Ida Mellqvist is living at the villa. She rents three rooms on the second floor from mamma and pappa. The old Mellqvist house has been changed to a guesthouse to accommodate those coming into the country from the city.

Espes´ Helena is in a hospital in Stockholm. She has had severe rheumatism for many years and cannot walk without using a walker. In summer, she is still able to use a bicycle, however. She finally has a warm heater in her forever cold apartment.

I hope this letter will reach you for Christmas. Our very best greetings to you and Lennart,
from Bror and Nelly

Nelly is Stina's younger sister.

Nelly's letter references the European theater prior to the United States' entry into World War II. Nelly informs Stina of the brave Swedes who are preparing to fight the Russians alongside their Finnish neighbors during the Winter War that began on November 30, 1939, just four days after Nelly wrote this letter. The tiny nation of Finland borders Russia. Stalin was determined to move Finland's border back 16 miles to create a buffer zone around the city of Leningrad. On November 30, 1939, Stalin sent 500,000 Soviet troops to invade Finland's border. Swedish volunteers aided Finland against the Soviet Union's invasion. *(Wikipedia: online resource.)*

The Carlander brothers enter the scene: Henrik and Arvid.

Twelve years pass between Nelly's letter of 1939 and the following
letter from Arvid Carlander dated October 10, 1951.
Arvid is the younger brother of Henrik. Henrik Carlander is a
possible identity of the Mystery Man from Alfta. However, there is
no mention of Henrik or Arvid in earlier letters. The brothers live in
Stockholm. Stina may have met Henrik during one of her visits.

Stina returned to Sweden in 1947 at the time of her father's death. I
believe Stina and Henrik were married during this visit. Stina and
Henrik must have had an earlier relationship, but we have no
evidence of this (unless he is the Mystery Man). Arvid's letter is
addressed to Mrs. Henrik Carlander. Arvid is Stina's brother-in-law.

Letter 76

10 October 1951. Typed letter to Stina, Minneapolis, from Arvid
Carlander, Stockholm.

Arvid mailed three large (8 ½" X 11") sports magazines to Stina.
He is on the cover of two. Articles of his 1946 record-breaking 530
lb. (240 kg) bluefin tuna caught in Øresund (The Sound) between
Denmark and Sweden in the Balltic Sea, appear in all three
magazines.

Envelope: Mrs. Henrik Carlander
               1806 Third Avenue South
               Minneapolis, Minnesota

Dear Stina,

Since I came home at the end of September, I've had some
things to do and also have been down in the Sound for a few days.
That is why I have not, until now, had the opportunity to thank You
for Your letter of 19 September.

It was fun to talk to you on the phone. Lisa and I were delighted
to hear how happy everything seems to be for you and Henrik.
It was also a great pleasure to hear that Henrik has a job. I hope it
develops favorably, although I understand there are many obstacles
for him to overcome in the beginning, especially regarding the
language. Even though he is not paid much, the most important
thing is that he has a job and has begun. He should be able to do
well on the salary he receives. Would you please let me know if the
money I'm lending him arrives from New York?

As I mentioned, I was down in The Sound fishing last week. Lisa was with me, and we had some wonderful days together with a couple of friends there.

I enclose some photographs. You can take one copy with the fish. Please send the second copy of the fish as well as the photograph with the king aboard the boat to sports journalist, Nick Kahler, in Minneapolis. I have lost his address, but I am quite confident that you can find him as he is well known. Nick is waiting for the photos. Please send him the photos as soon as possible.

All is good here at home. Lisa joins me in wishing the warmest greetings to you both.

Your affectionate brother-in-law,
Arvid C.

P.S. I will send you a photo of the boat and the king as soon as I get another copy of it.

Letter 77

14 December 1951. Letter to Stina and Henrik, Minneapolis, from Arvid, Stockholm.

Envelope: Mr. and Mrs. Henrik Carlander

1806 - 3rd Ave South #27

Minneapolis 4, Minnesota

U.S.A.

Envelope back: Arvid Carlander

Ericksbergsgatan 27

Stockholm

Sweden

Dear Stina and Henrik,

Unfortunately, I have not been able to fix Stina's rings. It is not allowed here to manufacture rings other than 14 karat, unless you, yourself, find your own 24 karat gold. I have not been able to find it. I could not get this done before Christmas, and I have not had anyone who could transport it to the U.S.A.

I send two pictures of the king onboard "Tonina." Has Nick Kahler received my photos? I have not heard anything from him.

Here everything is good. Peter will arrive on Tuesday and Johan on Wednesday. Then I suppose the Christmas hunting will start.

Here, we still have autumn weather. So far, there has not been any snow or ice. I had a bad hounding with the dogs this year, just 52 pheasants and 20 hares. However, it was a very windy day, and then things can easily go wrong.

Birgit has come home from Germany with her family. Her husband is working at Gustavsberg.

Lisa and I would like to wish you a Merry Christmas and a Happy New Year. I hope Henrik can stay home from work during the weekends.

Warmest greetings from us all.
Affectionately, Arvid

King Gutaf VI Adolf of Sweden enjoyed fishing with Arvid Carlander from Arvid's boat, the Tonina, in "The Sound."

King Gutaf VI Adolf (wearing a hat) sits at the stern.

Arvid is standing.

Letter 78

6 August 1954. Typed letter to Stina, Edsbyn, from Arvid
Carlander, Stockholm.

Envelope: Mrs. Stina Ohman
                Edsbyn
Envelope back: Arvid Carlander
                Eriksbergsgatan 27
                Stockholm

Dear Stina!

I hereby enclose a check for 1,000 crowns from the Sundvalls
Enskilda Bank.

I will not be in Stockholm Saturday, Sunday, or Monday, but
you can meet me at the office on Tuesday morning if you have the
time before your flight.

If you call from Edsbyn, you can reach me at the following
telephone No: Staket 42037. If you call from Stockholm, the No. is:
0758-42037.

Best greetings!

Yours sincerely,

Arvid

*Stina returned to Edsbyn in 1954. Her mission may have been to
search for 24 karat gold. This letter from Arvid was written a few
days prior to her return flight to the USA.*

Reflections

Letters 51 – 78

The letters end abruptly. We'd like to know more.

Sven

Sven's eloquent love letters will be missed. We have come to know Sven well through his letters, and we have a better understanding of Stina's character through Sven. Sven is a likeable guy. He is sincere and hard working. When he and Stina were a couple, he remained steadfast and faithful. Sven and Stina met one another four years before they became romantically involved. They were committed to one another (off and on) for eleven additional years.

Stina's decision to stay in Sweden vacillated often. On 26 July 1926 when Stina and Lennart were in Sweden, Stina wrote in her job application to The Fashion House Regent in Stockholm, "I have now decided to stay in Sweden." One year later on 17 July 1927, Stina explained her love for her new country to Sven. There was a gnawing in her heart for the U.S. that was impossible for her to ignore. Sven again pledged his love to Stina and Lennart and asked her to again reconsider their life together as a family in Sweden and not to return to the United States. He writes, "Love is the gold you are searching for, this richness you have here, and you can get it from me anytime." Sven was persistent. His hopes of persuading Stina to stay and become his wife never waned.

In August 1927, Stina apparently changed her mind again and agreed to marry Sven. He ecstatically calls her his Wife and signs his name, "Your Husband," (letter of 15 September 1927). They have much to discuss and decide regarding their new home. Sven shopped for furnishings. "Should they be birch or pine?" he asks, and sends her photos of the buffet, kitchen table, and chairs to assure Stina that all will fit nicely together with the wall hanging she has made. Sven asks Stina if she has registered a change of residency from Edsbyn to Orsa. He calls her his fiancé-wife. They exchange rings and Sven is elated by Stina's sincerity and acceptance of marriage.

However, in 1928, Stina and Lennart leave Sweden and return to the USA. Stina once again rejected Sven. It is a travesty. It is a tragedy. Sven is psychologically destroyed and develops a gastric ulcer. How could this have happened again? Did Sven imagine Stina's affection and misinterpret her intent regarding marriage? It appears, when Stina was with Sven, she loved him, but when she was alone, the lure of the United States was simply too great and controlling. She mentioned to many in Edsbyn her love for her new country. The U.S. was young and thriving, full of opportunity. She knew she had a thrilling and vibrant life awaiting her in the U.S. After all, it was the Roaring 20s! Stina wanted freedom from conventional norms. She arrived in the U.S. the same year that women were given the right to vote. There was a wave of loosened independence sweeping the U.S. This attraction was too strong; she found she could not commit to a life in Orsa with Sven where her income was needed for household expenses. As much as she loved Sven, Stina loved her freedom more, especially her freedom in the United States. It is difficult to understand how Sven could not sense her anguished indecisiveness and allowed himself to again suffer Stina's rejection.

A year later, 22 April 1929, Stina received a letter from Sven. He has found a new love, a young, sweet girl who appreciates and loves him. They are parents of a baby girl born on April 1. Sven is delighted, contented, and in love with his two girls. Sven requests Stina to "Please leave my happiness alone." We can infer that Stina may have chastised Sven for marrying another.

I support Sven's final letter to Stina, 7 July 1929, and agree that Stina, alone, is to blame for her unhappiness. Her sorrow is caused by her inability to commit to a permanent and secure love of one, and one alone. Sven informs Stina that he is leaving her. He asks for her friendship forever, but only that.

Stina

I have often wondered if Stina, during her three years in Sweden with Lennart, ever considered a permanent arrangement for him to live with his grandparents or an aunt or uncle and receive formal education in Edsbyn. She may have considered him an inconvenience in the U.S. as she needed fulltime employment to support them both, and young Leonard needed daily care. Single parenting was difficult and definitely a detriment to Stina's independence.

There were three opportunities for Stina to permanently remain in Sweden. Stina seriously considered each. Option #4 would have allowed her to reside in the USA.

1) Marry Sven and move to Orsa.

2) Manage a Fur and Fashion shop in Edsbyn or elsewhere in Sweden (her father's wishes).

3) Work at The Fashion House Regent in Stockholm (or find work elsewhere).

4) Marry H.? and live in South America or the USA (letter 51 and letter 60).

For my father's sake, I would like to think that my grandmother regretted not marrying Sven. I am sure my father would have welcomed and supported their union. Lennart's life would have been more stable and complete. Stina's life with a devoted husband may also have been happier, more secure, and ultimately easier in the long run. I believe her unhappiness was not a question of "who" but rather a question of "where." The United States lured Stina and was a greater power of attraction than any love for a prospective husband.

It must have been a difficult, gnawing decision for Stina, "Do I stay in Sweden, or do I return to the States?" Stina's father, Carl, sensed her torn love and indecision. He refers to her "new country" as opposed to her "old country." Stina decided to follow her dream in the United States and become an American citizen. She found no satisfying alternative. I am amazed at Stina's lust for a new life and also her courage and determination.

H?, Alfta.

Henrik Carlander or Henning Persson or Hugo Larsson

The identity of H? is uncertain. It is impossible to decipher the illegible hand written initials at the bottom of his letters. Letter 24 September 1926, reveals a first initial, "H," that is somewhat legible, perhaps for Henrik or Henning or Hugo. Sven mentions Henning Persson in his letter to Stina's mother in September 1918.

"She (Stina) is still seeing this most abominable young man in Edsbyn, the metal smith, Henning Persson, a person whom I would never like to know . . . " Henning is certainly a possible candidate as he is a metalsmith and was courting Stina eight years earlier. Sven and Henning were competing suitors in 1918, just as they are again in 1926-1927.

Among Stina's keepsakes was a Gott Nytt År (Happy New Year) card from Hugo Larsson sent in 1918. We know nothing of Hugo. It is surprising, however, that Hugo's handwritten address to Stina on the New Year's card (1918) and H?'s handwritten addresses to Stina on the Chicago Motor Club envelopes (1926-27) are quite similar. Hugo signed the card with a full signature. Hugo's script "H"and the script initial, "H" on the Chicago Motor Club stationery are very similar. However, the beginning letter "L" in Hugo's last name and the surname script initial on the Chicago Motor Club letters bear no resemblance.

Whomever H? is, Henning or Henrik or Hugo, he is in Alfta on business and quickly becomes a suitor of Stina's when he hears she has returned to Edsbyn from the United States. H? investigated job opportunities in South America and wanted Stina to move there with him.

Neither H? nor Sven had a problem with others knowing Stina "belonged" to them. Both "unnaturally longed" for her, wanted to see her every day, and wanted the whole world to know about it. H? went to great lengths to plan secretive meetings with Stina to the precise time (minute of the day) and place. He pinpoints (nearly by coordinates!) the location for their rendezvous and attempts to put

Stina's mind at ease by promising to "put the hood up and also the side panels at the front seats, so no one will know who is in the car."

Often, when anticipating a meeting, each suitor experienced a long wait of hours with the disappointing outcome of Stina's "no show." Their meetings were secretive because Stina did not want either of them to know of the other. She did not want her family or friends to observe her in two serious relationships with two different men. Both relationships escalated out of her control. Stina felt smothered. Perhaps she hoped to elude both suitors by moving to Stockholm, or better yet, fleeing the country just as she had eight years prior in 1920. Stina, being the independent woman she was, did not want to be "owned" by either man.

I was initially bothered by the term "own you." Both Sven and H? used this term to describe their exclusive relationship with Stina. Each expected Stina to honor and return this fidelity. It is a term of endearment, meaning you are mine to love and no one else's, yet it suggests servitude.

Henrik Carlander

Henrik could also be H?. The two photos dated 11 August 1947 are evidence that Henrik and Stina saw one another during her 1947 visit to Sweden. We can assume they were married during this visit as well. Stina was in her mid 50s at the time of her first and only marriage. Henrik was a year or two older; he had been married before.

You will notice that Stina is wearing a wedding ring in the 1949 Christmas photo of her holding me on her lap. Arvid Carlander, Henrik's brother, sent a Christmas letter on 16 December 1951 addressed to Mr. and Mrs. Henrik Carlander in Minneapolis. Note also, the photos of Stina, my father, my mother, and me (age 2) on Christmas Eve 1951, and the partial image of a man's arm and edge of his face in the far right of the photos. I believe this must be Henrik. I did not know him in 1951, nor did I remember him from that Christmas, as I was too young. He was a stranger and I was probably fearful of him.

Stina and Henrik's marriage was hot and cold as they lived together sporadically. The marriage ended after a few years. Stina had lived alone too long to accept a new partner in the small living space of her apartment. She considered Henrik a free-loader. She didn't want to support him, and encouraged him to get a job in Minneapolis. He was a capable worker; however, the language barrier was an insurmountable detriment.

As a child, I knew Henrik had dealings in South America. It was this South American connection and also the discernible initial "H" in one of the letters that led me to conclude that Henrik Carlander could be H?. However, while looking through my grandmother's memorabilia, I found a signed photograph of Henrik. When comparing his full signature to the scribbled initials at the end of the letters, I could not with certainty conclude that he was H?.

I met Henrik for the first time (that I remember) when I was five years old (1954). My parents explained the marriage to me in the car on our way to visit Grandma Stina. They told me there would be a man at her apartment and that the two of them were married. My father said he was a friend of hers from Sweden and his name was Henrik. This surprised me. At the time I thought the wedding had just occurred, and I expected there to be a big wedding reception party. I did not realize my grandmother and Henrik had been married for several years, and that I, very simply, had not been informed. Henrik was out of the picture in my younger years. I knew my grandmother well; however, to my recollection, I had never met nor seen Henrik.

Henrik had a daughter from an earlier marriage living in San Antonio, Texas. He left Minneapolis and went to live near his daughter. I have fond memories of Henrik. He was thoughtful and kind to my parents and me; he gave me a couple of cuddly stuffed animals. My parents regretted that Stina and Henrik's marriage failed as they knew Stina was lonely. Henrik arrived in Minneapolis, stayed a short time, and left. I never saw him again. He died in Texas, and his daughter called to inform my grandmother of his death. She also asked if there were any belongings of his in Minneapolis. There were none.

Kristina Evelyn Ohman, age 32.

Edsbyn, Sweden, 1926.

Engagement photograph August 12, 1917. Stina (age 23) and Sven
Bengtzon (age 22); Karl (Kalle) Klang and Stina's sister Emma (age
28). Both couples are wearing engagement rings.

Stina and Sven

Sven Bengtzon (with pipe) and railroad cronies.

Stina

Stina

The family pose in their new Model T Ford.
Stina's father, Carl Ohman, was the first to own a car in Edsbyn.
Stina, age 15, wears the white hat.

The Ohman family in 1905. Kerstin, sitting in the center, continuing
clockwise: Emma (black dress); Carl; Nelly (with flowers in her
hair); Gustav; Stina (in dark dress); Justina; Anna (sitting); Göthe
(baby boy). Carl and Kerstin were married on December 26, 1882.
Carl was 16 and Kerstin was 17.

Carl E. Ohman, Stina's father, my great grandfather.

Karl Ohman (B May 31, 1866. D Jan 2, 1947)

Gustaf	Emma	Torsten	Erik	Kristina Evelyn (Stina)	Justina
B 1887	B 1889	B 1926	B 1891	B 1894	B 1897
D 1947	D 1965	D 2017	D 1891	D 1984	D 1983

Lennart
B 1918
D 1998

Leonard
B 1920
D 2010

Janet   Ross
B 1949   B 1958

Ake
B 1937

Kerstin Ersdotter (B March 13, 1865. D Nov. 1, 1952)

Anna	Nelly	Gothe	Ake
B 1899	B 1903	B 1905	B 1908
D 1957	D 1987	D 1981	D 1959

Jan
B 1940
D 1995

Eva   Bo
B 1950   B 1941
         D 2003

Agneta
B 1944

Three sisters, 1926: Nelly (age 23), Anna (age 27), Stina (age 32).

Stina

Newsweek

Volume XXVIII Number 18   *The Magazine of News Significance*   October 28, 1946

· NATIONAL AFFAIRS ·

THE UNION: Dollars and Cents Crossroad

For the man who jingled a few coins in his pocket last week, the question was not so much how many he jingled, but what they were worth. Whether he was schooled in the complexities of economics or not, his plain horse sense told him that the nation's economy was at a vital turning point:

❡ In line with President Truman's message to the nation directing a general removal of price controls (NEWSWEEK, Oct. 21), a suddenly freed commodities market had first shot skyward and then abruptly broken.

❡ Likewise in step with the White House position, labor leaders were hastily reforming their lines in anticipation of the complete removal of wage controls forecast by the President in his speech.

To the man with the coins, the break in commodity prices was a hopeful sign; whether it was a harbinger of an end to the price spiral or not, at least he could hope. But the impending removal of wage controls puzzled him: Would it touch off another series of strikes for higher wages and again start prices upward? In his predicament he was not alone; even the labor leaders were not sure what their course would be (see page 79).

Out of it all, there was one measure of relief. The removal of meat from price control had overnight started livestock once more to market (see page 24). Even the Mrs. was grinning about this one.

Prices by Appetite

The high cost of living went over the postwar peak and started downhill in the past 48 hours . . . It's on the way—cheaper clothes, cheaper food.

Just when President Truman's decontrol edict was prompting dire warnings of an inflationary spiral last week, the normally restrained Wall Street Journal on Friday, Oct. 18, climbed out on its long limb. Whether The Journal was right or wrong could be proved by time alone. But what led to its conclusion was fact, not fancy: the sharpest break in the nation's commodity markets since the 1932 depression.

To be exact, meat decontrol touched off frenzied bidding in the nation's near-empty stockyards. Overnight, livestock prices made their highest leap in history: hogs from the $16.25 OPA ceiling per hundred pounds to $27.50, an all-time high; cattle from the $20.25 OPA maximum to $28.75.

That was just a starter. Hogs later hit $30 at Indianapolis. One carload of fifteen Hereford steers brought an unheard-of $38.50 at Kansas City to Karl Hoffman, a feeder of show cattle from Ida Grove, Iowa.

Then the inexorable law of supply and demand took over. The flood of livestock which these prices siphoned from the farm (see page 24) broke the market. The year's heaviest receipts on Thursday tumbled hog prices by $4 to $7 and cattle prices by $2 to $4 per hundredweight.

"Pax Vobiscum": Now that the government's hold-the-line policy was doomed, the OPA's Washington head-

garine, shortening, mayonnaise, and salad dressing) were decontrolled during the week.

Price controls would be retained on what OPA Administrator Paul Porter called "important commodities and services where demand is still in excess of supply." Specifically, they were sugar, rent, autos, building materials, household appliances, farm equipment, leather and shoes, and basic clothing.

Even the Price Decontrol Board, which precipitated the crisis by recontrolling meat last August, caught on quickly. It refused to recontrol dairy products, even though it considered prices "unreasonably high." After three months of life, the board was already a historical relic. Last week it fired half of its staff. Two of its three members declined their $12,000-a-year salaries. The lifting of controls on wages as well as prices was only a matter of time (see page 79).

The Break: It was in the nation's commodities markets that the astonishing paradox of a ceilingless downward spiral occurred: prices fell sharply in the first

Steak! Only bison, but beef was on its way   *Acme*

quarters was as gloomy as a morgue. A wreath of black carbon paper inscribed *pax vobiscum*—peace be with you—was hung over the door of Arval Erickson, chief of the OPA's meat branch. Almost lethargically the agency's 34,728 officials and employes set about carrying out Mr. Truman's general order to decontrol other items.

Scheduled for the free list were virtually all foods except sugar. Coffee and vegetable fats and oils (including mar-

week that the lid was off. Initially, of course, meat price rises sent The New York Journal of Commerce's index of 30 sensitive commodity prices (Aug. 15, 1939, equals 100) zooming from 232.9 the day of the Truman speech to an all-time high of 266.6 on Wednesday, Oct. 16. The previous peak, 242.8, had been hit Aug. 23, just before meat recontrol.

Then came the crash. The price of meat substitutes such as poultry and eggs skidded by the hour as cattle moved to

Bollnäs, August 11, 1947. Honeymoon (?).

Stina and Henrik have married;

Mr. and Mrs. Henrik Carlander.

A wedding ring is visible on Henrik's left hand.

Stina and Henrik dining in Stockholm, 1947.

Henrik (center) and Arvid (right), Henrik's younger brother,
were avid hunters.

Cross country skiing on a warm day in Edsbyn, 1947-1948.
In earlier years, Stina skied to and from work.

Grandma Stina and
Janet, 1949.
Stina is wearing a
wedding ring.

Below: Christmas 1951.
Leonard, Fae, Grandma
Stina, and Janet.
Henrik's arm (?) is in
right bottom corner of
both photos.

1955

It's A Small World . . .

COMPARING GOLD BRACELETS from Sweden, Stina Ohman (Oval Room Millinery) and Hillevi Rombin, Miss Universe, chat about Sweden and their many mutual friends.

When Miss Universe was chosen, Stina Ohman's (Oval Room Millinery) friends from Sweden wrote her about the lovely girl, Hillevi Rombin, who came from Miss Ohman's home town. Then Hillevi came here to model bathing suits and Miss Ohman met her.

But to discover that she had known Hillevi's mother was almost unbelievable! "Thirty-five years ago I came to America from the small town of Alfta in Sweden." Miss Ohman recalled. "In our county there was a beautiful young girl whom everyone called 'Beautiful Anna' —All knew her through her beauty, and I also knew her personally." That girl was Hillevi's mother.

To make the discovery even more exciting Miss Ohman found that Miss Universe was a friend of her brother Ake, a violinist in Sweden.

"Dear Mother:"

Leonard's Story
Part Four

To the Reader

Preface

Letters 1 - 17

September 2, 1938—March 25, 1939

Fall/Spring Semester

Pillsbury Academy

Minneapolis

Reflections

To the Reader

My father, Leonard Ohman (Lennart), never had a children's book read to him. He never owned a children's book. His inadequate early learning of English literacy basic skills was a detriment to his education and life.

Stina was educated in Sweden from an early age. She entered public school with the other five year olds in her small town. She graduated from high school with her classmates. She learned the fundamentals of reading (decoding, syllabication, vocabulary, comprehension) and writing (grammar, spelling, punctuation, composition) naturally. She mastered the mechanics of literacy in her native language, Swedish.

Lennart was denied the advantage of early literacy in a formal setting that most of us take for granted. His first language was Swedish. His mother and he spoke Swedish to one another with ease from his birth. Mother and son lived in a Swedish community in Minneapolis where the residents spoke Swedish. Lennart acquired English skills simply by living in the United States as he heard it being spoken, but rarely spoke it himself because speaking Swedish was easier and natural. In Minneapolis, at age five, when his playmates were heading to school for the first time, rather than enroll Lennart, Stina took him to Sweden to meet his family. This was a convenient time to go because Stina wasn't sure in which country, language, or culture she preferred to raise her son.

Arriving in Edsbyn, Lennart felt an immediate sense of belonging and acceptance with his new family. He had cousins, aunts and uncles, and grandparents who welcomed him. Stina, too, was happy to be back in Sweden. If a book was ever read to

Lennart, it would have been in Edsbyn, alongside his cousins. Lennart's sense of family, however, was short lived, as Stina decided they would return to the USA in 1928.

Lennart entered his first year of school in Minneapolis at age eight. He was several years older and larger than the other students in his class. He had few friends. We can assume he and his mother returned to the U.S. in the fall as school was starting or, perhaps, midyear. My father told me that his mother dropped him off on his first day of school. He said he sat at the back of the classroom and looked out the window most of the day because he didn't know what the teacher was saying. School ended that first day, and he didn't know how to tell anyone that he didn't know where he lived or how to get home. He said he sat on the steps of the school for hours. His mother finally came looking for him.

My father was behind before he began. He had not been nurtured in the English language. He arrived and enrolled in a strange school where it was assumed he could count to 100 in English and he knew the English alphabet. It was a sink or swim situation, and my father sank. Yes, he eventually learned to read English, but not well. Yes, he eventually learned to write and spell in English, but not well. Not only had he missed the basics of English literacy, he also missed the basics in his native Swedish language as well. He left Sweden and returned to the U.S. at a crucial time when his educational wellbeing was not considered. Had it been, Stina and Lennart may have remained in Sweden where he would have systematically and formally learned the essentials of literacy in his preferred language, Swedish.

My father mastered verbal speech in both languages. He could neither read Swedish nor write it. He read and wrote in English, but not well. Lennart was a victim of inadequate schooling. He "fell through the cracks" in the public school system. He needed specific instruction in the mechanics of English (or Swedish) and never received it. I attribute his deficiencies in both languages to having been uprooted twice, once in each country at the critical age when he would begin learning the necessary and fundamental literacy skills for fluency. He was disadvantaged in both languages and mastered neither.

Janet Ohman Lindsay
April 2020

Preface

There is not much known about my father's early schooling. Stina discovered soon after she and Lennart returned to the U.S. that her son remembered little from his early years in Minneapolis at age three and four. Lennart's learning in an English-speaking school proved to be a difficult challenge. His young life was in constant change and upheaval: a new language, new friends, a new community. Lennart needed a place to belong. He needed stability.

Stina also found it difficult to parent an adolescent youth. My mother told me that Stina did not like Lennart's choice of schoolyard friends in the neighborhood. At age thirteen and in 7th grade, my father had a cigarette burn on his chest, a distinguished scar of gang membership. Stina rationalized that Lennart would have a better learning experience in a different part of the city, miles away. She decided Lennart needed a more traditional living arrangement in a home with supportive family members and a functional family environment. Stina was working fulltime, and with her social life, found it hard to care for a young teenager. This mindset firmed her decision in Lennart's move to the Emil Lundquist home in Northeast Minneapolis. Lennart lived with the Lundquist family for six years, beginning in seventh grade through his years at Pillsbury Academy. Mr. and Mrs. Lundquist were conservative and devout, never missing a Sunday morning church service. The couple had two older daughters, Laura and Eva, who were married and no longer lived at home. This was a stable environment, but established teaching norms at the middle school level did not work for Lennart. He needed literacy basics. Lennart had never begun at the beginning. Without an early learning sequence of skill sets, reading and learning continued to be difficult.

Lennart's earliest report card (that I found) was from the second semester of 7th grade at Pillsbury Elementary School. Lennart Ohman is the name on the report card. There are no grades for first semester, which leads me to speculate that he entered this school the second semester, perhaps when he moved to the Lundquist's home. His second semester 7th grade report card showed failing grades. He was retained and repeated 7th grade, no doubt the oldest and physically largest student in the class at age fourteen. Mrs. Lundquist signed his report card each grading term.

Students from Pillsbury Elementary School fed into Edison High School. Among my father's keepsakes was an Edison High School course of study list for ninth, tenth, eleventh, and twelfth grades with check marks of required subjects for graduation at each level. I believe this affirms Stina's and Lennart's intent that he would continue to live with the Lundquists and graduate from Edison High School.

Lennart, however, fought and succumbed to the impossible challenge. He failed again and withdrew from Edison High School with two years of course work remaining. At the age of eighteen, Lennart enrolled at Pillsbury Military Academy in Owatonna, Minnesota, a residential, private high school. We can assume his enrollment at the Academy was his mother's wishes.

Lennart, again, lacked belonging and was a victim of inconsistency. Learning a new set of rules and norms, making new friends, and learning the ropes in a military environment, he again, was behind before he began. Lennart grew accustomed to failure.

He was a kid with tough breaks and a painful school history. Failure was the norm. His learning suffered, but his emotional stability suffered more. His self worth was near zero. It was at Pillsbury Military Academy that Lennart changed his name to Leonard.

Leonard's Learning Experiences:

Childhood play in the USA

Childhood play in Sweden

Elementary school, inner city Minneapolis (Lennart failed to learn basic literacy)

Pillsbury Elementary School, Northeast Minneapolis (Lennart failed; retention)

Edison High School, Northeast Minneapolis (Lennart failed; withdrew)

Pillsbury Academy, Owatonna, Minnesota

Note of Clarification

The spelling, grammar, and mechanics in the letters Leonard wrote to his mother while a cadet at Pillsbury Academy were not corrected. The letters remain in the original form in which they were written.

Owatonna, Minnesota is 65 miles south of Minneapolis.

OFFICE OF
MILO B. PRICE, PH. D.
HEADMASTER

September 2, 1938

Mrs. Stina Ohman,
Young Quinlan Store,
Minneapolis, Minnesota.

Dear Mrs. Ohman:

I had a very pleasant visit with your son, Leonard, last night.
I like the boy. I think he would be very happy to know
definitely that he is coming to Pillsbury, and I suggest that
you fill in the application and let us have it an an early
date. I expect to be in Minneapolis next Thursday, but am
not sure that I shall get to see you. I may not be able to
stay until five o'clock. However, let me say that I hope
we may have the privilege of serving you in connection with
the education of this boy. The rate I offer you is so low that
I hope you will not mention it to any one for it would be
embarrassing to us to have it known. I shall be very glad if
you do not say anything to the lad about the rate which we are
making you. Leonard assures me that he would be willing to do
such work as we assign to him to help offset the reduction in
rate.

With best regards, I am.

Very truly yours,

Milo B. Price

MBP:H

244

Sept. 8, 1938

Received of Mrs. Stina Ohman
Eighty five ($85.00) toward tuition
of Leonard Ohman.

Milo B. Price

PILLSBURY

Sept. 19, 1938
Owatonna, Minn.

Dear Mother:

I'm sorry that I did write ~~you~~ before
but the reason is that I was expecting to
come home last Sunday with a fellow
that was driving up and finally he couldn't
go so that's how it is and an other thing
is that I haven't had time ~~they keep you~~
going all the time. I'll write again soon and
tell you when I'm going to hitch hike home
so you and Emil can take me back beer. ~~I~~
~~wish you would send me a bath robe, a~~
~~fountain pen, my powder my post cards belt.~~
The school isn't so bad but they are so strict
and the only time a fellow can go out is on
Fri. and Sat. nites till 10 o'clock and Sun. after
noons. I can go out Sat. nites because I'm on
the foot ball team, but we really get it nice
Gerry and I, Gerry is a fellow who has the room
next to mine. We met a couple of girls while
roller skating one nite and they have a 37
Ford coach and we have a swell time,

246

I've got my room in Kelly Hall and down in the basement there is a smoking room for the fellows and a gang of us always have ~~a swell time down there.~~ The only ~~thing is I'm~~ running short of money. We have to get up at 6:30 in the morning and I'm not used to that. Every day we have drill and we have to carry a 14 pound 30 cal. endfield army rifle for 3 hours, and march. I hope your taking good care of yourself while I'm gone. I've got my uniform and it fits me good. I tried to get my ~~stuff~~ second hand but I couldn't so I had to get a little of it new. You'll have to excuse my writing I'm no good at it. ~~Please write me soon and often because~~ I'm lonesome for you.

P.S.
I want you to write me and give me permission to come home Sat. noon because I can get a ride home and back with some people I know here. __Please__ write me and give me per-mission, because it is required.

Yours as always,

Love

Lenny

P.S.
I got the box you sent.

Letter 1

September 19, 1938, Monday.

Envelope: Miss Stina Ohman

              1806 3rd Ave So

              Mpls. Minn.

Pillsbury Academy

Owatonna, Minnesota

Dear Mother:

I'm sorry that I did write you before but the reason is that I was expecting to come home last Sunday with a fellow that was driving up and finally he couldn't go so thats how it is, and an other thing is that I haven't had time they keep you going all the time. I'll write again soon and tell you when I'm going to hitch hike home so you and Emil can take me back heer. I wish you would send me a bath robe, a fountain pen, my corduroy pants, and a belt. The school isn't so bad but they are so strict and the only time a fellow cane go out is on Fri. and Sat. nites till 10 o'clock and Sun afternoons. I cane go out Sat. nites because I'm on the foot ball team, but we really got it nice Gerry and I, Gerry is a fellow who has the room next to mine. We met a couple of girls while roller skating one nite and they have a 37 Ford coach and we have a swell time. I've got my room in Kelly Hall and down in the basement there is a smoking room for the fellows and a gang of us always have a swell time down there. The only thing is I'm running short of money. We have to get up at 6:30 in the morning and I'm not used to that. Every day we have drill and we have to carry a 14 pound 30 cal. endfield army rifle for 3 hours, and march. I hope your taking good care of yourself while I'm gone. I've got my uniform and it fits me good. I tried to get my stuff second hand but I couldn't so I had to get a little of it new. You'll have to excuse my writing I'm no good at it. Please write me soon and often because I'm lonesome for you.

Yours as always,
Love, Lenny

P.S. I want you to write me and give me permission to come home Sat. noon because I can get a ride home and back with some people I know here. Please write me and give me permission, because it is required.

P.S. I got the box you sent.

Emil Berglund is the gentleman Stina is seeing at the time of this letter. Emil has a car.

Stina's address, 1806 3rd Avenue South, remained the same throughout Leonard's tenure at Pillsbury Academy. Her typed address will not appear on subsequent letters. All letters from Leonard were written on Pillsbury Academy letterhead and mailed from Owatonna.

Letter 2

September 21, 1938, Wednesday.

Dear Mother:

I wrote to you before I don't know if you got it or not. I want you to write back giving me permission to come because I can get a ride both ways with some people I know hear so write back right away so I can get it by Sat. noon when I'm leaving. We have to have parents permission to go home so <u>don't</u> get Emile to take you down hear next, but a week from Sunday maybe. Please write me and give me the permission.

Love, Lenny

Letter 3

September 29, 1938, Thursday.

Dear Mother:

I got home all right that Sunday. I hitch hike home Fri. Oct. 7 and then I'll ride back here with you and Emil on the following Sun. morning, but write me permission, and if you can spare some money please send it. I must get a hair cut. I got a letter from Fred & Eva today. Some kids get permission to come home every week, and Dr. Price doesn't care. Please send me a pen soap certains* a jacket and my tennis shoes & basketball pants. If you have any stamps please send them I'm feeling kind of stiff from football but outside of that I feel swell I hope your alright too. I got a camera from Gerry now all I need is some film. Say "Hello" to Lundquists, Emil, the Dr. and every body for me. Please write sone and more often. I want to hear from you. Tell me if any ting exciting is going off. To-day I'm cadet on color guard, and a couple of days ago I was cadet on guard. I'm get to like it more and more as the days go by. There are an awfull lot of meskestoses* out here. We (the foot ball team) went to Medford to play football and had a swell time riding in an old truck.

Love, Lenny

P.S. Don't forget to send me permission.

*curtains

* mosquitoes

Letter 4
October 5, 1938, Wednesday.

Dear Mother:

I might come home next weekend enstead of this one. I haven't much time to write because I must hurry. I'm taking good care of my self so don't worry about me. I must go now so long.

Please write,

Love, Lenny

P.S. If I don't come Fri don't worry about me. It'll be because I change my mind, and will come next week.

Letter 5

October 7, 1938, Friday.

Dear Mother:

After this you will have write Price asking him to let me go home. I'll tell you when to write him and tell him that you said I could go home. Don't forget you have to write a letter addressed to him asking if I can go home but I tell you when to write. He just made that rule for everybody. I'm all right and I hope you are the same. I'm dying to come home. Please write to Price permission when I ask you to, and put it in an envelope in the same letter as you write to me. Only leave the envelope on Dr. Price's letter open so I can read it and see if it is written alright. Boy! I'm tilling you my room looks alot better after I put the curtains and things in my room. Thanks a lot for making them.

Love,

Lenny

Letter 6

October 10, 1938, Monday.

Dear Mother:

Please write Dr. Price and tell him I have permission to go home. Gerry and I will hitch hike home Fri. afternoon. I'm dying to come home and see you. I've got a lot of durty cloths to bring home too. Write Dr Price as soon as possible. I got my hair cut as you told me. Some kids hitch hiked home last week end and they got a ride right away both ways. When I come home I might have a metal on me I'm not sure. The metal is for being a good shot with a rifle.

I'll be awarded with it sometime within ten days. Last Fri. night we played Owatonna High School but we lost. 12 to 6. Most people thought we would lose by more than that. They have a lot of kids to pick from when we only have a few. Don't forget to write Dr. Price the permission for me to come home, write it as soon as possible. because I want to be sure to go home.

Love

Lenny

OFFICE OF
MILO B. PRICE, PH.D.
HEADMASTER

October 15, 1938

Mrs. Stina Ohman,
1806 - Third Avenue #27,
Minneapolis, Minnesota.

Dear Mrs. Ohman:

This acknowledges receipt of yours of the 14th inst. enclosing
a Money Order for $25.00 to apply on the tuition account of your
son, Cadet Leonard Ohman. Thank you kindly for this remittance.
Our receipt is herewith enclosed.

Leonard went home last night, and I hope you will have a
pleasant visit with him. The boy seems to me to be starting
nicely. About the 25th of this month, you will receive a
report showing his standings in his various classes and in
military work and deportment. These reports go out every six
weeks.

Very truly yours,

Milo B. Price

MBP:H

254

Letter 7

October 17, 1938, Monday.

Dear Mother:

I got home to school O.K. but I was a little late I got seven rides on the way home here. You write me and tell me if your are coming down. I think it would be best if you made it the 30 that's up to you. I'd like to go hunting with you as you know. When you come down bring my crystel set down too. And some time when you have time please look in those boxes for my basketball pants. It sure was a lucky thing that Herry came over Sunday afternoon wasn't it? When I was going to the city limits I looked for a street car line but I didn't see any. Laura sent me a postcard I got it to-day. One of the teachers wifes had a heart attact Sunday. I forgot to take that shoe brush with me too. Boy! I'm telling you if I had a car I'd be home every week end almost. I suposes the next I come home there will be snow on the ground. If you find any thing that you think I can use to occupy space please bring it down. Don't buy a rug yet because I think I can get one up here to use. Take good care of your self while I'm gone. Please send me some stamps if you have any extras. I don't know what I did with the others.

Love,
Lenny

PILLSBURY ACADEMY

Owatonna, Minnesota

MILO B. PRICE, Headmaster

Mrs. Stina Ohman,
1806 - 3rd Avenue South,
Minneapolis, Minnesota.

Report of   Leonard Ohman

For six weeks ending   October 21, 1938

SUBJECTS

	Six Wks.	Sem.
English 2	79	
Modern History	80	
Algebra 1	70	
Mechanical Drawing	75	
Military Drill	74	
Deportment	80	

Passing Grade: 70.

_____
                                 Headmaster

Deportment is citizenship.

256

Letter 8

October 26, 1938, Wednesday.

Dear Mother:

I probable told you I got my first medal, well I did, and I'm getting another one Saturday. Last Sunday Ray, Herry, Murphy, Cliff and Red came down here to see me. Boy was I glad to see them. Please write Doc. Price the permission for me to come home one week from Friday the forth of Nov. You won't have to write him till the first of next week by that time I'll have my other metal to show you. If Gerry has any money he will come home with me. When I get home we'll have to try to find some time to take pictures all the kids in Mpls are asking me for some. And I'd like to have some for my self too. When I get home I'll have some good news for you. When I get home I'm going to pick out a lot of my winter cloths and take back here with me. Then you can proable get Emil to take me back down here so you can see the school too. If you can spare some money I can sure use it.

Love,

Lenny

P.S. Don't forget to write the permission next week.

Letter 9

Oct 29, 1938, Saturday.

Dear Mother:

Why haven't you been writing me. I been worried about you. Every day I've been expecting a letter from you. Please and tell me how things are going along back there. Your not sick are you, I hope not. I can't wait till I get home. This place gets so tire sone after a while I'll feel a lot more like working after a week end at home. There are a few fellows here that go home to Mpls every week end, and they hitch hike to, and Dr. Price never says any thing to them about staying here. But when you told him you didn't want me to come home to often

Leonard did not finish this letter. It was included in the envelope along with the letter he sent to his mother on November 19, 1938.

Letter 10

November 7, 1938, Monday.

Dear Mother:

    I got my radio conected now and it doesn't work bad a all. I was kind of cold going home to school, but I got there on time any way. The fellows might come down here the last part of this week, they were kinda talking about it when I was home. I just wish that the school wasn't so far from Mpls so it would be easier to get home. You know I would be home for Thanksgiving don't you? The next holiday which at the end of this, will be something new for me because we will have to march down town with our rifles. I wonder how I'll like it. I can't think of the name of the holiday. If you happen to see any of the kids tell them to be sure to come down because we have to march. I'm listening to my radio now and it doesn't work bad at all. Please send me some stamps if you have any laying around, I can sure use them.

Love

Lenny

PILLSBURY ACADEMY
OWATONNA, MINN.

OFFICE OF
MILO B. PRICE, PH.D.
HEADMASTER

November 17, 1938

Mrs. S. Ohman,
1806 Third Avenue South,
Minneapolis, Minnesota.

Dear Mrs. Ohman:

This acknowledges receipt this morning of your Money Order
for $25.00, which has been credited as per the enclosed
receipt. Thank you kindly for your remittance.

Leonard appears to be happy and doing his work in satisfactory
fashion. We shall know more about his work when the grades
come in about two or three weeks from now, showing his standings
for the second six weeks period of the year. I feel confident
the boy is making satisfactory progress.

With best regards, I am

Very truly yours,

MBP:H

260

Letter 11

November 19, 1938, Saturday.

Pillsbury Academy

Owatonna, Minnesota

Dear Mother:

Please send me the permission to come home next Friday night, because I want so much to come home. Yesterday I got a letter from Lundquist (Laura) and she told me they were going to send me a box. That night I got a box that was full of peanuts, candy, pear, and cookies. We sure have learned a lot of new cammands lately, I'll be a professional souldier before long. I just wish I could come home every week. I've got a good surprise for you too. As soon as I finish letter I'll have to write to Lundquist, Eva & Fred, and the kids up northeast. The next time you send a package send me some vasoline, talcm power and some after saving lotion. When Laura wrote me she said that if I came home for Thanksgiving that you and I should go over there for dinner. Don't for get to send me the permission to go home, send it so it will get here by Wed.

Love

Lenny

PILLSBURY ACADEMY

Owatonna, Minnesota

MILO B. PRICE, Headmaster

Mrs. Stina Ohman,
1806 - 3rd Avenue South,
Minneapolis, Minnesota.

Report of ᴸeonard Ohman

For six weeks ending December 2, 1938

SUBJECTS

	Six Wks.	Sem.
English	Inc.	
History	65	
Algebra	75	
Mech. Dr.	78	
Military Drill	76	
Deportment	88	

Passing Grade: 70.

Milo B Price
Headmaster

Letter 12

December 3, 1938, Saturday.

Pillsbury Academy

Owatonna, Minnesota

Dear Mother:

I'm in study hall right now and I haven't any other paper to write on so this will have to do. I got home O.K. and I didn't get any squad so thats all O.K. Boy I'm realy hard up I need about $2.00 bad. I have a radio service bill for $1.00 when I had to get my radio fixed. And I have to get a hair cut that's 50 cents and I owe some money to Gerry so that won't leave me much left, but please try to spare $2.00.

You'll be getting my marks perty soon now. Yesterday I joined the Cadence Squad I don't think I'll make it but I'll try. It isn't very often that a new man will make the cadence. We've had nice weather right along it hasn't even been freezing. I realy am anxious to get home for Xmas vacation. I can't think of any thing to write about. So good night.

Love,

Lenny

PILLSBURY ACADEMY
OWATONNA, MINN.

OFFICE OF
MILO B. PRICE, PH. D.
HEADMASTER

December 16, 1938

Mrs. Stina Ohman,
1806 Third Avenue South,
Minneapolis, Minnesota.

Dear Mrs. Ohman:

This acknowledges receipt of your Money Order for $25.00,
which has been credited on the tuition account of your
son, Cadet Leonard Ohman, as per the enclosed receipt.
Thank you very much for this remittance.

Leonard has left for home and will you kindly see that he
returns to be at the Academy by seven P. M., on Tuesday
evening, January 3rd.   I hope you will feel that it
has been worth while to send the boy to the Academy. We
are pleased with him and want him to return.

With the Season's Greetings, I am

Very truly yours,

Milo B. Price

MBP:H
ENCL.

264

Letter 13

January 4, 1939, Wednesday.

Dear Mother:

It's been raining every day down here since I've been back. Boy this is realy terrible compared with the fun I had when I was home. You were realy swell to me when I was home I'll never forget that. Gerry's aunt wants me to take him with me the next time I hitch hike home, that will be in about 3 or 4 weeks. I got back all right last Tue. but I've got something to tell you about the ride I got, I haven't enough time to tell you now because I'm supposed to be in bed, but I'll tell you later.

Thank Emil for the $5.00 I got from him you know I ment to thank him but I never saw him, and I called him a couple of times but he wasn't in. I'm writing fast thats why I'm writing so poorly. Love, Lenny

Letter 14

January 10, 1939, Tuesday.

Dear Mother:

It has been raining an awful lot down here and the temperature has been around 45 all the time. Did you thank Emil for the $5.00 for me. A new fellow started school the first day after vacation his name is Hoban, he went to North High School and he knows a girl that I know that goes there too. So Gerry, Hoban, and I are going to hitch hike into Mpls. the 27 of Jan. Hoban has a car in Mpls. so we are going out together when we get there. I could use some money very nicely if you can spare it. I've been taking good care of myself here I feel swell, I putting on weight, and I've been brushing my teeth every day, I wish you would send down some tooth paste and a couple of my pocket combs.

Love, Lenny

Letter 15
January 12, 1939, Wednesday.

Dear Mother:

    I ve haven't gotten any money since I got here after vacation. I relly need some pertty bad, I have to get both of my hats cleaned and I have to get my long pants cleaned too, so if you can apare any money please it.

    I hope your taking care of yourself while I'm away. Rember I'm coming home the 27th of this month, so please send me the permission about the 23 or the 24 of Jan, so I'll get it about Tue. or Wed. before Fri. the 27, so it will be in on time. I'm running out of stamps and envolopes, so if you have any extra ones please send them to me. My lights are suposed to be out, and I'm supoed to be in bed, so I better quit, "so long."

Love, Lenny

Letter 16

January 23, 1939, Monday.

Dear Mother:

Please send me the permission to go home right away so Dr. Price will have it in plenty time because I want to be sure to get home the 27 because it's been a month now sence I've been home, and I'm realy getting home sick, another reason is because a bunch of us fellows are going to have a party at Eddy Hoban's house and I want to be along, you wouldn't want me to miss this would you. Our Cach Squad is going to have an exhabition at the Winter Carnaval in St Paul on the 28th of this month , that's another thing I want to see, you should see it too. I wish you would send me some money for a hair cut and you know I'm on the bowling team up at school and that cost a little money too. I got the money you sent me the last time "thanks" but I got my hats cleaned and got my pants cleaned two. I can't think of anything more to say so good night.

Love, Lenny

P.S. Don't for get to take care of your self. Please send the permission as soon as possible. I'm taking good care of myself.

Leonard wrote to his mother a month later,

February 22, 1939, on Owatonna Hotel letterhead.

I questioned why an 18 year-old young man

would write a letter to his mother from a hotel room.

It seemed odd.

I cautiously proceeded to read my father's letter.

Letter 17

February 22, 1939, Wednesday.

Hotel Owatonna

Owatonna Minnesota

Dear Mother:

I sorry I didn't write or send you a letter or a card for your birthday, but I've been so busy trying to get settled that I haven't had time to write to you. It has been kind of hard getting settled. I'll write you more often now. I lost my certains and two rugs one of those wall hangs, a pair of rubbers, a pair of shoes, hair oil, vasoline, talcum powder and some underware, a couple of white shirts got schorchld by the smoke. We got some new furniture and it really looks nice. The only thing I don't like is that there are three kids in one room and it makes it kind of crowded. I wish you would send me a laundry kit so I can send my laundry home. We're having school six days a week to make up for the school we missed so I can't go home until the middle of March. I'm all right. Please send me about a dozen of 3-cent stamps I need them. Take care of yourself.

Love

Lenny

Leonard's words, "schorchld by the smoke"
suggested what may have happened
between January 23 - February 22.

At a loss and perplexed to a frenzy,
I needed more information.

In searching the archives
of the Minneapolis Star Tribune newspaper,
I entered the keywords:
"fire, Pillsbury Academy, Owatonna, Minnesota,
January 23 - February 22, 1939."

Three articles surfaced.

A devastating fire occurred
on the Pillsbury Academy campus on February 3.
Kelly Hall dormitory was destroyed.

My father was in this fire.
He lost all his possessions.

Leonard and other cadets
were housed at the Owatonna Hotel
until lodging could be found elsewhere on campus.

The Minneapolis Star
Friday, February 3, 1939, page 1

Flames Raze Landmark at Boys' School

Pillsbury Is Closed Until Housing Is Arranged

Owatonna, Minn.—(UP)— Kelly hall, historic landmark on campus of Pillsbury academy, was razed by fire early today.

The flames drove approximately 60 persons from the building into below-zero temperatures, but the residents were warned of the blaze in time to don clothing and save some personal effects. No injuries were reported.

* * *

Firemen were probing the ruins to determine what caused the blaze. Preliminary investigation indicated bad wiring was at fault.

* * *

Loss was estimated at between $60,000 and $70,000.

* * *

The hall, used as a dormitory and furnishing living quarters for five faculty members and their families, was built in 1909. It was isolated from most of the other buildings.

* * *

The entire student body of boys was leaving for home today, as college authorities were unable to arrange housing for the 45 students whose rooms were destroyed. Officials indicated the school would remain closed until some plan was arranged for housing.

* * *

The blaze was discovered practically simultaneously by nearly a dozen students. They warned other residents immediately.

* * *

Only the walls of the brick building remained standing, and part of the rear wall collapsed.

271

The Minneapolis Tribune
Saturday, February 4, 1939 - page 13

This is a view of Kelly Hall, at Pillsbury academy at Owatonna, in the late stages of the fire which destroyed the building early Friday. Fifty-five boys and five instructors escaped.

Belching smoke and flames during an early morning fire, Kelly Hall, at Pillsbury academy at Owatonna, was a charred mass of ruins Friday.

The Minneapolis Tribune
February 4, 1939; p.13
Most of the Pillsbury Students Return to Homes
Pending Arrival of New Equipment at Owatonna

Classes were suspended at Pillsbury academy at Owatonna, Minn., Friday following a $50,000 fire that early Friday morning routed 61 persons in the main dormitory at the school. Headmaster Owen B. Price said classes probably will not be resumed until late next week.

Fifty-two boys, 24 of them from Minneapolis, were in the building when the fire broke out. There also were four teachers and their wives and a seven-year-old boy, William McDonald, Jr., son of the coach at the school.

Mr. Price said most of the boys went to their various homes, but that about 15 or 20 who stayed in Owatonna are being cared for in other dormitories at the school.

Built in 1904.

Mr. and Mrs. McDonald and their son were in their suite on the fourth floor of the building, near the place where the fire broke out, but got to the street without injury, as did all the occupants of the building.

Mr. Price said new equipment must be purchased before classes can be resumed, and that this will take several days.

The dormitory burned was Kelly hall, built in 1904. Owatonna firemen were unable to save the dormitory, but prevented the blaze from spreading to other buildings.

Boys Give Alarm.

The fire was discovered at 3:30 a. m. by John Draggoman, 16, of International Falls, Minn. Draggoman roused his roommate, John Anderson, 5712 Forty-sixth avenue south, Minneapolis, and the two boys raced through the dormitory awakening the others. Most of the students and faculty members ran out of their rooms clad only in their night clothes and carrying a few of their valuables.

Most of the dormitory equipment and household goods in the three-story structure were destroyed. At 8 a. m. nothing but the brick walls and a heap of smouldering ruins remained.

Minneapolis Students.

Minneapolis students at Pillsbury academy, all of whom were housed in the razed dormitory, are John Anderson, son of Mrs. Sarah Anderson; Merle Anderson, son of Mr. and Mrs. M. O. Anderson; Rodney Antonsen, brother of Mrs. Evelyn Antonsen Albinson; Melvin Barnard, grandson of Mr. and Mrs. M. W. Barnard; William Bartlett, son of Mrs. Ruth Bartlett; Richard Berry, son of Captain and Mrs. Charles J. Berry; John Calvin Bleecker, son of Mr. and Mrs. J. D. Bleecker; Walter Burg, son of Mrs. Mayme W. Burg; Earl Cowan, son of Mrs. Janita Cowan; Charles Freidheim, son of Mr. and Mrs. Charles M. Freidheim; Donald Haven, son of Mrs. Vera Haven; Wilbur Johnson, son of Mr. and Mrs. Paul E. Johnson; William Johnson, son of Mr. and Mrs. E. M. Johnson; Lee Jones, son of Mr. and Mrs. Malcolm Jones; Donald Knutson, son of Mr. and Mrs. Thor Knutson; Gerald Kronberg, nephew of Miss Nan Kronberg; John Nichols, son of Mrs. G. A. Schildknecht; Leonard Ohman, son of Mrs. Stina Ohman; Wesley Pearson, son of Mr. and Mrs. Nels Pearson; Harrison Perl, son of Mr. and Mrs. E. Grant Perl; Robert Pratt, son of Mr. and Mrs. Alden Pratt; Ernest Rider, son of Dr. and Mrs. Ernest B. Rider; Doran Unschuld, son of Mr. and Mrs. Henry Unschuld, and Kenneth Wong, son of Mr. Wong Hing.

273

Pillsbury Academy

Owatonna, Minnesota

February 6, 1939

Cadets of Pillsbury Academy are asked to report at the
Academy on Saturday, February 11th, as early in the day as
possible. New equipment has been purchased and will be in
place by next Saturday. Cadets should report at the office
upon arrival at the school and they will then be directed
to their new quarters.

Cadet property salvaged from Kelly Hall is locked up in the
Armory and the Gymnasium. It will be necessary for each
cadet to claim and care for his own things and see that they
are removed to his new quarters, hence the need of early
arrival on Saturday. Readjustment of quarters in Pillsbury
Hall makes it imperative that Pillsbury Hall cadets return
as early as others.

It is proposed to resume school work with study hours at
seven o'clock on Sunday evening, February 12th, and regular
class work will proceed as usual beginning Monday morning,
February 13th.

Very truly yours,

MILO B. PRICE, Headmaster

274

The fire was a disparaging setback for Leonard.

He walked away from Pillsbury Academy
three days after writing the February 22 letter to his mother.

He left.

In the dead of winter, with little clothing or possessions of any kind,
Leonard ran away.

There is no indication as to where he went or what he did.

Leonard completed the first semester (ending January 28) of the
academic year at Pillsbury Academy.
He was truant the remainder of the second semester.

Leonard's life and learning were disrupted again.

OFFICE OF
MILO B. PRICE, PH. D.
HEADMASTER

March 7, 1939

Mrs. Stina Ohman,
1806 Third Avenue South,
Minneapolis, Minnesota.

Dear Mrs. Ohman:

The Principal of Edison High School called me this morning
to inquire about the reason for Leonard's departure from
Pillsbury Academy. I had to tell him the truth. I doubt
very much if he will receive the boy into the High School.

It occurs to me that you might find it possible to get
Leonard into a C.C.C. Camp. I don't know whom to refer
you to in that connection, but I do know that those camps
are made up of young men who get a pretty valuable training
in industry and deportment, and I know of several parents
who have been greatly pleased with the results of C. C.
Camp experience. It might be worth your while to look into
it.

Very truly yours,

Milo B. Price

MB:N

276

OFFICE OF
MILO B. PRICE, PH.D.
HEADMASTER

March 25, 1939

Mrs. Stina Ohman,
1806 Third Avenue South,
Minneapolis, Minnesota.

Dear Mrs. Ohman:

When Leonard left here about February 25th, we ceased all
charges against him on account of tuition, board, and room.
The amount due us up to the 25th of February is $102.38.
$65.98 is charged incident to the first semester of the
school year, which semester ended January 28th.

We are desperately in need of funds to meet our own bills,
Mrs. Ohman, and shall greatly appreciate it if you will continue your installment paying until you have this obligation
settled up. The total amount due us is $102.38. If we could
have $25.00 a month, the account would be cleaned up in a
short time. May I hear from you about it?

Very truly yours,

Milo B. Price

MBP:H

Reflections

Letters 1 – 17

Fall Semester 1938 – Spring Semester 1939

Why did Leonard leave Pillsbury Academy? Was he emotionally traumatized by the fire and could not maintain a focus on learning and classwork? Did he leave due to his lack of money? Was he tired of school? Or had he simply reached the breaking point of defeat?

I believe my father was not fond of sharing a hotel room with two other boys. When mandatory attendance at the Academy changed to six days per week to make up for the days missed due to the fire and when Leonard realized that it would be three weeks before he could go home, he hit a vulnerable breaking point. Leonard left. Once gone, his choice was not to return.

After Leonard's departure from Pillsbury Academy, there is evidence in Dr. Price's letter to Stina on March 7, 1939, that Leonard (or more likely, Stina) approached the Edison High School principal to request Leonard's re-enrollment at Edison for the remainder of the 1939 school year (three months). This proposal was rejected by the high school principal. It would have been difficult for Leonard, now 18 years of age, to pick up the fragments and be successful in an institution he had dropped out of a year earlier. Also, does Stina's request for Leonard's re-enrollment then imply that Leonard would return in the fall of 1939, at the age of 19, to complete his senior year at Edison?

You will note that Leonard and Stina's names appear in the *The Minneapolis Tribune*, February 4, 1939 article, "Most of Pillsbury Students Return to Homes Pending Arrival of New Equipment at Owatonna." I had no idea my father had survived a residence hall fire while a student at Pillsbury Academy. He had never mentioned this tragic event. I am sad. I wish he had shared this very serious and devastating experience.

"Dear Mother:"

Leonard's Story

Part Five

Letters 18 - 29

September 16, 1939 — December 12, 1939

Fall Semester

Pillsbury Academy

Hard Times

Reflections

Letter 18

September 16, 1939, Saturday.

Dear Mother:

Most of the kids down here are planning on going home every other week, but I want to go home every three weeks. Please send me some stamps a hole pile of them because I need a bunch of them. Did you get that picture made, and did you send it to Ruth? I got another shirt and it's all most new but I've got to get it refitted or in other words altered and I need some paper and things so maybe you better send me some more money for the altering of the coat or shirt. I want you to send me the permission to come Sept. 30. Then I been down here three weeks. Be sure to send me a bunch of stamps because I need them. And send me some candy and cookies and stuff. But be sure to send Strayer the permission for me to come home. Because I going home that day wether you send the permission or not so you might just as well send it, and I should have the shirt altered be fore that time so I'll have something to wear home. And don't for get to send Ruth that picture. When I come home I'll spend some time with you two. I've got to go now but I'll write again soon. I don't like it down here so let me come home when I want to.

Love

Lenny

Leonard returned to Pillsbury Academy in the fall of 1939, three semesters short of the required graduation requirements in his two-year program. There are no additional details.

Letter 19

September 18, 1939, Monday.

Dear Mother:

Don't come up Sunday because some of the kids from up N. E. are coming up and I can't see you both at the same time. And anyway I'm coming home a week from Friday the 29 of this month so I'll see you then. Some of the kids (about 5) have gone home all ready so send the permission for me to come home. I asked some kids what his folks write when they wrote to Strayer to let the kids go home, they said just write,

I want Leonard Ohman to come home this week end it is important. *(This sentence is circled.)*

so please write Strayer so I can come home. I'll see you too.

Love

Lenny

P.S. and if you don't I'll come home anyway.

P.S. send some stamps

Letter 20

September 20, 1939, Wednesday.

Dear Mother:

Why don't you write more often I want to here from you. I got
my new shirt refitted and now I'm broke, but Boy does it look good
on me. Remmber don't come down here Sunday because some of
the kids from up N. E. are coming down and then I won't be able to
spend any time with you, and an other reason is because if you
come down Sunday then it'll look funny when I go home on the 29th
and I'm going home for sure the 29th so tell Strayer to let me go.
Some kids went home last Friday, and some are going home next
Friday but, I want to go home the 29th of this month. Some kids are
planning on going home every week end. and I want to go home
perrty often before it gets two cold, because then I wont be able to. I
wish you would send me some money. And that knot book and
some paper. Send me a hole bunch of stamps I need them. And send
me my tennis shose too. I would like some candy too. Have you
sent Ruth that Picture yet. be sure to write Strayer about me coming
home because I'll go even if you don't write. I should have been in
bed a long time ago so good-night or good-by

Love

Leonard.

Letter 21

October 5, 1939, Thursday.

Dear Mother:

Be sure to send me the permission to come home the 13th of Oct. so I can see that game, all the kids are going up then. Don't tell Strayer that I just going up to see the game because that isn't a big enough reason. Just write I want my son to come home the 13th of October. Because I just run away from here for good if you don't, and you wouldn't want me to do that would you. I'm doing everything right and I'm working hard so I can finish, now you do me a favor and let me come home. I got the two packages, thanks a lot dear mother. I'm being a real good Boy as please let me come home. I can't stand to stay down here too long at one time. I could stand some money if you can spare it, I'm broke. Tell Strayer that you want me to come home. I just can't think of anything more to say, except that I'll do every think I can for you if you will let me come home when I want to. I'm working hard every day. Take care of your self mother dear. Please write often.

Love

Lenny

Letter 22

October 10, 1939, Tuesday.

Dear Mother:

Be sure to send me permission to come home because everyone is going to Mpls Friday the 13th of Oct. Because if don't I'll just run away from here and never come back. I've made plans with a lot of the kids down here, for Sat. night so I've got to come home, and because of other plans too. I've worked hard every sence I came down here, so you can do me a favor now, I haven't had any squad either I've been real good. If you love me you won't make me stay down here when I want to go home. Stayer fixed so the kids could go home more often. I had ran out of stamps so I had to borrow some. I'm broke too. I've got something to tell you when I get home.

Why didn't you send that picture to Ruth. All the kids are going to Mpls Friday some are going and they don't even live in Mpls, so their going to live in Hotels over the week end. They mad a lot of changes in the vacations we have and I think there for the best too.

Love

Lenny

P.S. Please send the permission.

Letter 23

October 18, 1939, Wednesday.

Dear Mother:

I sorry I didn't get to see you when I was home, I especial got up early Sun morning so I could see you and then Mrs. Lundquist told me you had gone hunting. Please send me some stamps I need some bad. And I haven't got a penny to my name either. I've got to get my uniform cleaned and pressed. And I need money bad. I've got to get a hair cut too. and I won't be home for a few weeks either, so please send me some money. I felt so bad when I couldn't see you. I wish you would press my black suit for the next time I come home. I'm beginning to feel so blue. Please write soon, and please send Ruth that picture. She's asking for it because I promised her it.

Love

Lenny

P.S. Please send some stamps.

xxxx

PILLSBURY ACADEMY

Owatonna, Minnesota

MILO B. PRICE, Headmaster

Mrs. Stina Ohman,
1806 - 3rd Avenue South,
Minneapolis, Minnesota.

Report of   Leonard Ohman

For six weeks ending   October 20, 1939

SUBJECTS

	Six Wks.	Sem.
English 4	70	
American History	70	
Economics	73	
Plane Geometry	78	
Mechanical Drawing	88	
Military Drill	81	
Deportment	90	

Passing Grade: 70.

F R Strayer
Headmaster

Letter 24

October 26, 1939, Thursday.

Dear Mother:

I passed in all 5 subjects and got some real good marks. I wish you would send me some envelopes and writing paper I'm all out. And the thing I need most is stamps please send me a bunch of stamps. I get the package yesterday thanks for it. I want to come home the 3rd of Nov. that is a week from Friday. It is very very important that I see you then. I have some very important things to tell you about school and about some money I got in the mail that I had to give the school for toishion. And I have also made some plans. Please let me come home then because it is very important. I want to come home then because I won't be able to come home again until Thanks giving. unless I come home then. All the kids are going home the 3rd of Nov, and I'll run away if I can't.

It will be all most a month then since I was home last. Tell Strayer that it is important that you see me. I'm getting along swell down here but I haven't any money and I can't go roller skating with the other kids from school so I don't feel so happy. If I had some money I would go roller skating too. Thanksgiving is a long way off so please let me come home. It has been a long time since I was home last. Have you sent Ruth that picture yet? Why don't you write more often. I would but I haven't any stamps, I had to borrow this one I feel all right, I mean I'm healthy I have put on some weight too. Please send me some stamps and money. And by all means let me come home Nov. 3rd.

I love you a lot. so please be good to me. I also need envolopes and writing paper.

Love

Lenny

P.S. Please write.

Letter 25

October 30, 1939, Monday.

Dear Mother:

I wasn't lying to you when I said I had some thing important to see you about. I have three important things to see you about so I have to come home Friday. All most all the kids are going home so why can't I anyway. I came down here on the condition that you would let me come home anyway. All the other kids go home and I want to also. Your the only one I can have a heart to heart talk with, and if you won't talk to me I'll just leave this place for good and never come back. I've got to see you Friday. So send the permission right away.

Love

Lenny

Letter 26

November 12, 1939, Sunday.

Dear Mother:

Why don't you ever write, don't you think I get lonesome for you and want to hear from you. Has any think new happened up there lately.

Ruth sure did like that picture I gave her, she's been writting me and telling me that her whole family likes it. but don't call her up and say anything will you, because I wouldn't like that I got a hair cut last week and now I'm broke so please send me some money, because I could sure use it.

all the kids are getting there graduation rings I sure wish I could get mine before Xmas or else get it now and call it my Xmas present. Some kids are getting them and there not graduating for 2 or 3 years yet.

I haven't any cloths to wear. I have wore the same shirt for three weeks now. Please send me some money so I can get my radio fixed up too. I need money bad.

Please write soon dear, and send my cloths too. Take care of your self.

Love
Lenny

Letter 27

November 22, 1939, Wednesday.

Dear Mother:

I have to get a hair cut and I have to buy a Geometry book for school, the book costs 85 cents and I need some more money to pay my debts. Please send me some money because I need it bad. I had to get four service stripes sewed on my uniform So I owe out a lot of money.

I'll be home Wed. and I wish you press the pants for my black suit, because I want to wear that every day. I'm getting along swell down here, I haven't had a day of squad yet, so that proves I've been good.

I sure would like to get my graduation ring soon. I hope your taking care of your self. I've been down here so long now that its almost driving me crazy. Why haven't you written me I've been waiting for you to write me.

I had to borrow some money so I could get some soap. I wish you would send me some stamps too. I can hardly wait till I can come home again. Please write soon.

Love
Lenny

PILLSBURY ACADEMY

Owatonna, Minnesota

MILO B. PRICE, Headmaster

Mrs. Stina Ohman,
1806 - 3rd Avenue South,
Minneapolis, Minnesota.

Report of   Leonard XXX Ohman

For six weeks ending   November 29, 1939

SUBJECTS

	Six Wks.	Sem.
English	65	
History	70	
Economics	74	
Geometry	78	
Mech. Drawing	85	
Military Drill	84	
Deportment	94	

Passing Grade: 70.

F R Strayer
                                                Headmaster

294

Letter 28

December 8, 1939, Friday.

Dear Mother:

I had to lend Gerry 85 cents so he would have enough to pay for his hotel bill, and now I'm broke please send me some money, but don't say anything to Gerry's aunt about it. He hasn't payed me back yet, and I don't know when I'll get it.

Don't let that mark on my report card worry you, because it doesn't mean anything. I'll explain every thing about it when I get home. There's about 17 in our English class and 8 of us got 65% and some got lower so don't worry about it.

Be sure to send me the permission to come home, because if you don't I'll come home any way, because its important, and theres nothing that can hold me back.

Please send me some stamps I'm all out of them, and I do need some money. The 15th is when I want to come home that's on a Friday.

Please take care of yourself.

Love

Lenny

Letter 29

December 12, 1939, Thursday.

Postmarked, Owatonna, Minn., Dec. 21, 1939, 4:30pm.

Dear Mother:

You've got to send me the permission to go home Dec 15. because I want to go to that banquet, and I don't care how much squad I get if I go without permission, because its important that I go.

If you don't send me the permission to come home I'll never forgive you for it. And if you send me permission I wont get squad. We've made a lot of plans about the banquet, Ruth, Earl, Harriet and me, so I've got to go.

I'll never speak to you again if you don't send the permission. I'll give you the last warning, I'll run away if you don't send the permission. I mean business. There is a lot of kids going home this weekend.

Love

Lenny

Reflections

Letters 18 – 29

Fall Semester 1939

We learn of Leonard's special friend, Ruth, in his letter of
September 16, 1939. He speaks of her often throughout the fall
semester and wants his mother to send her a photograph of himself.
Among my father's collection of mementos was a three-ring binder
of biology notes. The endsheets of the binder were covered with
doodling and caricature drawings surely etched during deep
moments of dull lectures. "R. O. + L. O." appears everywhere on
these endpapers. I learned in my recent research that Ruth Olson
was my mother's friend. Both were members of the same 1940
graduating class from Columbia Heights High School. Ruth, Doris,
Lois, Mary Jane, Kitt, and Fae were girlfriends who formed a
"club" and were inseparable. My father and Ruth became
acquainted during the summer of 1939.

All of Leonard's letters have a common thread: "I want to come
home for the weekend," and, "I need money." Both requests are
reasonable, since the depression had ended just a few years earlier.
Financial stress was still high in 1939 as the U.S. economy was in a
recession. Stina worked as a milliner in an upscale department store
in downtown Minneapolis. Her wages were low, and she had a
monthly outlay to Pillsbury Academy for Leonard's tuition. It was a
financially difficult time for her with little money to spare.

Nine of the twelve letters in this section contain threats that
Leonard made toward his mother. I was disturbed by my father's
manipulative words to gain leverage for his desired outcome.
Leonard knew his mother's ultimate wish was that he graduate from

high school. He used threats of quitting school to accomplish this goal of approved weekends home. All of his threats insinuate that if his mother did not send Mr. Strayer a fictitious note requesting Leonard come home, that the payback would be Leonard's departure from the Academy, never to return. In Letter 29, Leonard writes, "I'll never speak to you again . . . I'll never forgive you if you don't send the permission." His approach is childish. Leonard's choice of words and tone of voice are shocking. Neither my brother nor I would have ever considered using such a ploy and ultimatum with either of our parents. This type of behavior was unacceptable. It must have worked for Leonard, however, or he would have stopped using it.

As evidenced by Letter 23 (October 18, 1939), the Lundquist home remained Leonard's home base on weekend furloughs to Minneapolis. Leonard remained under the Lundquists' care. This allowed Stina free weekends of relaxing pleasure and social opportunities without parental responsibility. Leonard writes, "I sorry I didn't get to see you when I was home, I especial got up early Sun morning so I could see you and then Mrs. Lundquist told me you had gone hunting . . ." He continued near the end of the letter, "I felt so bad when I couldn't see you . . . I'm beginning to feel so blue."

Stina distanced herself from Leonard and enjoyed living in her own private world. Leonard was a financial burden. Even though Leonard was a young adult at age nineteen, he needed Stina's affirmation. He wanted his mother's support and reassurance, and craved his mother's love and attention. Leonard felt she did not write to him often enough. In his letters, he frequently asked his mother to please write to him more often.

Stina exhibited selfish tendencies in her decision that Leonard live with foster parents and attend a boarding school 65 miles away from their home. Stina was often absent both emotionally and physically in Leonard's life. It could be said that Leonard was a victim of maternal neglect and abandonment.

In the fall of 1939, Leonard did not relish his return to Pillsbury Academy nor did he feel a part of the student body. Being readmitted to a school after a three-month truancy was not well received by the administration, the instructors, nor his cadet peers. Letter 18 (September 16, 1939) was likely written during his first week back to school. In this letter Leonard discloses his dislike for Pillsbury, "I don't like it down here so let me come home when I want to." Leonard felt he no longer belonged.

"Dear Mother:"

Leonard's Story

Part Six

Letters 30 - 48

January 10, 1940 — June 17, 1940

Spring Semester

Pillsbury Academy

Harder Times

Reflections

Photos

Letter 30

January 10, 1940, Wednesday.

L. G. Ohman

P. A.

Owatonna, Minnesota

Dear Mother:

I got down here about 3:00 safe and sound. I talked to this kid about letting me borrow his ring so I could get one made like it and he said I could. So the ring buisness is all settled I'm anxious to work hard and be sure to graduate this May, for a matter of fact I'm going to work real hard. I just hope I'll be something that you will be proud of because I want you to be proud of me, so I'm going to work real hard.

And the next time I come I won't spend so much money. I'd like to come home the 27th thats three weeks from know. And then I bring you that Christmas present too. Boy it's the nicest thing you've ever seen. Im anxious to show it to you.

I just wrote Fred and Eva and thank them for the tie and cookies they sent me. Write me as soon as you can and often because you have to make for the letters that Ruth used to write.

Love

Lenny

Letter 31

January 19, 1940, Friday.

Dear Mother:

Why don't you ever write, don't you think I wont to hear from you? Please send me some money I spent all the money I had buying books for next semester.

All the kids are going home the 26 of Jan. because it is the end of the first semester, and I want to come home too. Its been a long time since I was home last and Its very important that I come home the 26 of Jan.

I got the box you sent me but it was all torn apart and it looks like something might have gotten lost. Write me and tell me what you sent me. I wish you would send me some shaving cream and tooth paste and some stamps because I need them badly.

You've got to let me come home the 26 of Jan. when our last marks for this first semester come out. I can hardly wait until May when I graduate, It will be so swell to be out of school for good. Then I hope I can get a good job and help you out.

Its been pretty cold down here lately its been between 10 and 26 degrees below zero all last night. But don't worry about me I'm O.K.

Love

Lenny

P.S. Please send those things to me.

Letter 32

February 3, 1940, Saturday.

L. G. O.

P. A.

Owatonna, Minnesota

Dear Mother:

I'm sorry I didnt write you before but I've been perty busy
lately. I'm badly in need of money so badly that I'm worried about
it I can't sleep nights on account of it. Every body had to order
white pants for spring The new ones cost about $6 for two. We have
to have two pair but I got two pair of second hand pants and the kid
wants $3 for them and he wants it right away. I tryed to put it on the
bill but Mr. Strayer said I couldn't do that and told me to write you
and ask you for it. I also need a hair cut and a pair of gloves, some
one stold the pair I had. I hate to ask you for any money but I have
to, because I can't get it from any one else.

I hope your all right. I feel swell, I hope you'll take care of
yourself. We had swell weather down hear lately but it snowing
down here right now and its snowing perrty hard too.

Please write me soon and I'll answer you right away and send
me the money <u>Please</u> because I need it and send me some stamps
too.

Love

Lenny

Letter 33

February 10, 1940, Saturday.

P. A.

Owatonna, Minnesota

Dear Mother:

I got your letter with the money it, thanks alot I really needed it.

I think I got a good by on those pants, there were two pair. I'll by those gloves here because they have to be regalation type.

It'll be three weeks since I was home last so I want to come home next Friday the 16 of Feb. It is very necessary that I do. I'll try not to spend much money when I come home this time. Mrs. Lundquist it going to make an appointment for me with that guy who was going to help me get a job. And I've got to go to the dentist also.

I hope you will take care of your self and get better real soon because I worry about you.

Please write and send me the permission to come home and see you the 16 of Feb. And I've got some business to attend to. I'm feeling swell and I weigh 155 lbs now. Please take care of yourself.

Love

Lenny

P.S. Don't forget the permission send it about 14 or 15.

Letter 34

February 13, 1940, Tuesday.

L. G. O.

P. A.

Owatonna, Minnesota

Dear Mother:

I got the backage with my shirt and stockings in it, Please don't buy any more black stockings I got so many now that it will take me five years to wear them out.

It is very necessary that I come home Friday the 16 of this month so don't for get to send me the permission because it is very necessary.

I got a letter from Fred and Eva and I got a box from Lundquist it was a box of candy and it was good. I wrote Mrs Lundquist a letter telling he to make an appointment with Mr Holmquist for Sat. afternoon, now I have to come home for sure so be sure to send the permission right away.

I can't think of any thing else to say.

Love

Lenny

P.S.   Take care of yourself.

Letter 35

February 20, 1940, Tuesday.

L.G. Ohman

P. A.

Owatonna, Minnesota

Dear Mother:

I got down here all right and I had perrty good luck too. Dr Priece died a couple of days ago so the whole school is going to the Funeral Services.

When you send my cloths down send down some writting paper and envolopes I haven't any, and I could use some stamps too, and don't for get to send some hair oil. I can't spend any money because I have to pay the rest of the money on the car or else they'll take both the car and the money, you know they can do that when you buy a car on time payments. I've only got $4.75 left to pay and then I'm all done.

I got a letter from Ruth today, boy, was I surprised. If youve got any extra money please send it so I can get the car pay for. They sent that card, I was telling you about, so as soon as you get it write me and let me know, it is very important that I know when you get it. When I bring it home you'll be so surprised because its a swell car and it work so nice, I know you'll be glad I bought it. I'll be home to see you again the 8th of next month. Take good care of your self now. I'm going to work my hardest now.

Love

Lenny

P.S. Write soon.

Letter 36

February 28, 1940, Wednesday.

L.G. Ohman

P. A.

Owatonna, Minnesota

Dear Mother:

I've got a big suprise for you when I come home next time, then you will be happy to see me I'm sure. Boy, I'm thrilled about it. I need some money for something for my uniform. I can't tell you what it is yet but you'll see when I come home. It won't be long now until I graduate and I'll need a job then so I want to talk to that guy I know down at the Northern Pump Co. as soon as I can, and thats why I want to come home the 8th of March which is a week from Friday thats the only time that I'll be able to come home for a long time. And I have to see Dr. Thorandaul too. And there is some else that I have to see you about. I got a letter from Ruth and see wants to see me to. You've got to let me come home then, It'll be 3 weeks sence I was home and there so many things I have to take care of then. I feel swell and I'm working hard every day. I hope your taking good care of your self. I need some money to fix my shose too.

I wish you'd send me that stuff you said you were, and send me some stamps too. I wish you'd write more often. I have to close now.

Love

Lenny

P.S. Please send me some spare money.

Letter 37

March 3, 1940, Sunday.

Dear Mother:

   I want to come home home Friday for sure, because I have
several reasons, one of the main reasons is to show you something
and give you a big supprise, its biger than I ever expected. I told Mr.
Strayer that when I went home on week ends I'd put in my
applications at different companies he said that was a good idea,
and thats what I'm going to do when I come home Friday. I'm
going down to The Northern pump company and see that guy I
know that works there, And I'm going to some other factories to,
I've got a lot of things to take care of. Why haven't you written me
lately? I've been expecting a letter from you for a long time. I hope
your not sick, are you? Don't for get you got to take care of your
self, because I wouldn't want any thing to happen to you. How is
the weather up there? Its swell down here. Has anything new
happened up there. We won't get our spring vacation until the last
part of this month. I'm as healthy and as happy as can be, but I wont
to come home Friday, so don't forget to to send me the permission.
I can't think of any thing else to say.
Love, Lenny
P.S. Please send me some stamps.

*Leonard drove his newly purchased car home the weekend of
March 8th and left it parked in Minneapolis. He had no money for
gasoline. He continued to hitchhike from Owatonna to Minneapolis
and back again on his weekend visits home.*

PILLSBURY ACADEMY

Owatonna, Minnesota

MILO B. PRICE, Headmaster

Mrs. Stina Ohman,
1806 - 3rd Avenue South,
Minneapolis, Minnesota.

Report of   Leonard Ohman

For six weeks ending   March 8, 1940

SUBJECTS

	Six Wks.	Sem.
English	D -	
History 4	C -	
Economics	D +	
Plane Geom.	B -	
Mech. Drawing.	B -	
Military Drill	B +	
Deportment	a	

Passing Grade: 70.

G. R. Strayer
                                    Headmaster

311

Letter 38

March 14, 1940, Thursday.

L.G. Ohman

Pillsbury Academy

Owatonna, Minnesota

Dear Mother:

I need some money to get a hair cut, and we're have a dance before our vacation. It cost $1.00 per couple or else $1.00 per stag. I wont to go to this dance and I haven't any money. I don't think I'll be able to hitch hike to Mpls because there is so much snow down here. The snow is about 2 and a half feet deep and some drifts are 3 feet deep. I wish you would send me some stamps too. Has there been much snow up there? We have to have a large attendance at this dance or else we won't be able to have a formal for graduation, and I want to go to it so bad. I got down here all right the last time. My hair is terribly long so I have to have it cut before the dance. The kids have so much fun at those dances so I want to have some fun to I haven't been able to go to any of the rest of the dances because I was saving my money.

I'm looking forward to the vacation we're going to have, because some of the kids from Duluth are going to stay at Mpls.

Love

Lenny

P.S. Please write soon, right away or else I won't get it in time

Letter 39

March 28, 1940, Thursday.

Owatonna, Minnesota

Dear Mother:

I didn't get into Owatonna until 1:30 Wed. morning and Mr Strayer asked me why I was late and I told him that I started out from Mpls hitch hiking but I didn't get a ride because there wasn't any traffic because of the snow. And I told him that after trying to hitch hike and didn't get a ride I took the next train to Owatonna, and it didn't get into Owatonna until 1:30, so I think every thing will be all right know.

I hope that Mrs Seberg will talk to that fellow so I will get a job from him because that would be swell. I want you to leave one white shirt there at home so the next time I come home I will have something to change into to take back to Owatonna. because I have some white shirts down here.

Half of the kids aren't back here yet. Don't for get to take care of yourself while I'm gone, you can send down some Vixs vaper rub for my cold if you want to. I'm really looking forward to graduation now.

Take care of yourself now.

Love

Lenny

P.S. Please write soon.

Letter 40

April 9, 1940, Tuesday.

L.G. Ohman

Pillsbury Academy

Owatonna, Minnesota

Dear Mother:

I got a letter from Vern and he said that I would have to move my car so please let me come home Friday the 12 of April and some other kids from school are going up to Mpls to so I want to come home, One of the kids is the one with the ring and he said he would meet Sat morning down town and then we would go up there. I haven't been home for 3 weeks now so be sure to let me go home. We've had some swell weather down here lately its really been just like summer

Thanks for the letters, Boy! Was I supprised to get two letters in the same day and get them both from you. I'm sorry I didn't write before but I wasn't able to, It seem like Ive been down he so long I'm terribly anixous to get home Friday.

If you could spare a dollar I could make use of it when I'm on the road home its always nice to have something to eat on the road you really get hungry. If any thing new has happened tell me about it. Take good care of yourself, and I'll see you Friday.

Love

Lenny

Letter 41

April 16, 1940, Tuesday.

L.G. Ohman

Pillsbury Academy

Owatonna, Minnesota

Dear Mother:

I was very disapointed when I couldn't come up last week, and if you don't let me come up this week I'll come with out your permission, even if I loss my office. Be sure to send the permission wright now because I have to talk over some thing with you. If you don't send the permission this time I'll never for give you for it. There are a lot of reasons why I have to come up, one is my shoes are all worn out there are holes in the soles. and there are many other things too.

I've been down here for a whole month, 4 weeks and haven't been home once. I was suppose to me a kid last Sat. in Mpls and we were going down to see about the ring.

I went to a dance that the Gradatin Socity had last Sat. night and know I haven't any money to get a hair cut and I need it bad. So if you send me some money I'll get a hair cut and I'll have some money to eat with on the way up to Mpls.

Be sure to send me the permission.

Love

Lenny

Letter 42

April 30, 1940, Tuesday.

L.G. Ohman

Pillsbury Academy

Owatonna, Minnesota

Dear Mother:

Mr Strayer is giving a formal doing for the Senior class and I sure could use that some money, anyway you said when I was home that you would send me some money right away, and I didn't get any.

Don't for get I have to come home a week from Friday so I can go up to the Lincoln Employment Agency again the way she told me. so they can line me up with a job, because I want to have more than one prospect for a job because it wont be long now before I'm out. I have to go down Wednsday and have the proofs taken for my pictures I'll get a half a dozen then. Boy am I getting excited about the graduation and every thing. And I hope this formal we're going the the 25 will be some thing I'll remember the rest of my life. The Formal Mr. Strayer is giving will be Sat. this is a big doing just for the Seniors. If you could spare a couple dollars I would sure appreciated it.

Love

Lenny

Letter 43

May 7, 1940, Tuesday.

L. G. Ohman

Pillsbury Academy

Owatonna, Minnesota

Dear Mother:

I've been down here for 3 weeks now and I have to come home for several reasons, one is because I have to go down the Lincoln Employment Agency that is when I'm supposed to go down there and see about that job. And I have to see if that girl is still going to the our Formal Military Ball before I buy the tickets and there are many other reasons why I have to come home. Be sure to send me the permission to come home this Friday. It is very necessary that I come home I just have to come home so don't for get to send the permission right away and its Mother's day Sunday so I want to be home with you then.

How have you been while I've been gone O.K. I hope. We had a swell time at the dance. When you write I'd appreciate it if you would send down some money, I've a lot of debts to pay and I'd like to have some money on the way home to eat on. Take care of your self, and be sure to send the permission.

Love

Lenny

Letter 44

May 15, 1940, Wednesday.

Dear Mother:

I meant to write you before and tell you that I got down here all right, but I haven't had time, because I've had so much to do before I graduate.

I have to get a hair cut because my hair is pretty long, and the senior class is going to pitch in some money and by the school something like all the other classes have done. (I have no money)

Some of the kids are send announcements to there friends about their graduation, but I dont think I will because it cost quite a bit of money.

Be sure to send the permission for me to come home the 25 that when the formal it, you know.

I've been working like the dickens every sence monday and I have to keep it up until graduation.

Try to get in touch with Bill Anderson about that job, because I just have to get a job right away thats all there is to it. And ask Mrs. Seaberg to talk to him to because that will help you know.

Just think how nice it will be after I've graduated and get a job, won't that be swell.

When you send the laundry if you have an extra cigarettes please send them.

Ask Emil if he can't fix me up with a job, he should be able to do that for me.

Love

Lenny

The Senior Class

of

Nineteen Hundred and Forty

Pillsbury Academy

announces its

Commencement Exercises

on Saturday afternoon, June the first

at three o'clock

First Baptist Church

Owatonna, Minnesota

Leonard G. Ohman

Letter 45
May 20, 1940, Monday.

L. G. Ohman
Pillsbury Academy
Owatonna, Minnesota
Dear Mother:

All the kids that a graduating are getting announcements to send to there friends, so I ordered some to. I'm badly in need of money I have to get my pants cleaned and I have to pitch in some money with the rest of the seniors and get something for the school I have to get all my clothes cleaned for the inspection, I have to get a hair cut too there are so many things I have to do but I can't because I haven't any money. I thought that was a durty trick of you not to answer my letter when you know I haven't any money.

Be sure to send me permission to come home this Friday the 24 because I have to. Don't send my clothes down now because I'll take them when I come back here Sunday.

If you don't send me the permission at a time like this when I need it so bad I'll never forgive you for it, I have to come home to pick up the girl for the Formal.

Please send me some money because I need it so bad. Answer right away

Love
Lenny

Letter 46
May 28, 1940, Tuesday.

L. G. Ohman
Pillsbury Academy
Owatonna, Minnesota
Dear Mother:

I got a letter from Emil and there was 10 dollars in it, I got it last
Monday. I gess he thinks I went to the formal, well let him keep on
thinking so, don't tell him I didn't go because he probly wouldn't
like that We'll have to stick to that story, because the next time he
see's me he'll most likely ask me, and I'll tell him I went, and you
tell him the same thing, but if you have told him already that I
didn't go write to me and tell me so, because we have to stick to the
same story.

That realy was swell of him alright. Don't let him see this letter,
for God's sake, but tell him thanks for me.

I hope I'll see the two of you Sat.

Don't worry about the money because I'm old enough to take
care of that I'm afraid I have to close now because I have to learn
my orations and I have to do a lot of work.

Love
Lenny

Letter 47

June 3, 1940, Monday.

L. G. Ohman

Pillsbury Academy

Owatonna, Minnesota

Dear Mr. Strayer:

I have been trying to get a job and have found it very hard. Last Saturday you told me that you would write to a company if gave you the address. I would appreciate it very much if you would write to the

The above letter was written in ink to Mr. Strayer, Headmaster, and Leonard's History/Government instructor. You will notice in the second sentence that Leonard omitted the word "I." He was unable to send this imperfect letter. It was discarded and Leonard wrote another. Stina recovered the tossed letter and kept it among her own letters from Leonard.

Office of the Headmaster

June 17, 1940

Mr. Leonard Ohman,
1806 Third Avenue South,
Minneapolis, Minnesota.

My dear Leonard:

I have written to the companies you suggested in your letter.
I hope you will be able to find a position.
Let us hear from you from time to time.

Very cordially yours,

GRS-h

G. R. Strayer

Northern Pump Company

920 18th Avenue N. E., Minneapolis, Minn.

SOCIAL SECURITY
NUMBER

APPLICATION FOR EMPLOYMENT

No.............................

PLEASE FILL OUT AS COMPLETE AS POSSIBLE

Name.. Date..................................., 19 ..... Phone { Res. ....

No. { Any other..........................

Address in full...

Age.................. Height.................. Weight.................. Nationality of Parents.......................

Citizenship.......................... Where born.......................... Date of birth..................

Married, single or widower?.................. Number of children?.................. Number dependent for support?..................

Ever employed here before?.................................. In what kind of work?..................

Kind of work wanted?.................................. Wages expected?.................. Do you object to piece work?..................

Sight?.................................. Hearing?..................................

Have you any disease or permanent disability or have you ever undergone any surgical operation, broken bones, etc.?

....

....

Accident—Notify: .... Address: ....

EDUCATION

Number of years in grade school?.................................. High School?..................

What other schooling have you had?..................................

NO CONSIDERATION GIVEN IF NOT FILLED OUT COMPLETELY

Kind of Job	Length of Time on Each	Kind of Job	Length of Time on Each	Kind of Job	Length of Time on Each
Engine Lathe........		Drill Press..........		Bench Work.........	
Turret Lathe (kind)..		Radial Drill........		Wet Grinder........	
Internal Grinder....		Warner & Swasey...		Assembly Work.....	
Screw Machine......		Blanchard Grinder..		Welding (Elec. Arc.)..	
Milling Machine....		Planer.............		Blacksmith.........	
Boring Mill.........		Horizontal Mill.....		Toolmaker..........	
				Inspector...........	

Give here any other experience not listed above: ....

....

Can you set up your own work: ....

Can you lay out your own work: ....

RECORD OF EMPLOYMENT FOR THE PAST FIVE YEARS

Experience—Kind of Work	From	To	Employer	Address

Least Salary to Start: Hour.................. Weekly.................. Monthly..................

Reason for leaving last position..................................

REMARKS: ....

....

....

FORM 150 2M 3-45 NP

324

Reflections

Letters 30 – 47

Spring Semester 1940

My father's grammar and sentence construction improved during the time he attended Pillsbury Academy. He failed English throughout his years of schooling, yet in his letters, there is evidence of growth.

Leonard's destitution permeated his letters. It is hard to imagine his level of poverty and also to accept the fact that he was one of the poorest students in his class.

When my father mentions in Letter 39 that he took the next train to Owatonna because he could not get a ride hitchhiking, I believe he hopped a freight. He did this from time to time in his youth although he didn't like to talk about it. On this occasion, he had no money. Hitching a ride on a freight train was certainly probable under the circumstances.

It is surprising that Leonard never attempted, to our knowledge, to forge a permission note allowing him to go home or forge his mother's signature. In every letter he begs her to send a note of permission so he could leave the campus. I'm sure the thought of forgery occurred to him. Perhaps Stina had distinguished stationery. A deviation in paper might have been recognized by Dr. Price or Mr. Strayer. Leonard's handwriting may have been easily discernible. Leonard must have decided forgery was not worth the risk.

I never heard my father use the word "swell."

I never saw a graduation ring from Pillsbury Academy.

It is unfortunate that my father did not attend his Senior Formal dance. Again, it was due to the lack of money. Neither he nor his mother could cover the graduation expenses that accumulated at the end of the school year. More than likely these expenses remained outstanding.

In 1940, Leonard's goal was to end his schooling experience for good and never return. He wanted nothing more than to just get through it, so that he could get a job and make some money. But the question remains, how was he granted a diploma lacking the semester credits from his spring 1939 truancy? Pillsbury Academy gave my father a gift. Perhaps he was forgiven his missing semester due to the fire. Maybe he did not receive a diploma; I did not find one. His situation needed special consideration. Had he been required to return to the Academy and make up his missing credits, he would have enrolled for the fall semester 1940 at the age of twenty. The committee chose mercy. Leonard had suffered schooling long enough. It was time he get on with his life.

Leonard's need for employment in June 1940 could not have come at a better time. Northern Pump Company needed workers. Even though the United States had not officially entered the war, the U.S. war effort was fully in gear. Great Britain and France needed tanks, planes, munitions, and heavy artillery. U.S. factories and workers ramped up production with factories running 24 hours a day with three shifts of workers. Hitler was on the move, and France was his target; Great Britain was next. Roosevelt and Churchill were in strategic talks. It was inevitable that the U.S. would enter the war. Leonard was offered a job at Northern Pump Company the same day he submitted his application.

326

Northern Pump Company later became Northern Ordinance, and then FMC, Northern Ordinance Division. The munitions plant was located in Fridley, Minnesota. Leonard retired from the same company 42 years later. He was hired as a draftsman and advanced into the engineering department. If asked what he did for a living, he always replied that he was a "mechanical design engineer" though he held no degree in engineering nor could he attain one. Leonard was actually a captive in his job at FMC, as he did not have the credentials to pursue another employer had he wanted (or needed) to. It is probable he had no high school diploma.

During World War II, Northern Ordinance held contracts with the U.S. Navy. Later, my father's team designed guided missile launching systems and gun mounts for U.S. Navy ships. My father did well at Northern Ordinance. He was a loyal employee with a strong work ethic. He was also keenly conscientious with his paycheck. It is interesting . . . Leonard had an innate ability in mechanical design. Of course he did—his grandfather, Carl, was an inventor. Certainly Leonard inherited the genetic tendencies of the Ohman lineage.

Leonard and my mother, Matie Faye (Fae) Moore, were married February 14, 1942. My mother was Leonard's lifeline. A new and happier life began for Leonard when he met Fae. She added purpose to my father's life. Smart and popular, Fae was vice president of her class. My mother came from a loving and hard working family of German descent. Fae was good at math, loved reading books, wrote poetry, and enjoyed crossword puzzles and Scrabble. She had what my father lacked, a thorough command of the English language in all aspects of usage. She was a bookkeeper at the Electric

Machinery Company in Minneapolis and later at Caswell Engineering Company in Brooklyn Park. Her parents, Clarence Raymond Moore and Selma Helena Ziegenhagen Moore owned property on Lake Pokegama near Pine City, Minnesota. Fae and Lenny spent many weekends at the lake, north of the Twin Cities. When I was in college, my parents purchased lake property on Big Sandy Lake near McGregor, Minnesota. Big Sandy is a large lake, many miles long and wide. This property was used for duck hunting and fishing.

My father lacked a loving family. He suffered much tribulation in his young life. He also lacked emotional well-being, acceptance, and belonging. My mother; her parents; her brother, Raymond; and her sister, Arla, helped to fill this void. Leonard was drawn to Fae's fun-loving family. Leonard's life improved when he met Fae though he still carried the scars of an unhappy childhood. His feeling of inadequacy never left him, however, with Fae, he had never been happier.

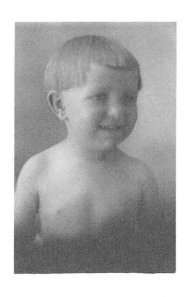

Lennart Gordon Ohman, age 3, Minneapolis, Minnesota, USA, 1923.

(*Right*): Stina wrote on the back of this photo, "Left for Sweden in 1925—I made this outfit, coat and cap! He was the darling on the ship."

Lennart, age 4 and his mother,

Lennart and the muskie are the same size, but the fish
probably weighs more!
Uncle Åke (Stina's youngest brother) caught this "big one."
Åke was a concert violinist.
He died at age 51 due to complications of diabetes.
Stina and Lennart are in Edsbyn, 1926.

Lennart, age 12, and friend.

This photograph was taken Easter Sunday, April 16, 1933.

Lennart, the WWI flying ace.

Lennart's eleventh birthday, August 15, 1931.

Graduation Day, Pillsbury Military Academy,
Owatonna, Minnesota, June 1, 1940.

Fae graduated January 18,
1940 from Columbia Heights
High School, Columbia
Heights, Minnesota.

Leonard and Fae's wedding, February 14, 1942.

Stina, Leonard, and Fae in the receiving line immediately following
the ceremony,
St. Matthew's Lutheran Church, Columbia Heights, Minnesota.

A night out with friends, Lenny and Fae, 1944.

Leonard sporting his brown, felt, trilby fedora.

Leonard at his desk at FMC Northern
Ordinance Division,
Fridley, Minnesota, 1967.

Leonard retired in December 1982 after 42 years 7 months at FMC Northern Ordinance, his lifetime employer.

Two Ohmans

Final Remarks

Of Interest

Timeline and Significant Dates

Contributors

References

About the Author

Two Ohmans

Final Remarks

Leonard

At an early age, Lennart lacked the emotional security of belonging.
Did he belong in Sweden, or did he belong in the U.S.? I have often
wondered if my father would have had an easier life, if, as a child,
he had remained in Sweden. In Edsbyn, Lennart had an extended
family, spoke the common language, and would have entered and
completed formal schooling with his cousins. I'm sure Lennart
found it difficult to leave Sweden, and once back in the USA,
yearned to return to Edsbyn.

My father experienced the love of family during Stina and his
3-year visit to Sweden. However, he was young and impressionable.
Later in life, he reflected on those years with inquiry, "What was
that all about? Why was I there? Why did I have to leave? Maybe
things were not as they seemed. Where are those people now? It's
all a bit of a blur." As Leonard matured, less was said about his
family in Sweden and he adjusted to life in the U.S. Stina may not
have shared correspondence or information about the family with
him. He distanced himself from those years in Sweden so long ago.
It was as if his visit never happened. He internalized the reasons for
the estrangement and his mind dwelled on the negative. "My mother
was not respected among the family members. She was sent away.
My mother is no longer loved. I am no longer loved because I am a
bastard. Those people mean nothing to us now." This is how I
regarded the family in Sweden. My father instilled this belief.

I regret that my father never knew his own lineage, as it was not spoken about. He was never told the story of his real father. He respected his mother's right to privacy. In never knowing the truth, however, my father regarded his birth as an unfortunate happenstance and himself as an undesirable.

When I was young, I remember my father wanting to answer the phone when it rang. I was taught that if someone on the phone asked for "Lennart," it was a person from his Swedish past, and the phone call was very important. My father believed that some day he would receive a call from his real father or a half brother or sister, or an attorney, informing him of an inheritance left to him.

When Jerry and I returned from our first visit to Sweden in 1974, my father was anxious to see us and question me about our trip. Leonard had not returned to Sweden. It had been 50 years since his initial trip at the age of five in 1925.

"Was there anything there for me?" he asked with his heart in his throat. I witnessed hopelessness.

"Did my father leave anything for me?" he asked a second time. I was shocked. I had no idea who his father was. Dad had not mentioned his wish for us to conduct investigative research while in Sweden. My father also asked if I had met any of his half brothers or sisters. I couldn't understand his imaginative logic and was saddened by his unrealistic expectations.

My father designed our house built in 1953 on Shingle Creek Drive in Brooklyn Park, Minnesota. It was a well-built sprawling ranch style home. It had a finished lower level and a walkout basement onto a large backyard with the creek beyond. My father inspected every board that was used in its construction and instructed the carpenters to place the floorboards closer together than code to eliminate squeaky floors. Several specific conveniences and safeguards were drawn into the plans. A built-in gun cabinet was in the master bedroom closet. My father drew the materials to scale with dimensions for every outlet, pipe, and vent. I can remember him studying the pages of blue prints and overlay sepias. He had a tall drafting table set up in one of the bedrooms in our house. I would watch him stand or sit on his stool and draw with his tools: a straightedge, compass, several triangles, and a T-square.

Leonard was an active member of the Northern Ordinance Gun Club. He shot trap and skeet every Wednesday after work. Dad was a marksman and would often shoot 25 out of 25 clay pigeons, using his own reloaded shotgun shells. Pheasant and duck hunting seasons were his favorite times of the year. We had an Irish setter named Toots. She was an excellent retriever. I remember Dad raving about her. One late season hunting trip Toots fell through thin ice while attempting to retrieve a duck that had landed on the surface. The ice bath did not stop her. She struggled, managed to climb out of the water, ran on top of the ice to retrieve the duck, jumped back into the ice bath, swam back to shore, and gently laid the duck at Dad's feet.

My father was also a trout fisherman and tied his own flies. The opening of trout fishing season on the last Saturday of April was always a big deal. This was serious business. The fishermen stood silently, so as not to scare the fish, elbow to elbow on both banks of a small tributary of the Root River (actually a small stream) with rods and lines ready, awaiting the noon signal that announced the season officially open. At the precise moment the noon alarm sounded, all flies and lines plopped into the stream at the same time. Surely the trout were startled by this commotion and took cover, remaining under rocks the remainder of the day! I accompanied my father several times, and later, my brother, Ross, was invited to go along and experience this very special weekend with Dad in April in Lanesboro, Minnesota.

People loved my mother; she was a friend magnet. She was light hearted and accepting. My mother and father would often disagree; my father was not an easy person to live with.

Leonard, on the other hand, had an unusual personality and few friends. He imagined people (myself included) were out to get him. He would internalize a malicious thought to the point of convincing himself that it was true, and then act by accusing others of wrongdoing. People considered him peculiar and would distance themselves from him. As mentioned earlier in the book, my father trusted no one.

One afternoon when my father and I were fishing from the boat, he told me about a defining incident in his life:

When he was a little boy, about the age of four or five, before their trip to Sweden, his mother took him to the Washington Avenue Bridge in Minneapolis. This bridge spans the Mississippi River. She began to coax him to walk with her across the bridge. He did not want to go, he was afraid to walk on the bridge, afraid of the rushing water below. She coaxed him again and again to walk with her. He was fearful and resisted her advances. Finally, he stepped forward onto the bridge. Proceeding cautiously, he walked several yards. At some point, his mother bent down and lunged toward him, scaring him frightfully. He screamed and ran a distance away from her. She pursued him and at some point, relented. He was sure her intent was to push him into the river.

Leonard never forgave his mother for what he perceived was an attempt on his life. He truly believed his mother's sole purpose and intent in taking him to the bridge that day was to end his life. He believed he was bothersome to his mother, cramping her style as a young and attractive debutant in the social-climbing Swedish community. My father was sure his mother wanted to get rid of him. He relived this incident in recurring nightmares throughout his life. My father looked back on this grievous act as the turning point that led to his distrust of all individuals. In his defense, why *would* a parent take their young child untethered to a bridge over a rushing river? It seems odd to me—a playground in the park, yes, there are no concerns. But, to a rushing river?— No. This frightful incident occurred just prior to the two of them leaving the U.S. to return to Sweden. I find Stina's actions puzzling and very concerning.

Leonard was mentally scarred. Most children find refuge, love, comfort, and strength in the arms of a parent. He felt he could not trust his mother, his one sole parent. His life's endeavor became a struggle for survival. Alone. He searched for support, love, and acceptance his entire life. Yet, he did not know how to procure it, as he could not give it. Throughout Leonard's life, he was unable to trust anyone or anything, including his wife and his two children.

I questioned the inclusion of this disturbing account in the book. It is alarming and heart-wrenching. However, I was urged to include it, as it revealed Stina's state of mind and helped to explain Leonard's deep-seated paranoia and distrust.

Leonard led an early life of broken promises and disappointments. He learned how to persevere hardship. I have written this book in my father's defense. I want my family and friends to know why he was the way he was. He would often say he grew up in the school of hard knocks. This was true; he did. My father was a hero, and he was a victim. Long may he be remembered.

Stina

Stina was a stylish, classy lady, always aware of her own presence and the presence of others. She worked at The Dayton Company department store in downtown Minneapolis. Dayton's Oval Room on the 8th floor carried the ultimate quality of high-priced women's wear available in Minnesota during the 1950s, 60s, and 70s. Stina was a sales clerk in The Oval Room where she constructed and altered clothing and made women's hats. Items of silk, imported wool, cashmere, and Persian lamb were among the varied line of one-of-a-kind items. The elite of Minneapolis wanting to shop at The Oval Room needed an appointment.

Stina was coy and reserved, always in control of her surroundings. Her laugh was ladylike; her actions were smooth movements. She was graceful, held her head high, and had superior posture. She was a proud woman and gave the impression of being well-bred from a noble family of distinction.

In reality, Stina had very little. She never owned a car. She did not have a driver's license. She used public transportation, the city bus line, to get to and from her job at Dayton's Department Store. Stina worked hard and clocked many hours in the Oval Room. She was an excellent seamstress. Her favorite clothing store was the Salvation Army resale shop. She had an eye for quality fabric and a vision for an attractive makeover. Her one extravagance was gold. What little money Stina had, she saved to buy gold. She preferred 28 karat, but it was hard to find. Most often she settled for 24 karat. Stina was not a fan of costume jewelry. What my grandmother lacked in possessions, she made up with in dignity and presence. One would never know she counted every penny.

Stina made friends easily with men, and they admired her. She had more men friends than women friends. Women did not care for her aura of arrogance and aloofness. Stina appeared in the October 28, 1946 issue of *Newsweek* magazine, page 23. It is an article about the post-war price of beef hitting an all-time high, so high, that beef was not available in many places in the U.S., only bison. President Truman and his "decontrol edict" are mentioned often. The photo with the article shows Stina at a meat counter with the caption, "Steak! Only bison, but beef was on its way."

I am grateful to Hillevi Kihlin for saving the letters that Stina wrote to her and Bo, Eva's brother, during the ten-year period from 1972-1982. Eva translated the letters.

(Quote from Stina's letter, December 16, 1981):

"I often think of my relatives and Sweden, my native country, but after 55 years in America this is now my country. You automatically adjust to the traditions and, without knowing it, you have become another person. So when you return to your home country, you will notice that you do not fit in so well. I am not alone in having this experience.

The year 1920 opened up a new world for me, and I was alone. Now my family consists of eight people* who have lots of love for each other.

I must say I have nothing to regret. It has not been easy sometimes, but you do have to plan your own life. Nobody is going to plan it for you. It's up to you, right?!"

After Stina's death, I read all of the letters she wrote to Hillevi. I responded by email on March 20, 2015 to both Eva and Hillevi:

"Thank you Eva, for translating Stina's letters! And Hillevi for saving them! I must tell you ... I am surprised by your translations. I had no idea Grandmother Stina had such high regard for our family. I was also shocked to hear that she was happy to be an American!! She was quite reserved with her affection and never told me she loved me. She didn't care for my mother. She was quite critical of us both. I always felt she would rather have been in Sweden. She adored her homeland and I thought she felt like she was somewhat estranged from the family and felt badly about it. I had the feeling (as a little girl) that my mother and I were just not as good as her Swedish family. Interesting isn't it?! And very surprising to me. Thank you for sending the translations.
Love, Janet"

* *Leonard, Fae, and Ross Ohman; Jerry, Janet, Lara, and Jeff Lindsay; and Stina.*

352

It is true, my grandmother was critical of my mother and me. She thought my mother was too heavy, had poor taste in clothing, was a poor housekeeper, and a bad cook. She never liked my hair style or my make-up (even though I wore very little) and always told me about it. It irritated my mother when my grandmother and father spoke in Swedish to one another as she was sure that they were talking about her. My mother tried to learn the Swedish language. She took lessons at the Swedish Art Institute. This venture, however, was short lived. My mother never really caught on. Stina complimented me once on my sewing. She praised the alterations I made on a pleated wool skirt that I had in high school. It still hangs in my closet. Grandma Stina resented my mother's functional family. Stina liked the Beatles because she thought they washed their hair every day. My grandmother showed little emotion and never said "sorry" or "please."

I have often questioned my right to reveal the personal intimacies of another person's life. My father knew about the Swedish letters, but he did not pursue their content while his mother was alive nor after her death. I am confident my grandmother, Stina, felt the letters were safe and her secrets would never be known. After all, her descendants were English speakers and unable to read them. She could not imagine a time when the family east of the Atlantic would meet the family west of it, and lessen the divide. Yet, the question remains, "Why did she keep the letters?" I believe they were very dear to her and grounded her. They gave her a satisfying sense of belonging, connecting her to family, lost loves, and her youth. Much too precious to destroy, they were her last connection to her homeland. She loved them, and they were a part of her. The letters are the bones of this book. They have taught me, and other family members much about people we never knew and now love.

I am passionate about this book. I lived close to the immigration my entire life as my grandmother and father spoke Swedish to one another, and I knew Stina traveled alone and pregnant to the United States. I so easily could have been a Swede had she or my father remained in their homeland. The details of the past were a mystery. Finding the 78 letters, 36 years ago after my grandmother's death, encouraged me to pursue their content. Eva's translations unlocked the extraordinary story, and I was driven to record the knowledge of facts and events that changed the course of my life.

Compiling Stina's and Leonard's life stories into one book has been a labor of love come to fruition. I was compelled to research, as I knew there was more to the Ohman story than was known. There are still unanswered questions; the unknown answers will remain through eternity with the key players themselves.

Assembling the two anthologies of letters along with the additional writings for the book, *Two Ohmans,* was a two year endeavor. The inspirations began on May 9, 2019, when Eva arrived in Macomb, Illinois, to translate the letters that Stina had received and saved and loved. This book reached completion during the Corona Virus (Covid19) pandemic of quarantine in November 2020. It is oddly ironic, that a disastrous epidemic could be an author's best friend. Confinement aided this book's completion in commemorating Stina's immigration one hundred years ago on March 16, 1920.

354

Author's Note

It was our intent to keep the original meaning of the letters intact.
However, Eva and I have some reservations, as parts of letters were
unintelligible and there is the possibility of our misunderstanding
concepts due to a letter's age, obscure linguistics, and the
complexity in reading, translating, and rewriting an original script
into another language. Checking facts was difficult since those who
could have verified accounts are no longer living.

Of Interest

Grandmother Stina's chiffon, heavily beaded,

"flapper" chemise dress hangs in our cedar closet.

It is a rich ruby red color.

It has a same color under-slip that is visible through the chiffon.

There is a tie-on head-piece accessory.

It is over 100 years old.

I have worn it once.

I have several pairs of Stina's shoes.

Gramdmother Stina did not spare a dime when purchasing shoes.

Her shoes are of high quality leather, classic style,

and remain in fashion.

Many were purchased in New York.

Stina would stop and shop in NY on her trips to and from Sweden.

Daughter Lara and I occasionally wear her shoes.

I wore one of Grandmother Stina's dresses

when Lara was married in 2005.

It was a most perfect "mother of the bride" dress.

Stina would have been pleased.

Also of Interest

Two tuxedos, circa 1918, also hang in our cedar closet.
Both have tags from Stockholm.
Both were hand tailored.

Both are black wool gabardine,
and both include a pair of trousers, a vest, and a jacket.

One jacket has 23-inch long tails.
The other jacket has a twill collar.

One pair of trousers is dark grey pin-stripe.

One tuxedo has a white vest.
The other has a vest of black.

Our son, Jeff, dabbled in magic in his younger years.
He performed magic tricks at children's birthday parties
and at family reunions.

He wore the tuxedo with tails.
It has deep pockets, perfect for the slight-of-hand.

Of Greater Interest

Åke was great grandfather Carl and great grandmother Kerstin's
youngest child, born in 1908.
Åke was Stina's youngest brother.

Agneta is Åke's daughter.
Agneta presently lives in Edsbyn.
Agneta is Eva's first cousin and my second cousin.

In July 2020, Agneta told Eva that she had found a relative
that is their grandfather, Carl Ohman's, son.

This gentleman, born in 1930,
is Carl's youngest child by his mistress.
The gentleman lives in a nearby community close to Edsbyn.

As this book goes to print,
my great grandfather's youngest child is alive and well.
Great grandfather Carl, born in 1866,
fathered his youngest child at the age of 65.

The gentleman never met his father, Carl.
His mother wrote a letter to him informing him
that his father was Carl Ohman.

Timeline and Significant Dates

(*)	Denotes the years Stina returned to Sweden.
	1925
	1947
	1954
	1969

(**)	Denotes the years Leonard traveled to Sweden.
	1925
	1978

(***)	Denotes years Janet and Jerry traveled to Sweden.
	1974
	2007
	2012
	20??

1894   February 12, Kristina Evelyn (Stina) is born to Carl and Kerstin Ohman.
She is the fourth child. Four more children follow Stina.

1895   September 4, Sven Bengtzon is born.

1913   Sven and Stina meet.

1916
Letter 1   December 21, to Stina, Edsbyn, from Sven Bengtzon, Edsbyn

1917
Letter 2   August 18, to Stina, Edsbyn, from Sven, Orsa, Dalarna
Letter 3   September 10, to Stina, Edsbyn, from Sven, Edsbyn
Letter 4   September 29, to Stina, Edsbyn, from Sven, Edsbyn
Letter 5   October 9, to Stina, Edsbyn, from Sven, Edsbyn
Letter 6   November 9, to Stina, Edsbyn, from W.T. Heintges, Göthenburg (Göteborg)
Letter 7   November 21, to Stina, Stockholm (at Moden's), from Sven, Bollnäs

| Letter 8 | November 24, to Stina, Stockholm (at Moden's), from Sven, Bollnäs |

Stina leaves Sweden March 3, 1920. She arrives in New York City on March 16, 1920.

Letter 18	April 20, to Stina, c/o Mr. Helgar Gustafsson, Rhinelander, Wisconsin, USA, from Karl Eriksson. No return address on the envelope. Karl's return address is enclosed inside the letter: Oskar Nilsson, Box 26, Edsbyn. Written on the front of the envelope is "Via Kristiania." (Kristiania is now named Oslo, Norway's capital, or we can assume it is the name of a ship, Kristiania).
Letter 19	May 15, to Stina, c/o Mr. E. Persson, Minneapolis, from Karl Eriksson. No return address on the envelope. Karl's return address is enclosed inside the letter: Oskar Nilsson c/o Dalkvist, Tundelgatan 1, Stockholm.

Lennart Gordon Ohman is born August 15, 1920. His mother speaks to him in Swedish, which becomes his first language.

Letter 20	November 30, to Stina, Minneapolis (new address), from Sven, Bollnäs
Letter 21	December 1, to Stina, Minneapolis, from Papa (Carl), Edsbyn

1921
Letter 22	February 22, to Stina, Minneapolis, from cousin Erik Ohman (and wife Berta), Edsbyn
Letter 23	February 25, to Stina, Minneapolis, from cousin Erik Ohman, Edsbyn
Letter 24	March 20, to Stina, Minneapolis, from Sven, Bollnäs
Letter 25	September 25, to Stina, Minneapolis, from Sven, Bollnäs

1922
Letter 26	June 5, to Stina, Minneapolis, from Papa, Edsbyn
Letter 27	August 13, to Stina, Minneapolis, from Sven, Bollnäs
Letter 28	October 9, to Stina, Minneapolis, from Sven, Bollnäs

1923
Letter 29	March 14, to Stina, Minneapolis, from Papa, Edsbyn

Letter 30	July 12, to Stina, Minneapolis, from Papa, Edsbyn

In the fall of 1925, Stina and Lennart return to Edsbyn. Lennart is 5 years old. He immediately connects with his cousins as they speak the same language. His cousin, Lennart Klang, who was two years older, becomes his first close friend.

362

Letter 50	May 27, to Stina, Edsbyn, from ??, Alfta
Letter 51	May 31, to Stina, Edsbyn, from ??, Alfta
Letter 52	June 6, to Stina, Edsbyn, from Mimmie Johansson, Stockholm (Wedding invitation)
Letter 53	June 15, to Stina, Edsbyn, from ??, Alfta
Letter 54	June 28, to Stina in Edsbyn, from ??, Alfta
Letter 55	July 3, to Stina, Edsbyn, from ??, Alfta
Letter 56	July 13, to Stina, Edsbyn, from cousin Oscar Nilsson, Stockholm
Letter 57	July 29, to Fashion House Regent, Stockholm, from Stina, Edsbyn (Job application and three letters of recommendation)
Letter 58	August 8, to Stina, Edsbyn, from ??, Alfta
Letter 59	August 12, to Fashion House Regent, Stockholm, from Stina, Edsbyn (Two photos of Stina)
Letter 60	September 24, to Stina, Edsbyn, from H ?, Alfta (First initial "H" is evident)
Letter 61	October 7, to Stina, Edsbyn, from H ?, Alfta
Letter 62	November 19, to Stina, c/o Karl Klang, Edsbyn, from H ?, Alfta
Letter 63	November 24, to Stina, Edsbyn (Box 41), from H ?, Alfta

1927

Letter 64	January 7, to Stina, Edsbyn, from H ?, Alfta
Letter 65	June 12, to Stina, Edsbyn, from Sven, Orsa
Letter 66	June 21, to Stina, Edsbyn, from Sven, Orsa
Letter 67	July 2, to Stina, Edsbyn, from Sven, Orsa
Letter 68	July 16, to Stina, Edsbyn, from Sven, Orsa
Letter 69	August 2, to Stina, Edsbyn, from Sven, Orsa
Letter 70	August 9, to Stina, Edsbyn, from Sven, Orsa
Letter 71	September 15, to Stina, Edsbyn, from Sven, Orsa
Letter 72	September 27, to Stina, Edsbyn, from Sven, Orsa

1928

Stina and Lennart return to Minneapolis in 1928. They lived in Edsbyn over three years. Lennart begins school in Minneapolis in 1928 at the age of eight. He knows little English and finds school difficult. His teachers think he is learning disabled. Lennart misses his cousins in Edsbyn and wants to return to Sweden.

1929	
Letter 73	April 22, to Stina, Minneapolis, from Sven, Orsa
Letter 74	July 7, to Stina, Minneapolis, from Sven, Orsa
	September 15, Sven marries Kerstin Danils.

1938	September 12, Leonard enrolls at Pillsbury Academy, Owatonna, Minnesota.

1939	February 3, Fire on the Pillsbury Academy campus destroys Kelly Hall. February 25, Leonard leaves Owatonna. September 11, Leonard re-enrolls at Pillsbury Academy, Owatonna, Minnesota.
Letter 75	November 26, to Stina, Minneapolis, from Nelly and Bror, Edsbyn

1940	January 18, Fae Moore graduates, mid-year commencement, from Columbia Heights High School. June 1, Leonard graduates from Pillsbury Academy, Owatonna, Minnesota.

1942	February 14, Leonard Ohman and Fae Moore are married at St. Matthew's Lutheran Church, Columbia Heights, Minnesota.

*1947	Stina's father, Carl, dies; she returns to Sweden. Stina and Henrik Carlander marry.

1948	October, Stina returns to the USA.

1949	February 20, Janet Kaye (Jan) is born to Leonard and Fae Ohman.

1951	
Letter 76	October 10, to Stina Carlander, Minneapolis, from Arvid Carlander, Stockholm
Letter 77	December 16, to Stina and Henrik Carlander, Minneapolis, from Arvid Carlander, Stockholm

*1954	Stina returns to Sweden.

Letter 78	August 6, to Mrs. Stina Ohman, Edsbyn, from Arvid Carlander, Stockholm; August 10, Stina returns to the USA.
1958	September 4, Ross Leonard is born, son of Leonard and Fae Ohman.
1959	Janet writes her first letter to Eva.
*1969	Sven dies at the age of 74.

Stina returned to Edsbyn the summer of 1969. It had been 15 years since her last visit. She stayed several months (perhaps a year) living with siblings: her brother Göthe and his wife, Singa (Eva's parents); her sister Justina; and her sister Nelly.

***1974

Jan and Jerry visited Edsbyn for the first time in August. We met Eva; Göthe (Stina's brother) and wife, Singa; Bo and Hillevi (Eva's brother and his wife); their daughters, Sofia, age three; and newborn baby girl, Jenny. We also met Nelly (Stina's sister) and her son, Jon (about 40 yrs old), who lived in the villa, the main house of the Carl Ohman homestead. We stayed two nights in Edsbyn.

**1978

Leonard returned to Edsbyn the summer of 1978 for a five-week visit. It had been 50 years since his last visit to Sweden with his mother, Stina. My mother Fae and my brother Ross accompanied him. It was their first visit to Europe. Leonard and Fae stayed with Göthe and Singa. Ross stayed with Bo and Hillevi.

1978-1980

Nisse, Ingrid, Jon, and Andreas Nilsson live in Plymouth, Minnesota, near Leonard and Fae. Nisse is a distant cousin of my father's from Edsbyn. He works for Edsbyverken Cross Country Ski Company.

1982

Leonard retires from FMC Northern Ordinance Division, Fridley, Minnesota. He worked 42 years 7 months for Northern Pump Company. He remained with his first employer his entire career.

1984   May 11, Stina Ohman Carlander dies at the age of 90.

1989

Bo and Hillevi's daughter, Sofia Ohman-Lisiderius (age 18) came to the USA for the first time in August. She lived with us in Macomb, Illinois, and was our nanny for eight months. She helped with the children and housework. We became very close. Her younger sister, Jenny (age 15) flew to Minneapolis for Christmas. Sofia, Jenny, my parents, Jerry and I and our children enjoyed the holidays. Jenny flew back to Sweden in early January. Sofia wanted to stay in Minneapolis, (a much larger and more active city than Macomb!) get a job, and make some money. She said she could stay with my parents. I told her she couldn't work in the USA because she did not have a social security number. She replied that she knew that a social security number had nine digits. She said she could enter any random nine digits to complete a job application. "By the time they catch me, I'll be gone," she added. Leonard and Fae were not too thrilled about an eighteen-year-old female living with them, someone they had just met for the first time. Sofia returned to Macomb, Illinois, with us the first week of January. During the twelve-hour drive in the van with our three children, Sofia collected job applications at every gas station and restaurant. The family went skiing in Colorado in March. Sofia was determined to take a Greyhound bus to California. We were not keen on this idea. But, Sofia's mother, Hillevi agreed to her plan, and we could not stop her. We said farewell to Sofia in the Denver bus depot. From California, Sofia went to Thailand and several months later returned to Stockholm.

2003   August 4, Fae Moore Ohman dies at the age of 80.

***2007

Jan and Jerry visit Sweden for the second time in July. We stay three weeks. Nisse Nilsson guides us through the small town of Edsbyn. We walk the path from the Villa (the Ohman home) to the store where Stina worked in 1919. I could imagine her cross country skiing through the snow to work each day (as she told me she had).

2010   June 14, Leonard Gordon Ohman dies at the age of 89.

366

***2012

Jan and Jerry, and also Jan's brother, Ross, and his wife, Julie, spend the last week of November and the first week of December in Stockholm. The Nilsson family joins us at the Rica Hotel. The Ohman-Lisiderius family invites us to an early Svenska Jul celebration hosted by Sofia and Fredrik in Stockholm. We visit our nephew Joel Ohman (Ross and Julie's son) who is studying at the University of Trondheim, Norway. Our daughter, Katie, joins us in Norway. It is our third visit to Sweden and first to Norway.

2014

Eva, Hillevi Kihlin, and Leif Ydnäs visit the USA and Macomb, Illinois, for the first time, April 29 through May 14. They translate parts of paragraphs from several of Stina's letters. They are the first to unlock content.

2019   Eva returns to the US and Macomb in May to translate the entire collection of Stina's Swedish letters.

2020   July, Agneta informs her cousin, Eva, that they have a half-uncle, Carl Ohman's youngest child, living near Edsbyn.

***20??

Jan and Jerry visit Sweden for the fourth time to hand deliver the book, *Two Ohmans*, to Eva, Ulf, Agneta, Sofia, Hillevi, Jenny, Nisse, Gunni, and Åke.

Thank You to My Contributors

I and generations of family to follow, are indebted to the first
readers of the letters: Eva, Hillevi, and Leif, who broke the silence
in 2014, on their first night in Macomb during their first visit to the
United States. They read and translated until the early morning
hours. I listened and wept; we were captivated by their content.

I am indebted to Eva Ohman Johansson, from Ostersund, Sweden,
my beloved second cousin, to whom I owe so much. Thank you for
translating the 78 letters.

I am indebted to Nisse Nilsson, from Edsbyn, Sweden, a distant
cousin who with his wife, Ingrid, and sons, Jon and Andreas, spent
two years (1978-1980) in Minneapolis, Minnesota, managing the
Edsbyverken Cross Country Ski Company. Thank you, Nisse, for
translating and gaining permission to include the article, "Edsbyn's
Bow-Saw Frame Factory: Karl Ohman."

I am indebted to Hillevi Kihlin, from Falun, Sweden, for saving the
letters Stina wrote to her. I am deeply grateful to be able to include
Stina's own words and reflections on her life in the manuscript.
Thank you, Hillevi.

I am indebted to Ulf Jansson, from Jonkoping, Sweden, a third
cousin whom I have never met. Thank you for your research in
finding Sven.

I am indebted to Agneta Ohman Bergstrand, from Edsbyn, Sweden, a second cousin I met while visiting Sweden in 2007. Thank you for finding the living direct descendant of Great Grandfather, Carl Ohman. Carl's youngest child, a son, was born in 1930.

I am indebted to Therese Trotochaud, a consultant, who came to know the intricacies of the book well. Thank you for reading, editing, and rereading my drafts and revisions. Your thoroughness and suggestions enriched the flow of content. Thank you for your hours of work.

I am indebted to Dawn Sweet for her graphic design and advanced formatting skills. Your patience guided me through the labyrinth of jpeg, docx, pdf, and USB. You were a crucial resource; the missing link between the written word and the reader and a godsend when I needed it most. Thank you for bringing the project to life and available to others.

I am indebted to John Hallwas, author and educator. It was your L.I.F.E. class in writing memoirs, your "On Community," April 2016, article in *The McDonough County Voice* entitled "Looking at your life as a meaningful story," and our phone conversation the summer of 2019 that pushed me to attempt such a project and put fingers to keyboard. Thank you.

I am indebted to Tim Roberts, author and history professor, Western Illinois University. Thank you for your encouragement and suggestions of publishers.

I am indebted to Michael Lorenzen, Western Illinois University, Malpass Library. Thank you for *The Minneapolis Tribune*, February 4, 1939 articles of the Kelly Hall fire on the campus of Pillsbury Academy, Owatonna, Minnesota.

I am indebted to John Wareham, Star Tribune News Research Dept. Minneapolis-St. Paul, Minnesota. Thank you for the enhanced copies of the Kelly Hall fire on the campus of Pillsbury Academy, Owatonna, Minnesota from *The Minneapolis Tribune*, February 4, 1939, archives.

I am indebted to Drew at Donor Services, Ellis Island National Monument. It was impossible to discern the words of the first query of Question #20 from my copy of the Manifest of Alien Passengers. I was resigned to the word "indiscernible" going to print. Drew researched the original Manifest and resolved the gap of knowledge. All thirty-three questions asked of Stina on March 16, 1920 are now intact, clear, and included in the book. Thank you, Drew, for your extra effort.

I am indebted to Duane Kuss, my first cousin on my mother's side. Thank you for the book on publishing and your words of encouragement in the early stages and throughout the process.

I am indebted to Mike Anderson, Macomb, Illinois. As struggling authors, we commiserated on our progress from time to time. Thank you for your suggestions, Mike.

I am indebted to my family and dear friends who were aware of my ambitious endeavor. Thank you for supporting my inexperienced efforts.

Above all, I am indebted to my husband, Jerold Jess Lindsay, my first editor, defender, and critic. Thank you for suggesting the succinct and perfectly appropriate title, "Two Ohmans." Thank you for understanding my appetite for writing and encouraging me with each word that I processed. Thank you for restoring my soul during those times when I found the book impossible to complete. You never questioned the hours and nights I spent at the computer nor my use of copy paper and ink. Thank you so much. I love you.

References

About G-man. History. (n.d.). G-man Tools. Nordic saw makers
(paragraph 6). Retrieved from http://www.g-mantools.se/

Dayton's Department Store. (Summer 1955). It's A Small World . . .
Dayton's Department Store Employee Newsletter. (700 Nicollet
Avenue, Minneapolis, Minnesota). Copy in possession of author.

Dormitory in ruins, Academy closes for week. (1939, February 4).
Star Tribune Archives. 13. (Minneapolis-St. Paul). Retrieved from
https://startribune.newspapers.com/image/180307711/?terms=fire%
2Bat%2Bpillsbury%2Bacademy%2Bfebruary

Elflein, J. (2020). Covid-19 cases worldwide. Also, Covid-19 deaths
worldwide. https://statista.com

Färnström, N. (Ed.) (1946, January). Fantastiskt tunafiske. *Sport
fiskaren*, 3-4. Höckenström, A. (Pub.) Stockholm. Copy in
possession of author.

Flames raze landmark at boys' school. (1939, February 3). *Star
Tribune Archives*. 1. (Minneapolis-St. Paul). Retrieved from
https://startribune.newspapers.com/image/178780499/?terms=fire%
2Bat%2Bpillsbury%2Bacademy%2Bfebruary

Gustavus Adolphus Day. (n.d.). *Wikipedia*. Retrieved from
https://en.wikipedia.org/wiki/Gustavus_Adolphus_Day

Jennings, P., & Brewster, T. (1999). Over the edge, 1936-1941. Stormy weather, 1929-1936. In *The century for young people* (1st. ed., pp. 82-97, and 65-81). New York: Doubleday.

Leading Edge Materials Corp. (n.d.). Technical report for the Woxna graphite project, central Sweden. *leadingedgematerials.com*. Google Search: Public Domain Map Edsbyn, Bollnäs, Voxna, Sweden. Retrieved from https://www.google.com/search?q=public+domain+map+edsbyn%2c+Bollnäs%2c+voxna+sweden&+bm+isch&ved=2ahUKEwjR1NCQ19nqAhUDbqwKHdsiB

List or manifest of alien passengers for the United States immigration officer at port of arrival. List 10, p. 32, (1920, March 16). Ellis Island, New York. Copy purchased and in possession of author.

Most of Pillsbury students return to homes pending arrival of new equipment at Owatonna. (1939, February 4). *Star Tribune Archives*. 13. (Minneapolis - St. Paul). 13. Retrieved from https://startribune.newspapers.com/image/180307711/?terms=most%2Bof%2Bpillsbury%2Bstudents%2Breturn%2Bto%2Bhomes%2Bpending%2Barrival%2Bof%2Bnew%2Bequipment%2Bat%2BOwatonna

Pettersson, H. (1995). Edsbyns Sågbågsfabrik (Edsbyn's Bow-Saw Frame Factory); Karl Öhman. In *När Industrin Kom Till Byn (When the Industry Came to the Village)*. (pp. 38-42). Edsbyn, Sweden:

Utgiven av Ovanåkers Hembygdsförening (Edited by Ovanåkers Homestead Properties). Copy in possession of author.

Sågrörbågens uppfinnare död (The Inventor of the Bow Saw is Dead). (1947, January 31). *Journal of the Organization of Blacksmith, Forging, and Mechanical Foundry.* Stockholm. 2(January 31), 43. Copy in possession of author.

Spanish flu. (2010, October 12). Retrieved from *history.com.* https://www.history.com/topics/world-war-i/1918-flu-pandemic

The Union: dollars and cents crossroad. (1946, October 28). *Newsweek.* New York. XXVIII: 18, 23. Copy in possession of author.

Vasaloppet. (n.d.). *Wikipedia.* Retrieved from https://en.wikipedia.org/wiki/Vasaloppet

Winter War. (n.d.). *Wikipedia.* Retrieved from https://en.wikipedia.org/wiki/Winter_War

About the Author

Janet K. Ohman Lindsay once lived among the lakes in Minneapolis, Minnesota. She now lives in Macomb, Illinois among the tall corn and is the mother of Lara, Jeff, and Katie, and the grandmother of Bodhi, Nina, Landon, and Logan. For 34 years she educated other people's children, instructing them in all subject areas, but she especially enjoyed teaching reading and literacy skills. She found the case study of her father's inept abilities in reading and writing perplexing. This is her first experience in writing a book. Janet reflects, "I wrote it because I had something to say. The story had to be told."

Janet graduated from Osseo High School, Osseo, Minnesota in 1967. She attended Luther College, Decorah, Iowa and graduated from Drake University, Des Moines, Iowa with a B.S. in Education. She received an M.S. in Education from Western Illinois University, Macomb, Illinois, and remains A.B.D. (all but dissertation), toward an EdD. in Curriculum and Instruction from the University of Illinois at Urbana Champaign. She also holds an administrative license.

Upon the completion of the book, *Two Ohmans,* Janet celebrates, "I take pride in knowing far more will read my book than would have read my dissertation."

I AM FROM
the past, the present, and less of a future than most.

I remember the first TV,
one channel and one program,
one-half hour of news.

I am from a time before microwaves, cell phones, GPS, and PCs.
I am from a time of dim light, quiet nights, puzzles, and books.

I am from Sunday night suppers of sardines and herring,
anchovies and smoked oysters.
I Jesu namn till bords vi gå.
Välsigna Gud, den mat vi få.
I am from köttbullar, risgrynsgröt,
lutfisk, filbunke, and ligonberries.
I am from an immigrant who traveled by ship
to a land of promise and new beginning,
to Ellis Island—to be checked in and checked out.
The wooden barrel held her life's possessions.

I am from up north at the cabin,
a land of lakes and boats, birch and pine,
frogs and fish, chipmunks eating peaches.
I fish with Grandpa from the boat.
Grandma fries my sunnies and bluegill.

I am from snow and cold—
ice-skating the days of winter
after school and on weekends, between Thanksgiving and Easter.
I fish in an icehouse. My line drops through vast layers of ice
to the depths of liquid water below.

I am from listening to elders, not speaking.
From cigarette smoke, card playing, and late Saturday nights.

I am a lover of thread and needles and fabric.
I am a lover of children, the innocents of the world.
I am a teacher of reading,
a mother of three,
a grandma of twins and two more.

Janet Ohman Lindsay, September 17, 2009

Made in the USA
Las Vegas, NV
30 January 2021